W9-ANH-168

Evidence-Based
PRACTICES AND PROGRAMS
for Early Childhood
Care and Education

Evidence-Based
Practices and Programs
for Early Childhood
Care and Education

editors Christina J. Groark • Kelly E. Mehaffie
Robert B. McCall • Mark T. Greenberg

CORWIN PRESS
A SAGE Publications Company
Thousand Oaks, CA 91320

No Longer
the Property of
Bluffton University

Bluffton University Library

Copyright © 2007 by Corwin Press

All rights reserved. When forms and sample documents are included, their use is authorized only by educators, local school sites, and/or noncommercial or nonprofit entities who have purchased the book. Except for that usage, no part of this book may be reproduced or utilized in any form or by any means, electronic or mechanical, including photocopying, recording, or by any information storage and retrieval system, without permission in writing from the publisher.

For information:

Corwin Press
A Sage Publications Company
2455 Teller Road
Thousand Oaks, California 91320
www.corwinpress.com

Sage Publications Ltd.
1 Oliver's Yard
55 City Road
London EC1Y 1SP
United Kingdom

Sage Publications India Pvt. Ltd.
B-42, Panchsheel Enclave
Post Box 4109
New Delhi 110 017 India

Printed in the United States of America

Library of Congress Cataloging-in-Publication Data

Evidence-based practices and programs for early childhood care
and education/Edited by Christina J. Groark . . . [et al.].
    p. cm.
Includes bibliographical references and index.
ISBN 1-4129-2614-9 (cloth)—ISBN 1-4129-2615-7 (pbk.)
   1. Early childhood education. 2. Child care. I. Groark, Christina J.
LB1139.23.E89 2007
372.21—dc22   2006001807

This book is printed on acid-free paper.

06   07   08   09   10   10   9   8   7   6   5   4   3   2   1

Acquisitions Editor:	Stacy Wagner
Production Editor:	Beth A. Bernstein
Copy Editor:	Karen E. Taylor
Typesetter:	C&M Digitals (P) Ltd.
Proofreader:	Annette Pagliaro
Indexer:	Rick Hurd
Cover Designer:	Scott Van Atta
Graphic Designer:	Monique Hahn

Contents

Acknowledgments ix

About the Editors xi

About the Contributors xv

Introduction xix

A Growing Interest in Early Childhood Care and Education xix
How This Book Can Help xx
Risk and Protective Factors xxi
Levels of Evidence Regarding Programs and Best Practices xxii
References xxiii

PART I. EVIDENCE-BASED PRACTICES

1. School Readiness: Definitions, Best Practices,
   Assessments, and Cost 3
   Kelly E. Mehaffie and Jeffery Fraser
   The Importance of Early Learning 3
   Definitions of School Readiness 4
   The Intersection of Readiness Factors 10
   Research Informing School Readiness Factors 10
   Assessing Readiness 17
   Costs and Savings of Being Ready for School 19
   Conclusions and Recommendations 20
   References 21

2. Early Intervention Practices for Children
   With and at Risk for Delays 25
   Louise Kaczmarek and Christina J. Groark
   Children at Risk for Delay Due to Poverty 26
   Characteristics of Successful Programs for
      Children in Poverty 29
   English Language Learners at Risk for Delay 32
   Children With Developmental Disabilities and Delays 39

Conclusions and Recommendations   44
References   49

3. Best Practices for Transitions Into Kindergarten   56
    Kelly E. Mehaffie and Mary Wolfson
    Transitions in Context   58
    Best Practices for Transitions   59
    Conclusions and Recommendations   62
    References   62

PART II. EVIDENCE-BASED PROGRAMS

4. Publicly Funded Programs and Their Benefits for Children   67
    Wendy M. Barnard
    Federal Programs   68
    State Programs   73
    Trends in Publicly Funded Early Childhood Programs   82
    Conclusions and Recommendations   84
    References   85

5. Demonstration Programs and Successful Outcomes   88
    Wendy M. Barnard and Christina J. Groark
    Randomized Experiments   89
    Quasi-Experimental Studies   92
    Characteristics of Successful Programs   96
    Conclusions and Recommendations   98
    References   100

6. Home-Based and Family Child Care:
   Characteristics and Quality Issues   102
    Richard Fiene and Martha Woodward Isler
    Categories of Home-Based Facilities   102
    Current Quality of Home-Based Facilities   103
    Obstacles to Improving the Quality of Family Child Care   105
    Characteristics of Improved Home-Based and
        Family Child Care Programs   105
    Relative and Neighbor Care   109
    Conclusions and Recommendations   109
    Appendix 1: Overviews and Descriptions of the
        Early Childhood Environment Rating Scale (ECERS)
        and the Family Day Care Rating Scale (FDCRS)   110
    References   112

7. School-Age Services: Programs That Extend the
   Benefits of Early Care and Education Services   114
      Suh-Ruu Ou and Arthur J. Reynolds
      Why Extend Early Childhood Programs?   115
      Existing Extended Early Childhood Programs   116
      Characteristics of Successful Programs   129
      Conclusions and Recommendations   130
      References   131

8. Out-of-School-Time Programs That Promote
   Academic and Behavioral Achievement
   for Children Ages Six to Eight   135
      Anne E. Farber
      Outcomes and Evaluations of Out-of-School-
         Time Programs   136
      Academically Focused Programs   137
      Reading and Mathematics Programs   142
      Tutoring Programs   143
      Summer Programs   144
      Mental Health Focused Programs   145
      Study of High Quality Programs   146
      Characteristics of Successful Programs   146
      Quality Enhancement Tools and Initiatives   149
      Conclusions and Recommendations   150
      References   152

PART III. THE FUTURE OF THE FIELD

9. Professional Development and Higher Education Systems
   to Develop Qualified Early Childhood Educators   159
      Gwen G. Morgan and Jeffery Fraser
      The Current State of Professional Development   160
      Credentials Across Early Childhood Systems   161
      Content of Credentials for Early Education and Care   166
      Emerging Issues   169
      Changes at the College Level   173
      Professional Development Planning Groups   174
      The Role of Professional Associations   176
      Conclusions and Recommendations   177
      References   177

Index   181

Acknowledgments

The editors would like to thank Charles Bruner, Executive Director of the Child and Family Policy Center and also the State Early Childhood Policy Technical Assistance Network, for his contribution and insight in *Chapter 1: School Readiness: Definitions, Best Practices, Assessments, and Cost.* The editors would also like to thank Rekha Shukla, Private Consultant, for her contribution to *Chapter 8: Out-Of-School-Time Programs That Promote Academic and Behavioral Achievement for Children Ages Six to Eight.* In addition, the editors would like to thank Mary Ellen Colella, Administrative Assistant at the University of Pittsburgh Office of Child Development, for her patience and attention to detail during all phases of this manuscript.

Corwin Press gratefully acknowledges the contributions of the following reviewers:

Mathieu Aubuchon
Preschool Coordinator
The Early Childhood Center at Gregory Hill
Adams County School District 50
Westminster, CO

Diane Baumstark
National Board Certified Teacher, Early Childhood Generalist
Priest Elementary School
Detroit Public Schools
Detroit, MI

Rolf Grafwallner
Coordinator
Early Learning Office
Maryland Department of Education
Baltimore, MD

Susan Hoff
Executive Director
Educational First Steps
Dallas, TX

John P. Scholten
Superintendent
Public Schools of Petoskey
Petoskey, MI

Carmen N. Schroeder
Local District 5 Superintendent
Los Angeles Unified School District
Los Angeles, CA

Kyle Snow
Director
Early Learning and School Readiness Program
Child Development and Behavior Branch
National Institute of Child Health and Human Development
Bethesda, MD

About the Editors

Christina J. Groark, PhD, is Associate Professor of Education at the University of Pittsburgh and Co-Director of the University's Office of Child Development (OCD), where she provides administrative oversight, management, and practical and scholarly guidance for the OCD's interdisciplinary projects. The Office of Child Development is a university-community collaborative devoted to applied issues of children, youth, and families, especially of those in urban and low-income communities.

Dr. Groark's career has been devoted to improving the lives of all children, including institutionalized children, children with severe mental and physical disabilities, and at-risk children, and, more recently, to helping children by focusing on the entire family and caregiving environment. Dr. Groark has designed and implemented innovative cutting-edge service demonstration programs, policy initiatives, needs assessments, experimental interventions, program evaluations, and research studies, many of which analyze, document, test, and determine strategies to improve services to children and their families. Internationally, she is working on examining caregiver behaviors that influence short- and long-term outcomes for children in orphanages through projects in the Russian Federation and El Salvador.

In addition, Dr. Groark has been a consultant to many national and international programs, funders, policymakers, and universities. She has served on dozens of governmental, educational, national, and local committees and advisory boards. She is the author of many articles and book chapters in the areas of university-community collaborations, improved interventions in orphanages, applied developmental psychology, and early intervention.

Kelly E. Mehaffie, MS, is a private consultant in the field of early childhood education and policy. She was formerly the Assistant to the Co-Director at the University of Pittsburgh Office of Child Development and also the Co-Coordinator for Allegheny County Pennsylvania's early childhood local planning and engagement group.

Ms. Mehaffie's primary experience lies in coordination, collaboration, evaluation, policy development, and proposal writing for programs that work with children and families—especially early childhood education programs. In addition to working on the Allegheny County Early Childhood Initiative Demonstration Project, she also conducted a statewide study of higher education institutions that prepare educators to work with children from birth to five years old and directed a review of a university-based early childhood program. Ms. Mehaffie assists in writing proposals for training, technical assistance, school readiness, and quality improvement initiatives for early childhood programs and educators. Ms. Mehaffie received her Masters Degree in Developmental Psychology from the University of Pittsburgh.

Robert B. McCall, PhD, is Co-Director of the Office of Child Development and a Professor in the Department of Psychology at the University of Pittsburgh. Dr. McCall has authored hundreds of books, chapters, and articles on infant mental development, age changes in general mental performance, the prediction of later IQ, early childhood care and education, developmental research design and analysis, issues in applied research methods and program evaluation, parenting and child development, science communications through the media, and university-community partnerships.

Dr. McCall has been an Associate Editor of *Child Development* and has served on the editorial boards of 10 other journals. He has also been a contributing editor, monthly columnist, and feature writer for *Parents* magazine. For his work communicating developmental psychology to the general public and helping to create the Office of Child Development, he has been given awards by the American Psychological Association (APA), the Society for Research in Child Development (SRCD), the American Academy of Pediatrics, and the National Council on Family Relations.

In 1998, Dr. McCall received two University of Pittsburgh Chancellor Awards, one for Research and one for Public Service, and, in 2003, he received the SRCD Award for Distinguished Contributions to Public Policy of Children. He has served on SRCD Social Policy and Public Information Committees; APA's Public Information Committee; APA's Division 7 Executive, Credential, Convention Program, Public Information and Policy and Planning Committees; the Board of Directors of *Psychology Today*; and he is currently a member of the Governing Council of SRCD. He received his BA at DePauw University and MA and PhD at the University of Illinois.

Mark T. Greenberg, PhD, holds The Bennett Endowed Chair in Prevention Research in Penn State's College of Health and Human

Development and directs the Prevention Research Center for the Promotion of Human Development. Since 1981, Dr. Greenberg has been examining the effectiveness of school-based curricula (The PATHS Curriculum) to improve the social, emotional, and cognitive competence of elementary-age children.

Dr. Greenberg is a senior investigator on a number of prevention projects in Pennsylvania including Fast Track (NIMH funded), PROSPER (NIDA funded), Communities That Care, and REACH (Kellogg Foundation). Dr. Greenberg is also a senior investigator on a number of intervention studies to improve the social, emotional, and academic outcomes of preschool children through Head Start programs. He consults with government agencies and foundations at the local, state, federal, and international level on topics related to child development and mental health promotion. In 2002, he was awarded the Distinguished Research Scientist Award of the Society for Prevention Research.

About the Contributors

Wendy M. Barnard, PhD, received her doctorate from the University of Wisconsin–Madison where she worked on the Chicago Longitudinal Study examining the effects of the Chicago Child-Parent Program on the long-term outcomes for youth. Her particular area of interest was the influence of parent involvement on youth's school success and she has several publications in that area. She has worked as an Evaluation and Research Specialist at the University of Pittsburgh's Office of Child Development since 2001 where her evaluation research focuses on educational programs and youth development programs.

Currently, Dr. Barnard is evaluating the regional Stars TA program examining technical assistance and Keystone Stars attainment, a local Early Head Start program promoting early literacy in children, an after-school program focusing on increasing academic achievement for elementary students in low-income communities, and a community-based adolescent pregnancy prevention program.

Anne E. Farber, PhD, is Director of Planning and Evaluation at the University of Pittsburgh Office of Child Development. In this capacity, she promotes a collaborative approach with human service and policy agencies to build organizational capacity and quality through program evaluation. In addition to conducting program evaluations and policy studies, Dr. Farber and her team provide technical assistance and training to agency professionals in monitoring and self-evaluation.

Previously, Dr. Farber served as Executive Director of the Louisiana State Planning Council on Developmental Disabilities, where she provided leadership in promoting inclusion through public policy analysis, technical assistance and training, legislative initiatives, project funding, and advocacy. She obtained her BA degree in psychology from the University of Pennsylvania and her MA and PhD degrees in Developmental Psychology from Peabody College of Vanderbilt University.

Richard Fiene, PhD, is the Director of the Capital Area Health and Human Development Institute and Associate Professor of Human

Development and Family Studies in the College of Health and Human Development at the Pennsylvania State University. As a research psychologist, he has spent his professional career conducting research on child care quality and community-based research. His research at the national and state levels has centered on child care licensing, early childhood program accreditation, and child care and early childhood development training systems and their impact on child care quality, in particular on infant child care.

Previously, Dr. Fiene was Director of the Division of Licensing Systems and Research in the Office of Licensing and Regulatory Management, Pennsylvania Department of Public Welfare; Special Assistant to the Deputy Secretary, Pennsylvania Office of Children, Youth and Families; Co-Chair of the Cross Systems Licensing Project in the Pennsylvania Departments of Public Welfare, Aging, and Health; and Training Director for the Child Care/Early Childhood Development Training System. He is a member of the American Psychological Society and the Society for Research in Child Development, and Fellow of the Pennsylvania Psychological Association.

Jeffery Fraser is a freelance writer and former newspaper journalist, based in Pittsburgh. He spent 17 years in journalism, including 10 years as an editor and reporter for the Pittsburgh Press, the city's leading newspaper at the time. As a freelance writer, he has written for major foundations, hospitals, state and local government, universities, newspapers, and magazines. His freelance work includes the final report of the Mayor's Commission on Public Education, an 18-month examination of the city's public school system; a comprehensive report on child welfare issues in Allegheny County based on a two-year investigation of Juvenile Court and improvements to its dependency branch; an investigative report on the effectiveness of a mental health court recently established in Allegheny County; and reports examining several early education issues for the Governor's Task Force on Early Care and Education. Since 1993, he has written extensively on children and family issues for the University of Pittsburgh Office of Child Development.

Martha Woodward Isler is currently the Director of Public Policy for the United Way of Westmoreland County School Readiness Initiative. She is also a Certified Trainer/Consultant for The National Association for Regulatory Administration (NARA). Previously, Ms. Isler directed The Early Childhood Initiative, a community project to help low-income preschool children succeed in school and beyond. Ms. Isler also directed Child Care Partnerships (CCP), the resource, referral, and administrative agency overseeing child subsidy for Allegheny County, and managed

Employers & Child Care, a project of the Greater Pittsburgh Chamber of Commerce.

Ms. Isler has also held positions in Pennsylvania as Executive Director of the Governor's Commonwealth Child Development Committee, and Director of the Bureau of Child Development Programs. She established the first training program for child care licensing staff and provided leadership for follow through on the application and enforcement of licensing and registration standards. Ms. Isler's educational background includes a Bachelor of Science degree from the Pennsylvania State University and a postgraduate permanent state teacher's certification.

Louise Kaczmarek, PhD, is Associate Professor of Special Education at the University of Pittsburgh. She coordinates the Early Intervention and the Early Childhood Education Programs. Her accomplishments include principle investigator or co-principle investigator on many federally funded research, inservice training, model demonstration, and personnel preparation projects; author and co-author of numerous journal articles and book chapters; co-author of a book on social-communication interventions; and presenter at numerous conferences and inservice workshops. Her research interests include family-centered practices, classroom-based language intervention, social skills interventions, and interdisciplinary teaming.

Gwen G. Morgan, MS, is Senior Fellow for Child Care Policy at Wheelock College, where she founded the Center for Career Development in Early Care and Education (1992) and also the Advanced Seminars for Child Care Administrators (1975).

Ms. Morgan is a co-founder of WFD (originally, Work/Family Directions), a Boston-based management and consulting firm that helps large multi-sited companies develop solutions to address work and family issues. As a senior consultant from 1982 to 1999, she helped to develop initiatives for several large companies and also for the American Business Collaboration for Quality Dependent Care Initiatives. Her interest in child care took root when starting an employer-sponsored work-site center at KLH in Cambridge, Massachusetts in 1966.

Suh-Ruu Ou, PhD, is Research Associate at the Institute of Child Development, University of Minnesota, Twin Cities. She has been on the staff of the Chicago Longitudinal Study (CLS) since 1998. Her areas of specialization are program evaluation, research methodology, educational attainment, and the effects of early childhood intervention. She received her PhD in Social Welfare from the University of Wisconsin–Madison.

Arthur J. Reynolds, PhD, is a professor of social work, educational psychology, and human development at the University of Wisconsin–Madison. He directs the Chicago Longitudinal Study, one of the largest studies of the effects of early childhood intervention. A focal point of the 20-year, on-going project is the long-term educational and social effects of the Child-Parent Centers, a Title I preschool and early school-age program. The study is now in the adult phase and is examining impacts on education, economic well-being, health, and family outcomes. He also studies the child and family predictors of adolescent and young adult development. Dr. Reynolds is interested more broadly in child development and social policy, evaluation research, and prevention science.

Mary Wolfson is a doctoral student at the University of Pittsburgh in the Department of Psychology in Education. Her research interests include teacher and student relationships, equity in education, and educational policy. Previously, she worked on learning research in the area of mathematics, as a member of the Dr. Robert S. Siegler laboratory at Carnegie Mellon University. Ms. Wolfson holds a Bachelor of Science in Education from Indiana University of Pennsylvania, where she graduated with the honor of Magna Cum Laude.

Introduction

Young children's experiences in the first five years of life can have a dramatic, long-term effect on their life-long functioning. These experiences not only affect children's readiness for school, but can also influence the quality of their relationships with others and their ability to grow up to be effective citizens (Bowman, Donovan, & Burns, 2001). Thus, the early childhood years have implications not only for the children and their families, but also are of central concern to the social and economic health of the country.

A GROWING INTEREST IN EARLY CHILDHOOD CARE AND EDUCATION

During the past few decades, a number of forces have created greater interest in the needs of young children and their families. First, developmental scientists have made major advances in understanding the developing child as well as what factors influence the child's development. These findings not only provide dramatic new information on the child's early brain and its growth, but, more important, they also have demonstrated that the quality of the child's relationships and the degree of cognitive stimulation in the early years have a profound impact on the child's later cognitive, emotional, and social growth. Sensitive, responsive care and quality education can establish an important foundation on which later academic achievement and success develop. The ability of stimulating early social and cognitive contexts to benefit subsequent developmental outcomes suggests that they pose tremendous opportunities to influence children's development during the first few years of life.

A second factor influences public interest in and concern for early care and education: Family life has changed dramatically over the past three decades. These changes include dramatic shifts in (1) the number of two-wage-earner families—an almost 100% increase in the number of mothers of young children who are employed; (2) a continuing rise in the number of children living in single-parent homes; (3) the persistence of poverty for many young children and the growing gap between the poor and the wealthy; (4) significant disparities in developmental outcomes for advantaged versus disadvantaged children as well as continuing ethnic and racial inequities in access to quality health and educational services; and (5) further devolution of funding and responsibilities from federal to state and local governments to develop policies, programs, and services for young children and their families. These changes have come at the same time that employability has been more strongly linked to education, and citizens and policymakers have shown greater attention to improving the quality of our nation's educational systems. As a result, many families are struggling with the tension of balancing work and family responsibilities. A consequence of these changes is that someone other than parents cares for children during much of the day. As a result, early care and education enrollments of children ages three to eight have grown dramatically.

Quality early care and education holds the promise of helping children start school "ready to learn," greatly improving their chances of enjoying success in the classroom and later in life. Conversely, entering school academically or socially behind places many children at risk of staying behind, doing poorly, eventually dropping out, earning less money, and needing more public support during their adult lives.

How can we invest in our children's early development to ensure subsequent academic, social, economic, and emotional success? This question has attracted widespread attention from early childhood professionals, program administrators, public school personnel, early childhood advocates, professionals in early childhood system development and coordination, the business community, and policymakers.

HOW THIS BOOK CAN HELP

This book provides descriptions of programs and practices in early childhood that show evidence of some success in answering this question. It is written in non-technical language that summarizes results and program details, and thus is designed for administrators, staff developers, teacher educators, and other educational professionals, as well as university-level educational faculty. The primary goal of this book is to provide an informative and user-friendly overview of evidence-based programs, practices, and policies with descriptions of exemplar programs and explanations of effective characteristics. As such, this book identifies programs that have demonstrated records of effectiveness, identifies characteristics of programs and services that have positively affected children's social and cognitive outcomes, reviews practices of related services (e.g., family services, transition practices, non-school-hour programs) that enhance and prolong the benefits of early care and education, and provides estimated costs of implementation. In addition, this book reviews what is needed to prepare professional personnel for the increased size and better skilled workforce that will be needed to fulfill the promise of early childhood care and education. Finally, it provides recommendations for programs, services, and policies that can facilitate the implementation of effective early services.

RISK AND PROTECTIVE FACTORS

To accomplish this goal, this book examines the full range of evidence-based school readiness strategies for early childhood care and education. The editors and authors used the concepts of risk and protective factors in understanding how the child's experiences may influence his or her cognitive and social development in the early years. Risk- and protective-factor models provide a broad framework for understanding how to target services that are likely to reduce academic and social problems in childhood. Many of the effective programs and practices reviewed in this book are intended to reduce risk and promote protective factors to improve the child's school and interpersonal success.

Risk Factors and Their Operation

A number of factors have been identified that are associated with increased risk for school failure and social-emotional problems. In the period of ages three to eight, major risk factors are

1. *Family circumstances:* low income and low social class, mental illness in the family, maternal depression, child abuse, stressful life events, family disorganization, and family conflict;

2. *Skill development delays:* low intelligence, attention difficulties, emotional dysregulation;

3. *Ecological risks:* neighborhood disorganization, extreme poverty, racial injustice, and unemployment.

Research supports a number of principles about the operation of risk factors. First, development is complex, and it is unlikely that there is a single cause or risk factor for later difficulties. Second, there are multiple pathways to later difficulties; different combinations of risk factors may lead to the same outcome. Third, risk factors occur not only at the level of individual children and families, but also at the neighborhood, school, and community levels. However, not all children who experience such risks develop later problems; some are resilient, and it is not clear what promotes this resiliency. Finally, culture influences many aspects of child development and is reflected in child rearing beliefs and practices; this is an area that is understudied and less well understood (Shonkoff & Phillips, 2000).

Most of the risk factors related to school readiness also predict later academic and social problems, such as delinquency and school drop-out. Efforts in early childhood to reduce the effects of risk should focus on reduction of multiple, interacting risk factors that may have direct effects on multiple outcomes (both academic and social).

Protective Factors and Their Operation

Protective factors reduce the likelihood of troublesome outcomes. Protective factors include

1. *Characteristics of the individual,* such as temperamental characteristics, cognitive skills, and social skills;

2. *Quality of the child's interactions with others,* including secure attachment to parents and supportive relationships with other adults;

3. *Characteristics of communities,* including quality early education and care, quality schools, and comprehensive supports for families in need.

Successful programs are often targeted at children with multiple risk factors and attempt to promote the development of protective factors.

LEVELS OF EVIDENCE REGARDING PROGRAMS AND BEST PRACTICES

This book covers a wide scope of programs, practices, and policies for children ages three to eight. It includes programs and practices for all children, as well as for those in need of more intensive intervention because of significant risk factors or specific disabilities. It covers programs that involve home visiting, comprehensive family services, parent education, family and center-based early care and education, follow-on programs for children ages six to eight, non-school-hour (afterschool) programs, and the transition to kindergarten.

There is great variability in the quality and extent of research evidence supporting the effectiveness of the wide variety and types of programs and practices that are reviewed in this volume. Programs having better evidence are given greater attention. However, it should be remembered that some topics in early childhood cannot easily be studied with standard experimental research designs and thus rely on less rigorous forms of analysis. The literature reviews rely on the highest levels of evidence available, and there is considerable variability in the levels of evidence from topic to topic. The literature presented in these chapters is illustrative, not exhaustive; it summarizes the most important programs, practices, and policies given the current state of the research.

REFERENCES

Bowman, B. T., Donovan, M. S., & Burns, M. S. (Eds.). (2001). *Eager to learn: Educating our preschoolers.* Washington, DC: National Academy Press.

Shonkoff, J. P., & Phillips, D. A. (Eds.). (2000). *From neurons to neighborhoods: The science of early childhood development.* Washington, DC: National Academy Press.

PART I

Evidence-Based Practices

1

School Readiness

Definitions, Best Practices, Assessments, and Cost

Kelly E. Mehaffie and Jeffery Fraser

S tarting school ready to learn gives children tremendous advantages that improve their chances of enjoying success in the classroom and later in life. Entering school behind, however, places many children at risk of staying behind, doing poorly, eventually dropping out, and enduring other troublesome outcomes. Research indicates that half of the achievement gap between poor and minority students, which the federal No Child Left Behind legislation has focused upon closing, is evident at the time of children's entry into school (Lee & Burkam, 2002). This gap is pronounced well before children start school, already evident in the infant and toddler years (Rothstein, 2004).

THE IMPORTANCE OF EARLY LEARNING

Recent brain and child development research demonstrates the importance of early learning for needed primary school skills as well as lifespan development. All infants and young children need a nurturing environment for physical, social, emotional, and cognitive development, particularly to develop trusting relationships with others—the foundation for a successful future. A nurturing environment, a common theme in the school readiness research, means an environment in which children receive constant and consistent parental caregiving; adequate food, nutrition, and health care; help in maximizing physical growth, preliteracy cognition, and socialization skills; and appropriate continuous supervision to safely explore their world. If these fundamental needs are not met, children may be at risk for not being ready for school and healthy life-long learning (Bruner, Floyd, & Copeman, 2003).

The future well-being of today's young children is not everything that is at stake. With a large number of today's working men and women set to retire over the next 20 years, the generation that has yet to enter school will account for a large share of the workforce and become a significant factor in determining the future economic strength and vitality of the United States. Business and community leaders are trying to cope with an unqualified workforce. The main complaint from this group is that too many job applicants simply do not have the interpersonal skills necessary to work in the business environment. More and more of these leaders are speaking out on the need to invest in early childhood services to improve the school readiness of young children (Committee for Economic Development, 2002; Rolnick & Gruenwald, 2003).

DEFINITIONS OF SCHOOL READINESS

There is broad consensus among scholars that school readiness is multidimensional–that health and physical development, social and emotional development, language and literacy, approaches to learning, and cognitive development all are independent and yet interrelated aspects of "what children know and can do" and that there is no single metric to determine a child's school readiness (National Education Goals Panel, 1991; Shonkoff & Phillips, 2000). At the same time, there is much debate over precisely what skills and supports should be part of public strategies to help children become ready for school (e.g., learning letters and numbers, learning how to take turns and sit still, eating healthy meals). Since President George W. Bush signed the No Child Left Behind Act (NCLB) into law in January 2002, the national focus on school readiness has been on helping children develop early literacy skills. Clearly, the focus of many public programs and services, and of the measurement and accountability systems for them, has been on the cognitive and literacy development dimensions.

Although these cognitive and early literacy skills are important components of readiness for school, other dimensions are equally important. Two prominent national groups have worked to define specifically the skills and supports necessary for school readiness: The National Education Goals Panel (NEGP) and the Head Start Child Outcomes Framework. Their definitions are discussed next.

The National Education Goals Panel

In 1991, the National Education Goals Panel (NEGP) developed a broad definition of school readiness based on child development research that includes a combination of three factors: (1) the readiness of children ("what children know and can do"), (2) the readiness of schools, and (3) the readiness of family and community supports (National Education Goals Panel, 1991).

Readiness of Children

The NEGP established its definition of readiness to include physical, social, and emotional well-being in addition to cognitive components, and it identified five dimensions of early development considered critical to preparing children to learn (Kagan, Moore, & Bredekamp, 1995):

Physical well-being and motor development. This category includes health; growth rate; physical abilities, such as fine motor skills; and conditions before and after birth, such as low birth weight and toxic environmental exposure.

Social and emotional development. Social development (the ability to interact with others) includes being able to take turns and enter play groups. Emotional development includes children's ability to understand the feelings of other people and express their own feelings.

Approaches to learning. Approaches to learning refer to a child's inclination and use of skills and knowledge and includes curiosity, enthusiasm, temperament, and cultural values.

Language development. Language development includes verbal language (listening, speaking, and vocabulary) and early literacy, such as being able to assign sounds to letter combinations and understand basic story structure.

Cognition and general knowledge. This category ranges from knowing about shapes and numbers to being able to identify similarities and differences in objects, events, and people.

Readiness of Schools

Schools themselves play a key role in the readiness of children to learn. Kindergarten teachers report that between 10% to more than 30% of their children do not have the skills necessary to be successful in school (Shore, 1998). Just as children need the opportunity to develop these skills, schools need to be ready to accept children with diverse backgrounds, abilities, and needs. The NEGP identified 10 key research-based practices of ready schools. Ready schools are prepared to receive children from diverse backgrounds and to support the learning and development of all young children. The following 10 practices are outlined in an NEGP publication (Shore, 1998).

1. *Ready schools smooth the transition between home and school.* For many children, the transition to school is stressful. Schools can work through this difficult time by connecting with parents and the community to understand each child and develop an appropriate school program. Despite the need for smooth transitions, few schools actively engage in adequate transition practices (Kraft-Sayre & Pianta, 2000).

2. *Ready schools strive for continuity between early care and education programs and elementary schools.* By reaching out and connecting to community early childhood programs, Head Start, families, etc., elementary schools can help to ease this transition for children. Joint planning and inservice training of staff between early childhood programs and schools can help promote a sense of continuity for education and learning philosophies for young children.

3. *Ready schools help children learn and make sense of their complex and exciting world.* Ready schools are able to help children use their new knowledge to make sense of their world and problem solve. Schools do this by using diverse curricula and instructional approaches, offering high quality instruction, using appropriate levels (pace and content) of instruction, creating incentives for learning, using time effectively, and learning in the context of relationships.

4. *Ready schools are committed to the success of every child.* Ready schools acknowledge children's individual needs; present an environment that is conducive to learning and exploration; exhibit an ongoing awareness of the impact of poverty and race; have the capacity to meet special needs in regular classrooms whenever possible; and ensure language-minority children age-appropriate, culturally sensitive, and challenging curricula and instruction.

5. *Ready schools are committed to the success of every teacher and every adult who interacts with children during the school day.* Ready schools hire knowledgeable staff and consistently offer opportunities for enhanced professional development, encourage mentoring and collaboration, support teachers in their lesson planning with time

and materials, foster teamwork, and encourage participation in performance-based assessments and national certification. In addition, ready schools encourage and host opportunities for school staff to interact and engage in professional development opportunities with staff from early childhood education programs as well as higher education institutions in the community.

6. *Ready schools introduce or expand approaches that have been shown to raise achievement.* Ready schools are aware of current research regarding educational strategies and use this information to provide prompt and supportive intervention; parent involvement strategies; flexible approaches to school and classroom organization, staffing, and grouping (class size, classroom staffing, and mixed-age grouping); and research and dissemination.

7. *Ready schools are learning organizations that alter practices and programs if they do not benefit children.* Ready schools avoid or eliminate the following common practices that do not show lasting benefits: retention and extra-year programs, "redshirting" (electing to delay kindergarten entry), denying school entry, and "pushing down" or "hothousing" (using the curriculum of an older grade in a younger grade classroom).

8. *Ready schools serve children in communities.* Ready schools form symbiotic relationships and collaborations with services and supports in the communities in which their children live (health, educational, social, etc.). These relationships allow a seamless system for referrals and out-of-school educational opportunities (e.g., museums, libraries), plus a sense of civic and community responsibility for all parties.

9. *Ready schools take responsibility for results.* Ready schools accept responsibility for individual children's learning and accomplishments by providing each child with the supports he or she needs to be successful in school. Ready schools also inform parents and communities of their mission and goals, how well they are being met, and how they are assessing them.

10. *Ready schools have strong leadership.* Leaders of ready schools have a vision that is based on the needs of the children and families in the community and on sound research, and they aspire to lead children to high standards of learning. Leaders of ready schools also are committed to guiding faculty and parents in obtaining the vision and communicating the ups and downs of success. Ready

schools require skilled teachers and maintenance of strong expectations and educational standards for all students (Blank, 2003; Rothstein, 2004).

Family and Community Supports

The NEGP underscored the importance of family and community supports in six key aspects of school readiness (National Education Goals Panel, 1997):

1. Access to high quality preschool increases children's chances of succeeding in school and later in life.

2. Decades of research have shown that high quality early childhood programming benefits children and communities.

3. Support and training for parents enhances their effectiveness as their children's first teacher.

4. Community supports are essential to family well-being.

5. Good health and nutrition allow children to enter school mentally alert and physically sound.

6. When children's physical needs are met, they are better able to explore and learn.

Head Start Child Outcomes Framework

The Head Start Child Outcomes Framework was released in 2000 to guide Head Start programs in planning assessments of their programs and children, rather than to prescribe a checklist to gauge children's progress. The Framework contains components similar to the NEGP definition of readiness. It encompasses eight general Domains, 27 Domain Elements, and Indicators of children's development and behaviors. The Domains, Elements, and Indicators comprise a framework showing what is necessary for children to be ready for school. Information from these Domains, Elements, and Indicators reveals children's progress in the form of teacher and home visitor observations, analysis of samples of children's work and performance, parent reports, or direct assessment of preschool-age children (U.S. Department of Health and Human Services Administration for Children and Families, 2003). The eight Head Start Domains and their Elements are listed in Box 1.1 and paired to the five NEGP dimensions of readiness in children.

**Box 1.1   The Five NEGP Dimensions and the Eight
Head Start Domains and Elements**

NEGP Dimensions	**Head Start Domains** **Head Start Domain Elements**

Physical Well-Being and Motor Development	Physical Health and Development
	  Gross Motor Skills
	  Fine Motor Skills
	  Health Status and Practices

Social and Emotional Development	Social and Emotional Development
	  Self-Concept
	  Self-Control
	  Cooperation
	  Social Relationship
	Knowledge of Families
	  and Communities

Approaches Toward Learning	Approaches to Learning
	  Initiative and Curiosity
	  Engagement and Persistence
	  Reasoning and Problem Solving

Language Development	Literacy
	  Phonological Awareness*
	  Book Knowledge and Appreciation*
	  Print Awareness and Concepts*
	  Early Writing
	  Alphabet Knowledge
	
	Language Development
	  Listening and Understanding
	  Speaking and Communicating

Cognition and General Knowledge	Mathematics
	  Numbers and Operations*
	  Geometry and Spatial Sense
	  Patterns and Measurement
	
	Science
	  Scientific Skills and Methods
	  Scientific Knowledge
	
	Creative Arts
	  Music
	  Art
	  Movement (also fits NEGP Motor Goal)
	  Dramatic Play

*NOTE: Indicates those Head Start Child Outcomes Framework Domain Elements that are legislatively mandated.

THE INTERSECTION OF READINESS FACTORS

Child Trends' analysis of the Early Childhood Longitudinal Study, Kindergarten Cohort (ECLS-K; Wertheimer, Croan, Moore, & Hair, 2003) showed that in 1998–1999, 56% of kindergarteners were lagging behind in health, social and emotional development, or cognition, and 37% of those lagging behind in at least one area (21% of all children) did so in more than one area. While the dimensions of school readiness are conceptually distinct, children often are behind on more than one dimension and, when behind on more than one dimension, face substantially more challenges in catching up with their peers.

Further, research and assessments have demonstrated that differences in children's socioeconomic background, experience of parenting behaviors, brain development, and health contribute to racial and ethic disparities in being ready for school. Best practices show that both parenting and preschool programs can benefit families and children in preparation for school (Haskins & Rouse, 2005).

RESEARCH INFORMING SCHOOL READINESS FACTORS

Age is the criterion most often used to determine eligibility for kindergarten in many states. In some states, local districts make decisions about how children should be assessed for readiness and kindergarten entry and how the data should be used (see below for information on readiness assessment; Saluja, Scott-Little, & Clifford, 2000). Some states have agreed upon and adopted a statewide definition of school readiness and begun to establish statewide measures across the five dimensions of school readiness (e.g., Maryland, Minnesota, Vermont, and Missouri). Most of these have adopted some form of work sampling to measure the five dimensions (Bruner & Copeman, 2003; Maryland State Department of Education, 2002).

As of 2003, twenty seven states had standards for preschool-age children covering at least one developmental domain or content area, and only four states had standards pertaining to infant and toddler-age children as well as preschoolers (Scott-Little, Kagan, & Frelow, 2003).

Many programs and methods to improve school readiness are multidimensional, but various initiatives sway more toward one dimension of readiness or development than another. For example, most of the states in the survey that developed early learning standards had a focus on language and literacy development. Social-emotional development was one of the areas of least focus (Scott-Little, Kagan, & Frelow, 2003).

The following sections represent examples of research perspectives on programs dedicated to improving early childhood outcomes in the indicated areas.

Health Development

The health of children during their early years can influence school readiness and school success. Good health and nutrition begins prenatally with parenting education and maternal health supports. Lack of prenatal care, low birth weight, inadequate nutrition, and lack of proper immunizations can affect a child's cognitive and behavioral development and thus readiness for and performance in school (Child Trends, 2000; Grantham-McGregor, 1995; Gross, Brooks-Gunn, Spiker, 1992; Korenman, Miller, & Sjaastad, 1995; Liaw & Brooks-Gunn, 1993). Further, lack of dental care can affect children's nutritional intake and physical growth (e.g., pain from tooth decay discourages eating) as well as their ability to concentrate and learn (Platt & Cabezas, 2000).

Several programs help to combat some of the heath risk associated with school readiness.

- Federal Special Supplement Nutrition Program for Women, Infants, and Children (WIC): provides nutrition to pregnant women
- Food Stamp program: provides nutrition to families
- Head Start program: provides children with dental screenings, preventive services, and offers parenting education
- Medicaid and State Child Health Insurance Programs (SCHIP): include an Early, Periodic Screening, Diagnosis, and Treatment (EPSDT) provision that can identify and address health needs. Now, more than one-quarter of the nation's children are enrolled in these programs.

Cognitive and other gains were seen among low birth weight babies in the Infant Health and Development Study, a randomized trial of an intervention that offered pediatric monitoring, home visits, access to a child development center, and other supports. At age 36 months, children had gains in cognitive, visual-motor, spatial skill, and language development (McCormick, McCarton, Tonascia, & Brooks-Gunn, 1993).

Vision

Nationally, it is estimated that 50% or more of minority and low-income children have vision problems that interfere with their ability to do academic work; this is double the rate among other children (Gould & Gould, 2003;

Orfield, Basa, & Yun, 2001). These visual deficits include difficulties with tracking, caused by insufficient activities that train the eye to develop hand-eye coordination, depth perception, and eye movement across a printed page—key elements for learning to read (Rothstein, 2004). Some simple activities, such as vision screening and corrective actions, have produced substantial gains in reading readiness (Rothstein, 2004).

Environmental Toxins

Exposure to environmental toxins, such as lead, also can inhibit development and limit children's school readiness. Lead exposure is higher for many children living in poverty. Eight percent of poor and minority children have highly problematic levels of lead in their blood (U.S. Department of Health and Human Services, 1999). Even low levels of lead exposure have been shown to cause cognitive deficits (e.g., IQ, reading, learning abilities), shortened attention spans, hyperactivity, and stunted physical growth (Child Trends, 2000). Prevention through parent and community education and proper lead abatement is the only treatment for lead exposure. Rhode Island recognized its high level of lead exposure among children and took a variety of corrective actions that dramatically reduced that exposure (Rhode Island Kids Count, 2003).

The Individuals With Disabilities Education Act, through its Part C Infant and Toddlers Program, provides early intervention services to address developmental delays. While these programs represent "entitlements to such services," state programs often are not well developed or comprehensive, and many eligible children do not receive early screening and follow-up services to address their health concerns.

Emotional Development

Children who are emotionally well adjusted have a much greater chance of early school success. On the other hand, children who struggle to pay attention, follow directions, get along with others, and control their anger do less well in school (McLelland, Morrison, & Holmes, 2000). However, emotional problems that threaten outcomes can be identified and their influence diminished through early treatment involving focused parenting education and training as well as through preventive interventions in preschool settings (Child Trends, 2000).

Studies using randomized experimental designs suggest that interventions addressing children's emotional problems both at home and school are effective in reducing disruptive behavior by improving social and emotional skills and reading readiness (Raver, 2002). The Kauffman

Foundation produced a major report on the social and emotional development of young children that identifies effective and promising practices and highlights the interrelationship between social and emotional development and language, literacy, and cognitive development (Kauffman Early Education Exchange, 2002).

Family and Home Environments

Strengthening families is another approach to improving school readiness. A large body of research underscores the importance of the family and home environment in early development. Economic status, particularly poverty, is associated with negative child outcomes. Poor children are more likely to have health problems and lower scores on measures of cognitive development than more affluent children (Brooks-Gunn, Britto, & Brady, 1999; Stipek & Ryan, 1997). Approaches to intervention include raising family income through jobs, income subsidies, and other means and providing quality child care and other services.

Studies suggest children do better in school when raised by both parents in a home in which conflict is minimal. However, in single-parent families, financial support from the absent parent, usually the father, has been associated with children's school success (Barber, Axinn, & Thornton, 1999; Huston et al., 2001; Moore et al., 1997; Morrison & Coiro, 1999).

Addressing any psychological problems of parents may benefit young children. Studies suggest children are at greater risk of emotional and behavior problems if their mothers are depressed or have other mental health problems (Child Trends, 2000).

Parents, particularly those who themselves lack strong educational backgrounds, need support and training to be able to help their children become ready for school. A good parent-child relationship shows children an important model of social relationships with others.

The earliest years of life (from birth to two) are exceedingly important to children's lifelong development, particularly in setting the social and emotional foundation and for early language acquisition; it is at these years that parental nurturing and support are critical to child growth and development (Kauffman Early Education Exchange, 2002; Shonkoff & Phillips, 2000). Further, increasing the supports

> The Parents as Teachers (PAT) program provides home visitors who help parents bring about the social-emotional development of their children (Wagner & Clayton, 1999), and many parenting education programs also help connect parents to social and emotional supports for themselves.

available for parents (e.g., mental health, physical health, occupational training, etc.) allows the family unit to function more efficiently, and thus increases the chances of positive child outcomes and school readiness.

Child Care and Early Education

Research shows that all children, and particularly low-income children, can benefit from high quality programming (Kagan & Cohen, 1997). Children whose families have lower levels of education and incomes are less likely to attend a high quality program (National Education Goals Panel, 1997), primarily because they are not available, not affordable, or not convenient for the family. Access to quality child care and preschool has emerged as a critical factor in the readiness of children to enter school, learn, and succeed. Quality programs offer children appropriate enrichment, small class sizes, and ample attention from well-trained, caring teachers and staff. Research shows that certain components of quality child care programs are crucial. (See Box 1.2.)

The research demonstrates that only high quality child care programs are able to produce lasting effects on children, and those effects are greatest for children in low-income families. In addition, low quality care can be detrimental to all children regardless of family income. Both the Cost and Quality Outcomes Study and the National Institute of Child Health and Human Development (NICHD) Study of Early Child Care show the important influence of quality care and education on children's overall development. Sadly, only a minority of child care settings in the United States now meets the criteria of good to excellent quality. Studies have shown that one key measure of quality is the training and credentials of the child care workforce (Ackerman, 2003).

The Carolina Abecedarian Project, a randomized experimental trial, reported significant gains among children given high quality child care and education from age three months to kindergarten. At 18 months, they had higher scores on IQ tests than nonprogram children, and, from elementary school to early adulthood, they had higher reading and math scores (Frank Porter Graham Child Development Center, 2001).

As efforts to improve quality of child care proceed, issues of diversity and cultural competence need to be recognized. Young children represent this country's most diverse age group in terms of race, ethnicity, and language. At the same time, the current credentialed early childhood workforce is not sufficiently diverse to meet the needs of the children it serves. Developing a culturally competent workforce requires investing in professional development that attracts this workforce.

**Box 1.2   Quality Characteristics of Early
Care and Education Services**

Well-educated staff specifically trained in the child development area and related fields.

Consistency of staff over time, often promoted by adequate salaries and benefits, reasonable workloads, and pleasant and supportive working conditions.

Low child-staff ratios and small group sizes are necessary for staff to interact effectively with individual children, develop relationships, and provide the "teachable moment" that defines developmentally appropriate practices.

Comprehensive educational and social services available or by referral that are directed specifically at each individual (e.g., parent, child) and domains of desired improvement (e.g., child cognitive, social-emotional, parenting skills, drug and alcohol problems).

Sufficient extent (e.g., hours per day, weeks per year, years in program) *and program intensity* (e.g., time on task, direct instruction on learning tasks, etc.) are necessary to produce benefits.

Supportive and regular supervision of staff by knowledgeable administrators. The benefits of training staff are often achieved only if there is supportive supervision.

Plans for developing a rapport with families based on mutual respect and support, for encouraging *the involvement of parents* (both custodial and non-custodial fathers and mothers) in the program, and for ensuring that staff and curriculum are culturally competent.

Systematic program monitoring and evaluation to continuously improve programs and benchmark progress.

In addition, a great deal of care provided to children is not in licensed or registered, formal care settings, but through family, friend, and neighbor care. There is promising work underway to support these caregivers and increase their capacity to enrich the development of the children under their care (Stahl, Sazer O'Donnell, Sprague, & Lopez, 2003). Up to half of all care provided to children while their parents work is provided in such nonregistered or licensed settings (Tout, Zaslow, Romano Papillo, & Vandivere, 2001).

There is a marked difference between many early care and education classrooms and kindergarten classrooms. With the advent of NCLB, focus in the classroom is even more pointed toward academic goals. For many children, these changes can be so intense that benefits gained from quality early childhood programming begin to fade in this new environment when the transition is harsh. States increasingly are working to align early childhood standards with early elementary school standards (Scott-Little, Kagan, & Frelow, 2003). In fact, the National School Readiness Indicators Initiative currently works with 17 states that developed sets of school readiness indicators for children from birth through age eight for the purposes of tracking progress in meeting key goals for children and to inform public policy (Rhode Island Kids Count, 2005).

Community

In general, the effects of neighborhoods are most often associated with the socioeconomic status (SES) of their residents. Studies consistently report that when children live among high-SES neighbors, they tend to be better prepared when they enter school and more likely to succeed, and this is over and above what would be expected on the basis of their family SES alone.

In the Infant Health and Development Program (IHDP), no neighborhood effects were seen until children turned three years old. Then, researchers noted, living in a high-SES neighborhood tended to have a positive effect on children's IQ scores (Brooks-Gunn, Duncan, Klebanov, & Sealand, 1993). Relocating families out of poor neighborhoods is associated with children doing better in school. In Chicago's Gautreaux Project, a study of quasi-experimental design, children who were moved from public housing to the more affluent suburbs were more likely to stay in school and to go on to college than their peers who remained in the city (Rosenbaum, Kulieke, & Rubinowitz, 1988). At the same time, relocating families can simply further impoverish the neighborhoods from which they have moved, placing children who remain in those neighborhoods at even greater risk of starting school behind or staying behind. There also is evidence that schools in poor neighborhoods, given needed supports, can succeed at much higher levels with the students they serve (Blank, 2003; Rothstein, 2004).

Many schools that are *not* "ready for children" by the NEGP definition are located in low-income areas and serve children who are more likely to be at risk because of family, community, or environmental factors. Further, many of these schools do not have the resources to hire qualified teachers and dedicate monies to addressing these children's specific needs (Lee & Burkam, 2002). Experts also agree that family and community supports are crucial to children's development and readiness.

> Communities need to encourage schools and early childhood programs to communicate with each other and with related community supports.

Communities need to organize, demand, and support high quality early childhood programs not only for the developmental needs of the children, but also as an investment in the future workforce and economy.

Families need, as well, to be educated on how to recognize and choose high quality care for their children.

ASSESSING READINESS

Although all children are born with the capacity for learning (Shonkoff & Phillips, 2000), assessing school readiness is important to the education of young children. Assessments help measure and monitor the current state of children's development and knowledge and can be used to guide classroom and individual kindergarten programming.

While there is general consensus that school readiness is multidimensional, how and whether to assess children at kindergarten entry is a controversial topic. The National Research Council (Bowman, Donovan, & Burns, 2001) cautions against the use of readiness assessments for determining whether children should enter kindergarten or for any "high stakes" testing that judges the performance of individual children. The Council stresses that development in children is highly individualized and there is a wide range of developmentally appropriate skills from child to child.

A child's development can progress faster or slower day to day, week to week rather than uniformly and consistently (Scott-Little, Kagan, Frelow, 2003), so assessments given *at only one point in time* can be very misleading about the future skills of a particular child.

Holding children back from school entry is considered poor educational practice, although it is still in use in some districts (Shonkoff & Phillips, 2000). At the same time, there are appropriate uses of assessments of young children at the time they enter school—for identification of special needs, for use in instruction, for program evaluation, and for broad-based tracking of trends. The NEGP recommends that assessments should be developed particular to these uses and warns against the dangers of misusing them.

Use of Assessments

Most assessments revolve around focused planning for the individual child's education and are completed for one or more of the following purposes: (1) to track a child into a particular program, (2) to diagnose a special need or special gift that would necessitate more individualized instruction, or (3) as a composite to determine appropriate curriculum and general instruction for the entire classroom (Bruner & Copeman, 2003). The national Good Start, Grow Smart initiative (2002) pushes the assessment of children's language and literacy development in preschool, thus raising existing issues of the use and administration of readiness assessment for this young population (Scott-Little, Kagan, Frelow, 2003).

Saluja and colleagues (2000) reviewed position statements of various early learning groups and organizations on documenting children's readiness and found common recommendations for assessments. Based on this review, a good readiness assessment should do the following:

- Benefit children and the adults who work with children.
- Be used for the purposes for which it is designed.
- Be valid and reliable.
- Be age appropriate, using naturalistic observations to collect information as children interact in "real-life" situations.
- Be holistic, collecting information on all developmental domains (physical, social, emotional, and cognitive).
- Be linguistically and culturally appropriate.
- Collect information through a variety of processes and multiple sources (collection of children's work, observations of children, interviews with children, parent reports, etc.).
- Be used to guide instruction and not to determine children's placement in school.

A survey of early childhood experts (Horton & Bowman, 2002) reported the three most important characteristics of an assessment system to be (1) having a matched curriculum and assessment of children's knowledge, (2) having teacher meetings to discuss the assessment and program, and (3) having a monitoring self-study process. Portfolios, developmental screenings, and parent evaluations were also rated highly with the disclaimer that these procedures need to be completed by well-trained personnel to be beneficial. These types of assessments do take considerable time for the teacher to conduct, but they seem to be the least intrusive and most helpful forms of assessment. For example, the Work Sampling System (Meisels, Jablon, Marsden, Dichtelmiller, & Dorfman, 1994) is a curriculum-integrated, performance-based assessment system that documents and assesses children's knowledge, skills, behavior, and accomplishments based on naturally occurring daily activities in the classroom over the course of the year. Teachers use three elements to record and evaluate children's development and performance: (1) developmental guidelines and checklists, (2) collections of children's work in portfolios, and (3) summary reports that integrate the checklists and portfolios.

In general, science supports the use of an assessment system to identify strengths and weaknesses of children for individualized education in the early years and to monitor child development from preschool to elementary school. Best practices suggest that information learned about children's development in preschool and shared with elementary school teachers can be used to guide each child's individual educational needs and capabilities in school. However, preschool and primary-aged children are still developing very rapidly and learning from their early environments, so such assessments should be conducted frequently (e.g., two to four times per year) to keep pace with the child's progress.

Assessment tools themselves must continually be evaluated for ethnic and racial disparities that may be contributing to the reported gaps in school readiness between different populations (Rock & Stenner, 2005).

Given the rapid changes in the preschool years, using these assessments to select children for special programming lasting more than one year should be avoided. Further, an ongoing plan for evaluating the school readiness of children is necessary to assess the effectiveness of newly implemented programs and policies on child development. By monitoring the school readiness of a random sample of children on a regular basis (every few years), it will be possible to assess the effectiveness of newly implemented programs and policies on child development and to monitor that the curriculum is meeting the needs of the children.

COSTS AND SAVINGS OF BEING READY FOR SCHOOL

A growing body of research is focused on assessing the costs of a lack of readiness and the savings of readiness to the community. Children who do not have the supports necessary for achieving the skills to be ready for school are placed at risk for a number of problems, including remedial schooling, special education, special health services, behavior management programs, juvenile delinquency, and dropping out of school, all of which are costly to the community both in dollars and in workforce potential of the child and of the parent who takes time out of work to provide special care for the child (Bruner, 2004).

Longitudinal early childhood research of several exemplary early childhood programs has returns on investment in the $4 to $8 range for every dollar invested (Bruner, 2004; Lynch, 2004).

The Return on Investment (ROI) is a tool that allows economists to assess the value of a new investment. Based on this method, economists can examine early childhood programs in three ways: returns related to child growth and development, returns related to economic activity, and returns related to adult human capital development. Analyzing these returns together provides influential information in making the case for investment in early childhood programming (Bruner, 2004). A study by the Economic Policy Institute (Lynch, 2004) shows that,

> Providing all 20% of the nation's three- and four-year-old children who live in poverty with a high-quality ECD [early childhood development] program would have a substantial payoff for governments and taxpayers in the future. As those children grow up, costs for remedial and special education, criminal justice, and welfare benefits would decline. Once in the labor force, their incomes would be higher, along with the taxes they would pay back to society. (p. vii–viii)

Further, the cost-benefit and public rates of return on investment in early childhood programming (a 12% return to the public), particularly for those most at risk, are better than the return on investments in physical capital or businesses. However, the public is not currently educated—let alone convinced—of this investment strategy. The benefits of such programs are gained in the distant future, which also adds to the difficulty in convincing the general public and legislators of the high rate of return (Klein, 2004).

The number of quality early childhood programs is so few in this nation that it would take a broad effort to increase quality across the country. Current governmental fiscal investment in early childhood education programs lags far behind what is spent per school-age child. A 12-state study recently showed that, for every public dollar invested in the education and development of school-aged children and every 70 cents invested in undergraduate-aged children, only 13.7 cents was invested in children in the early learning, preschool years (Bruner et al., 2003).

CONCLUSIONS AND RECOMMENDATIONS

Getting young children ready to learn puts them on track for enjoying success in school and later in life. School readiness is an issue that affects the workforce of the future and, to some degree, the strength of the economy.

Helping all children enter school ready to learn is a complex task. Research suggests many factors play a role. These include children's health; language, motor, social, and emotional development; cognition and general knowledge; how children make the transition to kindergarten; parents' income levels; neighborhood factors; SES; and access to quality early care and education. Studies suggest that many interventions addressing these issues can improve children's readiness. The following statements apply this research to practice:

- *The issue of school readiness should be addressed from the perspectives of the child, parent, school, and community.* Research has shown that successful preparation for school involves the developmental capabilities of the child and the commitment of the parents as their child's first teacher, the public school system to be ready for the individual needs of children, and the early childhood field and community to prepare children with the skills they need for success in school.
- *An assessment system should be implemented to identify strengths and weaknesses of children for individualized education and classroom programming in the early years and to monitor child development periodically from preschool to elementary school.* Research suggests that information learned about children's development in preschool, and shared with elementary school teachers, can better inform the school of each child's individual educational needs and capabilities at any given point in time.
- *Taking an economic perspective on the importance of early childhood programming is necessary for creating and increasing the number of quality programs for children.* Return on investment and rate of return studies demonstrate the benefits of quality early childhood programming for the public and our economy as a whole. Investing in early childhood will produce substantial savings for our nation that cannot be duplicated by business investment strategies.

REFERENCES

Ackerman, D. (2003). *States' efforts in improving the qualifications of early care and education teachers.* New Brunswick, NJ: National Institute for Early Education Research, Rutgers University Graduate School of Education.

Barber, J. S., Axinn, W. G., & Thornton, A. (1999). Unwanted childbearing, health, and mother-child relationships. *Journal of Health and Social Behavior, 40,* 231–257.

Blank, M. (2003). Reforming education: Developing 21st century community schools. In F. Jacobs, D. Wertlief, & R. Lerner (Eds.), *Handbook of applied developmental science: Promoting positive child, adolescent, and family development through research, policies, and programs: Vol. 2. Enhancing the life chances of youth and families* (pp. 291–310). Thousand Oaks, CA: Sage.

Bowman, B. T., Donovan, M. S., & Burns, M. S. (Eds.). (2001). *Eager to learn: Educating our preschoolers.* Washington, DC: National Academy Press.

Brooks-Gunn, J., Britto, P. R., & Brady, C. (1999). Struggling to make ends meet: Poverty and child development. In M. E. Lamb (Ed.), *Parenting and child development in "nontraditional" families* (pp. 279–304). Mahwah, NJ: Erlbaum.

Brooks-Gunn, J., Duncan, G. J., Klebanov, P. K., & Sealand, N. (1993). Do neighborhoods influence child and adolescent development? *American Journal of Sociology, 99,* 353–395.

Bruner, C. (2004). *Many happy returns: Three economic models that make the case for school readiness.* Des Moines, IA: State Early Childhood Policy Technical Assistance Network.

Bruner, C., & Copeman, A. (2003). *Measuring children's school readiness: Options for developing state baselines and benchmarks.* Des Moines, IA: State Early Childhood Policy Technical Assistance Network.

Bruner, C., Floyd, S., & Copeman, A. (2003). *Seven things legislators (and other policy makers) need to know about school readiness.* Des Moines, IA: State Early Childhood Policy Technical Assistance Network.

Child Trends. (2000). *Background for community-level work on school readiness: A review of definitions, assessments, and investment strategies. Final report to the Knight Foundation.* Washington, DC: Author.

Committee for Economic Development. (2002). *Preschool for all: Investing in a productive and just society.* Washington, DC: Author. (Available from http://www.ced.org/docs/report/report_preschool.pdf)

Frank Porter Graham Child Development Center. (2001). *Early learning, later success: The Abecedarian Study.* Retrieved August 8, 2000, from http://www.fpg.unc.edu/~abc/embargoed/executive_summary.htm

Gould, M, & Gould, H (2003). A clear vision for equity and opportunity. *Phi Delta Kappan, 85*(4), 324–329.

Grantham-McGregor, S. (1995). A review of studies of the effect of severe malnutrition on mental development. *Journal of Nutrition, 125,* 2233–2238.

Gross, R. T., Brooks-Gunn, J., & Spiker, D. (1992). Efficacy of comprehensive early intervention for low birth weight, premature infants and their families: The Infant Health and Development Program. In S. L. Friedman & M. D. Sigman (Eds.), *The psychological development of low-birthweight children: Annual advances in applied developmental psychology* (Vol. 6, pp. 411–433). Norwood, NJ: Ablex Publishing Corp.

Haskins, R., & Rouse, C. (2005). Closing achievement gaps: Policy brief [Supplement]. School readiness: Closing racial and ethnic gaps [Special issue]. *The Future of Children, 15*(1).

Horton, C., & Bowman, B. T. (2002). *Child assessment at the preprimary level: Expert opinion and state trends.* Chicago: Herr Research Center, Erikson Institute.

Huston, A. C., Duncan, G. J., Granger, R., Bos, J., McLoyd, V., Mistry, R., Crosby, D., Gibson, C., Magnuson, K., Romich, J., & Ventura, A. (2001). Work-based antipoverty programs for parents can enhance the school performance and social behavior of children. *Child Development, 72*(1), 318.

Kagan, S. L., & Cohen, N. E. (1997). *Not by chance: Creating an early care and education system for America's children.* New Haven, CT: Bush Center in Child Development and Social Policy, Yale University.

Kagan, S. L., Moore, E., & Bredekamp, S. (Eds.). (1995). *Reconsidering children's early development and learning: Toward common views and vocabulary* (Goal 1 Technical Planning Group Report 95–03). Washington, DC: National Education Goals Panel.

Kauffman Early Education Exchange. (2002). *Set for success: Building a strong foundation for school readiness based on the social-emotional development of young children, 1*(1). Kansas City, MO: The Ewing Marion Kauffman Foundation.

Klein, L. G. (2004). A conversation with Art Rolnick. *The Evaluation Exchange, 10*(2), 16–17.

Korenman, S., Miller, J. E., Sjaastad, J. E. (1995). Long-term poverty and child development in the United States: Results from the NLSY. *Children and Youth Services Review, 17*, 127–155.

Kraft-Sayre, M., & Pianta, R. (2000) *Enhancing the transition to kindergarten: Linking children, families, & schools.* Charlottesville: University of Virginia National Center for Early Development & Learning.

Lee, V. E., & Burkam, D. T. (2002). *Inequality at the starting gate: Social background differences in achievement as children begin school.* Washington, DC: Economic Policy Institute.

Liaw, F. R., & Brooks-Gunn, J. (1993). Patterns of low birth weight children's cognitive development and their determinants. *Developmental Psychology, 29*(6), 1024–1035.

Lynch, R. (2004). Exceptional returns: Economic, fiscal, and social benefits of early childhood interventions. Washington, DC: Economic Policy Institute.

Maryland State Department of Education (2002). *Maryland model for school readiness (MMSR).* Annapolis, MD: Author.

McCormick, M. C., McCarton, C., Tonascia, J., & Brooks-Gunn, J. (1993). Early educational intervention for very low birth weight infants: Results from the Infant Health and Development Program. *The Journal of Pediatrics, 123*(4), 527–533.

McLelland, M. M., Morrison, F. J., & Holmes, D. L. (2000). Children at risk for early academic problems: The role of learning-related social skills. *Early Childhood Research Quarterly, 15*, 307–329.

Meisels, S. J., Jablon, J. R., Marsden, D. B., Dichtelmiller, M. L., Dorfman, A. B. (1994). *The Work Sampling System.* Ann Arbor, MI: Rebus Inc.

Moore, K., Manlove, J., Richter, K., Halle, T., Le Menestrel, S., Zaslow, M., Greene, A. D., Mariner, C., Romano, A., & Child Trends, Inc. (1997). *A birth cohort study: Conceptual and design considerations and rationale* (Working Paper No. 1999–01). Washington, DC: National Center for Education Statistics.

Morrison, D. R., & Coiro, M. J. (1999). Parental conflict and marital disruption: Do children benefit when high-conflict marriages are dissolved? *Journal of Marriage and Family, 61*, 626–637.

National Center for Education Statistics (NCES). (1993). *Fast response survey system, kindergarten teacher survey on student readiness.* Washington, DC: U.S. Department of Education.

National Education Goals Panel. (1991). *The National Education Goals report: Building a nation of learners.* Washington, DC: Author.

National Education Goals Panel. (1997). *Special early childhood report 1997.* Washington, DC: Author.

Orfield, A., Basa, F., & Yun, J. (2001, Fall). Vision problems of children in poverty in an urban school clinic: Their epidemic numbers, impact on learning, and approaches to remediation. *Journal of Optometric Vision Development, 32*, 114–141.

Platt, L. J., & Cabezas, M. C. (2000). *Early childhood dental caries.* Los Angeles, CA: UCLA Center for Healthier Children, Families and Communities.

Raver, C. C. (2002). Emotions matter: Making the case for the role of young children's emotional development for early school readiness. *Society for the Research in Child Development Social Policy Report, 16*(3), 8–9.

Rhode Island Kids Count. (2003). *Issue brief: Childhood lead poisoning.* Providence, RI: Author.

Rhode Island Kids Count. (2005). *Getting ready: Findings from the National School Readiness Indicators Initiative, a 17 state partnership.* Providence, RI: Author.

Rock, D. A., & Stenner, A. J. (2005). Assessment issues in the testing of children at school entry. *The Future of Children, 15*(1), 15–34.

Rolnick, A., & Gruenwald, R. (2003, December). Early childhood development: Economic development with a high public return. *Fedgazette,* 6–12.

Rosenbaum, J. E., Kulieke, M. J., & Rubinowitz, L. S. (1988). White suburban schools' responses to low-income Black children: Sources of successes and problems. *Urban Review, 20,* 28–41.

Rothstein, R. (2004). Class and schools: Using social, economic, and educational reform to close the black-white achievement gap. Washington, DC: Economic Policy Institute.

Saluja, G., Scott-Little, C., & Clifford, R. M. (2000). Readiness for school: A survey of state policies and definitions. *Early Childhood Research and Practice, 2*(2). Retrieved June 22, 2005, from http://ecrp.uiuc.edu/v2n2/saluja.html

Scott-Little, C., Kagan, S. L., & Frelow, V. S. (2003). *Standards for preschool children's learning and development: Who has standards, how were they developed, and how are they used?* Greensboro, NC: SERVE Research Report.

Shonkoff, J. P., & Phillips, D. A. (Eds.). (2000). *From neurons to neighborhoods: The science of early childhood development.* Washington, DC: National Academy Press.

Shore, R. (1998). *Ready schools.* Washington, DC: U.S. Government Printing Office.

Stahl, D., Sazer O'Donnell, N., Sprague, P., & Lopez, M. (2003). *Sparking connections: Community-based strategies for helping family, friend and neighbor caregivers meet the needs of employees, their children, and their employers.* New York, NY: Families and Work Institute. (Available from http://www.familiesandwork.org/)

Stipek, D. J., & Ryan, R. H. (1997). Economically disadvantaged preschoolers: Ready to learn but further to go. *Developmental Psychology, 33*(4), 711–723.

Tout, K., Zaslow, M., Romano Papillo, A., & Vandivere, S. (2001). *Early care and education: Work support for families and developmental opportunities for children* (Assessing the New Federalism Project Occasional Paper No. 51). Washington, DC: Urban Institute Press.

U.S. Department of Health and Human Services. (1999). *Trends in the well-being of America's children and youth.* Washington, DC: Office of the Assistant Secretary for Planning and Evaluation, U.S. Department of Health and Human Services.

U.S. Department of Health and Human Services Administration for Children and Families. (2003). The Head Start Child Outcomes Framework. *Head Start Bulletin, 76.*

Wagner, M. M., & Clayton, S. L. (1999). The Parents as Teachers program: Results from two demonstrations. *The Future of Children, 9,* 91–189.

Wertheimer, R., Croan, T., Moore, K. A., & Hair, E. C. (2003). *Attending kindergarten and already behind: A statistical portrait of vulnerable young children* (Child Trends Research Brief No. 2003–20). Washington, DC: Child Trends. (Available from http://www.childtrends.org/Files/AttendingKindergartenRB.pdf)

Wesley, P. W., & Buysse, V. (2003). Making meaning of school readiness in schools and communities. *Early Childhood Research Quarterly, 18*(3), 351–375.

2

Early Intervention Practices for Children With and at Risk for Delays

Louise Kaczmarek and Christina J. Groark

In its broadest sense, early intervention refers to special services and supports for young children with a range of vulnerabilities and for their families. These vulnerabilities include biologically based risks that directly affect children and environmental risks that affect the caregiving environments that in turn potentially affect children. *Biologically based risks* include established developmental disabilities (e.g., Down's syndrome, autism, cerebral palsy), childhood psychopathologies, prematurity, low birth weight, and prenatal maternal substance abuse. *Environmentally based risks* include poverty, parental substance abuse, maternal depression, and child maltreatment. Environmental risks can lead to such biological risks as chronic health problems, poor birth outcomes, central nervous system damage, and post-neonatal mortality (Halpern, 2000).

Early intervention is based on the premise that formal services will improve child and family outcomes for these populations (Shonkoff & Phillips, 2000). Over the last 40 years, the focus of early intervention has shifted from primarily influencing the child to also indirectly influencing the child through interventions on families and the caregiving environment of the home (Brooks-Gunn, Berlin, & Fuligni, 2000; Farran, 2000).

The purpose of this chapter is to summarize what is known about the effectiveness of early intervention for preschool-age children. It will

- review children who are at risk for adverse developmental outcomes because of poverty;
- discuss what we know about young children who are learning English as a second language; and
- examine the status of early intervention and inclusion as an intervention model for children with established disabilities.

These reviews are then followed by a set of recommendations. Readers are referred to other more detailed reviews of this literature (e.g., Bowman, Donovan, & Burns, 2000; Guralnick, 1997a; Guralnick, 2001a; Shonkoff & Meisels, 2000; Shonkoff & Phillips, 2000; Vandall, 2004) that were used in the preparation of this chapter.

CHILDREN AT RISK FOR DELAY DUE TO POVERTY

Prevalence of Poverty

In the year 2003, one in six children (17.6%) was living below the poverty line, and the number of poor children in working families increased for the second year in a row (Children's Defense Fund, 2005). Today there are more children living in poverty than 30 years ago.

> The United States has more children living in poverty than any other industrialized nation.

Children who are poor are at greater risk for health problems, erratic parental care, negative birth outcomes, having mothers who smoke or use drugs during pregnancy, and being at risk of abuse and neglect by their caregivers (Children's Defense Fund, 2004; Shonkoff & Phillips, 2000). Poverty is associated with significant negative child outcomes, including greater risk for poor school performance, behavior problems, and disabilities (Brooks-Gunn & Duncan, 1997). Young children under five years of age living in poverty are more likely to meet the eligibility requirements for receiving disability services than those from higher socioeconomic status (SES) families. At least one-third of children with biological disabilities are doubly jeopardized because they also come from families that are economically disadvantaged (Bowe, 1995).

Effects on Child Outcomes

Children living in poverty have been the target of early intervention research since the early 1960s. Interventions conducted before 1987 were focused on providing children with cognitively enriched learning environments in center-based programs that were delivered by staff; little emphasis was placed on evaluating interventions with parents even though some programs included a parent component (Brooks-Gunn, Berlin, & Fuligni, 2000; Crnic & Stormshak, 1997). Since 1987, intervention programs have tended to have a dual emphasis on children as well as their families, including the addition of more home-focused interventions (Farran, 2000).

Most research reviewed in this section is from studies that randomly assigned children to intervention and control groups. The summary below is gleaned primarily from three National Research Council reports—*From Neurons to Neighborhoods: The Science of Early Childhood Development* (Shonkoff & Phillips, 2000); *Eager to Learn: Educating our Preschoolers* (Bowman, Donovan, & Burns, 2000); and *Working Families and Growing Kids: Caring for Children and Adolescents* (Smolensky & Gootman, 2003)—as well as from *The Handbook of Early Childhood Intervention* (Shonkoff & Meisels, 2000).

General Results

Thirty years of research have demonstrated that *well-designed and well-implemented early intervention enhances the short-term performance of children living in poverty* (Shonkoff & Phillips, 2000). Specific longitudinal investigations such as the Abecedarian Project (Ramey & Campbell, 1984) and the Perry Preschool Project (Schweinhart, Barnes, Weikart, Barnett, & Epstein, 1993) as well as more comprehensive literature reviews (Barnett, 1998; Farran, 2000; Guralnick, 1997a; Karoly, Greenwood, Everingham, Hoube, Kilburn, Rydell, Sanders, & Chiesa, 1998) have documented these effects. Effect sizes of up to 1.0 standard deviation in the preschool years were reported (Shonkoff & Phillips, 2000) with the average effect size for cognitive development at a half a standard deviation (Barnett, 1998).

Characteristics of Effectiveness

The impact of early intervention on the cognitive development of young children is associated with the *intensity and duration of the program* (Bowman et al., 2000). In addition, the effects observed were stronger when interventions were *goal directed and child focused* (Farran, 2000; Guralnick, 1997a). However, differences in gains between intervention and control groups, typically measured by IQ scores, were observed to dissipate during the middle

> There is some evidence to suggest that the cognitive effects of early intervention last longer when the intervention is carried beyond the preschool years into the primary grade levels.

childhood years (Bowman et al., 2000; Campbell & Ramey, 1994; Schweinhart et al., 1993; Shonkoff & Phillips, 2000).

However, evidence shows that children who received continued intervention beyond kindergarten had higher reading achievement scores through seventh grade when compared to those who did not (Reynolds & Temple, 1998).

Long-Term Gains

Despite the absence of sustained cognitive impact, early intervention does appear to produce a number of critical long-term gains for children living in poverty when compared to similar children who did not receive early intervention. These gains have included *higher academic achievement, lower grade retention rates, and decreased referral to special education services* (Bagnato, Suen, Brickley, Smith-Jones, & Dettore, 2002; Barnett, 1998; Karoly et al., 1998; Lazar, Darlington, Murray, Royce, & Snipper, 1982). Long-term effect sizes from 0.1 to 0.4 standard deviation have been reported (Shonkoff & Phillips, 2000). A small number of studies that have followed children into adolescence and adulthood (Karoly et al., 1998; Schweinhart et al., 1993; Yoshikawa, 1995) have revealed a number of promising social benefits for those children who received early intervention compared to those who did not. These benefits have included *higher graduation rates and incomes and less welfare dependence and criminal behavior.*

Parent Intervention and Indirect Effects on Children

Parent and family components are included in preschool programs to produce indirect benefits to children by improving parenting through teaching parenting or interaction skills directly or supporting family members in changing their life circumstances (e.g., employment, mental health). Support for this approach is grounded in the ecological (Bronfenbrenner, 1979) and transactional (Sameroff & Fiese, 2000) models of development. These programs are sometimes referred to as "two generation" programs.

Most of the two generation programs that measured maternal outcomes were begun in infancy; a minority of these programs continued through the preschool years (Brooks-Gunn et al., 2000). The 10 programs reviewed by Brooks-Gunn et al. represented a variety of service delivery formats (e.g., home visitor programs, parent education classes, resource identification and support including job training) and philosophical orientations (e.g., "whole person," pre/postnatal intervention, educational, therapeutic, parent-infant attachment). Nearly all programs that assessed parent-child interactions revealed positive treatment effects.

Parenting knowledge, attitudes, and quality of the home environment, however, were measured less frequently, and improvements in these areas seemed to be less successful.

Another comprehensive literature review (Crnic & Stormshak, 1997) presented evidence that some programs that

> Improvements in parent-child interactions included less harsh or negative parenting behaviors; more sensitive, supportive, or positive parenting behaviors; and greater likelihood of infant-parent attachment security.

offered social support to parents improved parent functioning, which in turn benefited children. In contrast, other programs (e.g., Burchinal, Campbell, Bryant, Wasik, & Ramey, 1997) found no such mediating effects. Bowman, Donovan, & Burns (2000) pointed out that very few programs for children living in poverty offer the level of parenting support of model programs and that several current efforts have not been reported as successful.

Farran (2000) cautioned that programs have not succeeded in changing *ecological* circumstances that interfere with parenting (e.g., maternal education level, employment status, stress). She concluded that low-income, minority single parents were more likely to leave programs than other groups, suggesting that programs have not succeeded in adequately addressing individual family needs. Another literature review of economically disadvantaged families (Olds, Henderson, Kitzman, Eckenrode, Cole, & Tatelbaum, 1999) sheds further light on the importance of individualizing intervention; their review, although focusing on infants, concluded that when parents perceived that they or their children needed help, parent-focused interventions were more successful.

CHARACTERISTICS OF SUCCESSFUL PROGRAMS FOR CHILDREN IN POVERTY

Essential features of successful center-based and school-based interventions have emerged through a combination of empirical findings and professional consensus (Shonkoff & Phillips, 2000). The features most commonly included are (1) quality of program implementation; (2) highly trained teachers; (3) timing, intensity, and duration of intervention; and (4) a family-centered, community-based, coordinated orientation. These points are summarized below.

Quality of Program Implementation

Research on child care has clearly substantiated that child outcomes (i.e., primarily cognitive performance and social competence) are related to program quality (Lamb, 1998; Vandell, 2004). Research and model demonstration projects, from which initial empirical findings of early intervention effectiveness were derived, offered well-trained staff and abundant resources to children from economically disadvantaged families (Frede, 1998). Generally speaking, however, children living in poverty are more likely to be placed in low quality child care programs that do not have the resources usually available in model programs (Phillips, McCartney, Scarr, & Howes, 1987; Smolensky & Gootman, 2003).

To obtain a better understanding of the natural variations in quality among early care and education programs available to the general population, two national multisite research programs were instituted. Both the NICHD Study of Early Child Care (Vandall, 2004) and the Cost, Quality, and Outcome Study (Peisner-Feinberg et al., 2001) have explored the relationship between program quality and child outcomes through correlational evidence. This examination of quality has generally been focused on structural and caregiver characteristics (i.e., adult-child ratios; teacher training and education) and process (i.e., children's experiences with caregivers, peers, and materials). More recently, with the emphasis on No Child Left Behind, accountability, and prekindergarten early learning standards, it is expected that studies relating to academics (i.e., literacy) and the instructional components of programs also will begin to emerge in the literature.

Teacher-Child Ratios and Class Size

Smaller class sizes and higher teacher-child ratios were found to be associated with higher process quality as evidenced by more complex language and play, more teacher-child interactions and child initiations, and less controlling teacher behaviors (Bowman, Donovan, & Burns, 2000).

Children in child care settings with more adults per child were more positive towards their peers and emotionally better adjusted; they displayed fewer problem behaviors (Smolensky & Gootman, 2003).

> Smaller class sizes and higher teacher-child ratios also have been shown to be related to improved child outcomes in IQ, achievement tests, school success, and social behaviors (Bowman et al., 2000).

Although we do not know enough at this point to identify optimal class sizes and ratios for preschool classrooms, evidence from primary grade studies have demonstrated significant child gains when class sizes were reduced to approximately 15 from 25 (Bowman et al., 2000). Bowman et al. (2000) also pointed out that a few studies demonstrated that, at the primary grade level, smaller class sizes are preferable to larger class sizes with the same teacher-child ratios.

Curriculum

Because of the heterogeneous nature of the different approaches used to teach young children, determining the effects of these approaches is methodologically difficult (Bowman et al., 2000). The few studies that are available have been riddled with methodological problems; consistent differential effects on cognition, socialization, and other related outcomes have not been revealed (Farran, 2000; Shonkoff & Phillips, 2000).

Teacher Education and Compensation

Studies on the relation between early childhood teacher quality and child outcomes demonstrate results that are similar to those in the larger literature on teacher quality (Bowman et al., 2000). Specifically, teachers with more formal education and more child-related training were shown to provide children with higher quality interactions and experiences (Bowman et al., 2000; Smolensky & Gootman, 2003; Vandall, 2004), manage classroom environments and children better, and display more positive and less negative affect in their interactions with children (Bowman et al., 2000). Children in classrooms with teachers who had higher levels of education displayed fewer behavior problems and received higher school readiness and language comprehension scores (Vandall, 2004). Higher levels of teacher education have also been linked to higher global measures of program quality. The most effective teachers are those with college degrees and specific training in early childhood education or development (Bowman et al., 2000). Engaging in reflective teaching practices (e.g., time spent planning, evaluating, and reflecting on individual children, program curriculum, and challenges) was another critical aspect of teacher quality that was shared by model programs (Frede, 1998) but which may be lacking in many programs available to the general population (Bowman et al., 2000).

Maintaining a stable, highly qualified staff is related to teacher compensation (Bowman et al., 2000; Smolensky & Gootman, 2003). Along with adult-child ratios and teacher education, wages have been found to be predictive of program quality; low wages are indicative of poor quality because of high rates of turnover in teachers. Teacher compensation comparisons are quite telling.

Whereas incomes for teachers from kindergarten through high school ranged from around $38,000 to $42,000 in 2000, the median incomes for prekindergarten teachers was less than $18,000 and those for child care teachers even less (Smolensky & Gootman, 2003).

Timing, Intensity, and Duration of Intervention

In an analysis of model programs for young children in poverty (Frede, 1998), one of the common elements identified was program intensity and coherence. Shonkoff and Phillips (2000) pointed out that, overall, the greater the intensity of intervention, the longer its duration, and the earlier its onset, the greater the gains. However, they further indicated that research is inconclusive concerning the need to have all three characteristics in place for the most gains to occur because, generally, each characteristic has been evaluated separately. For instance, if the program is very high quality and intensive, it may compensate for a shorter duration.

Family-Centered, Community-Based, Coordinated Orientation

Although there is virtually no research focused directly on features of a family-centered, community-based, coordinated orientation, these concepts are strongly rooted in the philosophical, theoretical, and experiential underpinnings of recent programs (Shonkoff & Phillips, 2000). Aspects of research on parent and family support do provide an initial, albeit indirect, foundation for the efficacy of a family-centered, individualized approach. Empirically, we know that interventions tailored to specific needs produced more desirable child and family outcomes than generic advice and support (Farran, 2000). Similarly, interventions that focused on everyday experiences or parent-child interactions were more effective than those that were generic (Brooks-Gunn et al., 2000; Farran, 2000).

> Family-centered care regards parents as the experts on identifying their own needs, and it seeks to build partnerships between professionals and parents or guardians that are built on mutual respect and collaboration to achieve family-driven goals for children and other family members.

Family-centered care requires that early intervention programs for children living in poverty must offer well-defined child and family goals matched specifically to the needs of individual children and their families. Community-based models offer services in nonstigmatizing normative environments so that children and families are a part of the total fabric of their communities and not isolated by the services they receive. Coordinated programming refers to working within and across agency and disciplinary boundaries so that families do not get caught up in the bureaucratic mire that can sometimes surround services.

ENGLISH LANGUAGE LEARNERS AT RISK FOR DELAY

In light of the changing demographics in the United States, it is imperative that all caregivers and educators of young children are aware of the issues and challenges in evaluating, assessing, and teaching young children who are culturally and linguistically diverse. Specifically, the percentage of children ages 5–17 in the United States who speak a language other than English at home has risen to 19% (or 9.9 million children) in 2003 from 9% in 1979. The number of children who spoke English less than "very well" increased as well to 5% (or 2.9 million) in 2003 from 3% in 1979 (U.S. Department of Education National Center for Education Statistics, 2005). Further, the U.S. Census Bureau (2000) predicts that by 2050 people of color and whites would make up equal parts of the U.S. population. Therefore, most teachers in the United States are likely to have students enrolled in their classrooms who are diverse in their ethnicity, race, and language, and this is true for all types of school districts and early care and education programs, whether in inner cities, rural, or suburban areas.

The relations and linkages among language, culture, ethnicity, and other family background issues are integral to children's future academic success. Consequently, the scope and complexity of the issues surrounding educating early English language learners (ELL) should be understood so that there is unbiased assessment and fair diagnosis of such children leading to appropriate and effective instructional strategies.

Screening and Assessment of Young English Language Learners

Screening and assessment of any child is key to matching instructional decisions to the child's needs. Through assessments, the teacher is better able to understand the child's individual talents and challenges, plan a more effective program of activities and experiences, and document progress of the child's skills and abilities.

A joint position statement of the National Association for the Education of Young Children (NAEYC) and the National Association of Early Childhood Specialists in State Departments of Education (NAECS/SDE) describes the characteristics of good assessments for young English language learners (NAEYC & NAECS/SDE, 2003). This statement presents testing considerations, similar to those necessary for effective programming, that are culturally and linguistically responsive to children who are ELLs.

There are also negative social consequences for the child who is misdiagnosed,

When screenings and assessments are inappropriate for the child's ethnic and cultural background, the results may be invalid, leading to inappropriate and ineffective instructional strategies and programs. Children might be identified inaccurately with delays that place them in unnecessary services and do not help them achieve success (McLean, 2001).

including the stigma of delay that the child might have to cope with for years to come. Moreover, once such mislabeling occurs, it may be difficult for children to "graduate" from special programs or become integrated into the social and academic fabric of the classroom. A summary of the draft recommendations of NAEYC and NAECS/SDE (2005) follows:

1. The purpose of assessments must be clear so that results are used primarily to guide and monitor learning strategies and to identify disabilities and other special needs.

2. Appropriate assessments should be administered periodically. Such assessments should be age appropriate and rarely standardized. Multiple methods and sources should be used.

3. Assessments should be linguistically and culturally appropriate for the child's history and language proficiency. Translated instruments should be carefully reviewed before being approved.

4. Assessors should be bilingual and culturally aware, and, as always, they should know the child.

5. Family members are important sources of information about a child; however, trained professionals should conduct the assessments and interpret the results.

It is also important to recognize that personal, familiar, oral communication is often the better means when initiating contact with culturally diverse families (Barrera, 2000). This would require a bilingual communicator or an interpreter.

This joint position statement of NAEYC and NAECS/SDE acknowledges that the field's current knowledge in assessing young English language learners is far from ideal, so it recommends that research and theory about second language acquisition be expanded. We refer the reader to the draft recommendations of NAEYC and NAECS/SDE (2005) for further details.

Characteristics of Effective Learning Environments

There are several comprehensive reviews of successful instructional strategies for linguistically and culturally diverse children (August & Hakuta, 1997; Garcia, 2001; Thomas & Collier, 1995). The characteristics of the reported strategies are similar to those of effective programs for other populations of children, such as children with disabilities or those at risk due to poverty.

For example, research supports the use of strategies that relate to the complete environment of the child including the child's family, school, and community. Specifically, August and Hakuta (1997) report that a mix of English language learners and fluent English speakers in the classroom as well as opportunities for the interaction of these two groups positively affects the social and language progress of the English language learners. Also, they have found that the attitudes and beliefs of the English speakers in the classroom make a critical difference in the atmosphere and, therefore, in the ability of the English language learner to participate in the opportunities for interaction that are an integral part of the classroom routine.

At the family and the community levels, Garcia (2001) reports that English language learners generally come from immigrant families that often have low levels of education and live in communities that lack educational resources. Therefore, these children may begin school at a substantial disadvantage compared to their peers whose first language is English. All children learn best when the new material relates to what they already know and what is familiar to them. For children who are ELLs, this means learning will be most successful if the new material relates to their native language, culture, and experience. A balance is necessary, of course, so that the children retain their ethnic identity while acquiring new academic skills through active and cognitively engaging instruction and learning activities.

> As in any good curriculum, curriculum that takes English language learners into account should be designed so that it includes explicit skill instruction, opportunities for practice, and experiences that assist in linking new skills to learners' backgrounds and existing knowledge base.

One way culturally appropriate curriculum can be accomplished is by enlisting the parents or guardians to help connect and extend the curriculum to the child's home and community experiences.

More specifically, Thomas and Collier (1995) list several factors that can help to relate curricula to ethnic and home experiences:

1. Begin by using the child's native language for as long as possible in the school day, then introduce English for a small part of the day, and later gradually increase the amount of English.

2. Combine a child's first language with English through activities that promote exploration, experimentation, and innovative experiences. For instance, use "hands-on" activities and explain concepts and instructions in the first language, and then blend English throughout the implementation of the activities.

3. Engage English speakers to help integrate the bilingual child into classroom activities by examining their respective instructional goals. For example, match an ELL and an English speaker who have complementary goals, and have this mixed pair work on a project together. However, it is important to note that all English language learner specialists do not agree on what strategies produce success. For example, some specialists do not teach English directly but emphasize nonlinguistic activities, such as using pictures, group projects, music, and drama (Garcia, 2005).

Research is skimpy at best as to which methods are most effective, but it is believed that using the child's native language is beneficial as a tool in assisting the child to achieve English skills, especially when the child is at substantial risk of poor literacy. The authorities in this field seem to agree that teachers must have patience, understanding, and flexibility and that it will take years for a child to learn English as a second language at a level that begins to match that of a child whose first language is English.

The Migrant and Seasonal Head Start Program

An example of a program that deals with all the issues related to English language learners is the Migrant and Seasonal Head Start program (Stechuk & Burns, 2005). Most children enrolled in this program speak Spanish as their first language and migrate with their families several times in a calendar year. The MSHS program must fulfill all Head Start program performance standards (Administration for Children and Families, 1996), which include supporting children's development of their first language as well as supporting their acquisition of English (Stechuk & Burns, 2005). Stechuk and Burns (2005) believe that a child should not lose the first language. To do so, they believe, can harm the child's relationship with his or her parents, make identifying with the family's culture more difficult, slow the development of thinking and reasoning skills, and harm the child's self concept.

Stipek, Ryan, and Alarcon (2001) found that children who attended a bilingual program from preschool through second grade were essentially similar in academic achievement to native bilingual English/Spanish-speaking children as well as to native English-speaking children who were taught entirely in English.

There is some research support for these principles, at least that a high quality bilingual preschool program can produce positive outcomes. For example, Winsler, Días, Espinosa, and Rodríguez

(1999) showed that Spanish-speaking children attending high quality and truly bilingual preschool programs (i.e., equal exposure to Spanish- and English-speaking teachers) showed significant gains in both Spanish and English acquisition compared to similar children who remained at home.

This and other studies are helping to dispel earlier notions that children would become confused if they were exposed to both languages; instead, research shows that exposure to two languages from early childhood has cognitive and social benefits (Hakuta, 1986).

Simultaneous and Sequential Learning

Although children develop spoken communication in similar ways regardless of the specific language, there are two types of language acquisition strategies for children learning more than one language: *simultaneous* (exposure to both languages at the same time from a very early age) and *sequential* (exposure to a second language after first-language learning has been initiated). Learning language is different in these two strategies because in learning a second language a child knows "what language *is*" but needs to discover "what *this* language is" (Tabors, 1997, p 12).

Most early childhood programs are inherently sequential because most ELL children arrive at such programs having been exposed to a primary language other than English at home. Nevertheless, early childhood programs typically follow one of three strategies that are variations on the sequential vs. simultaneous strategies (Tabors, 1997):

1. *First language classrooms* (e.g., Campos & Rosenberg, 1995). All teachers and children are native speakers of a language (L1) other than English and all interactions are carried out in this language. English is not taught directly in these classes. The focus is on the developmental curriculum, including the development of L1, rather than learning English, with the belief that a solid foundation in one language is necessary for learning English when the children start elementary school.

2. *Bilingual classrooms* (e.g., August & Hakuta, 1997). The teaching staff may be bilingual or may include a combination of English-speaking and native-speaking teachers. Typically, children are speakers of L1 or represent a mix of L1 and English speakers. Interactions are split between L1 and English. The classroom focuses on maintaining and/or developing the L1 as well as developing English.

3. *English-language classrooms* (e.g., Rice & Wilcox, 1995). All teachers are native speakers of English. The children may be speakers of a single foreign language or different foreign languages along with others who are native English speakers. All interaction takes place in English with a focus on learning English.

All three types of programs have been demonstrated to have positive effects on children, but no studies comparing the relative benefits of one versus another are currently available (Bowman et al., 2000). In contrast, English language learners who are in an environment that is not culturally supportive can be at somewhat greater risk for developmental delays (particularly socially) than other young children (Hanson, 2002; Shaw, Goode, Ringwalt, & Ayankoya, 2005; Tabors, 1997, 2003).

International English Language Learners Who Have Been Adopted

A special group of children who are ELLs have been adopted internationally, from countries such as Russia, China, Romania, or Korea, and this group includes those who have spent a portion of their early lives in institutions (Glennen & Masters, 2002; Groza & Ileana, 1996; Gunnar, 2001; MacLean, 2003; Rutter, & English-Romanian Adoption Study Team, 1998). In addition to the risks related to institutionalization, the experiences of these children once they are brought to the United States, Canada, Great Britain, and other countries is different from those who live in families in which the native language is spoken at home (Hough, 2005). They experience an "abrupt language shift" (Hough, 2005) in which they leave one linguistic environment and enter a totally different one, perhaps hearing only a few isolated words from their first language in the new environment.

> To determine if a dual language learner has a developmental disability following an adjustment period, it may be necessary to assess the child in both languages and to be aware that the child's inability to understand or use English may have implications for ongoing cognitive and social development (Shaw et al., 2005; Tabors, 1997).

Consequently, it is not uncommon for children adopted internationally to display a "silent period" in which they speak very little in either language, apparently losing their first language more rapidly than they are acquiring English. Fortunately, a disproportionate number of international children are adopted by very advantaged families who provide a rich home experience and readily use whatever educational and mental health services are needed to promote the development of their children (Peters, Atkins, & McKay, 1999).

Determining if a Disability Is Present

Ultimately, most dual language learners and all children adopted internationally will be enrolled in English-language classrooms when they reach school age. Of course, nearly all children need some time to adjust to new surroundings, but some will have more specific limitations.

For a few children adopted internationally from orphanages, more careful developmental monitoring may be necessary beyond the adjustment period. Determining whether a disability is present for these children may be more difficult because usually limited information is known about a child's social history and even less about cognitive, language, and social abilities prior to adoption.

CHILDREN WITH DEVELOPMENTAL DISABILITIES AND DELAYS

It is widely believed that the earlier the intervention for children with disabilities, the greater the benefits to children and families, including the prevention or reduction of additional developmental problems (Guralnick, 1997b). As the child grows older, early intervention is also believed to reduce the need for special education services, residential schooling, and the costs associated with these services (Pennsylvania Partnerships for Children, 2002).

Beginning in the 1980s, intervention efforts began to shift from programs that were primarily center based, staff delivered, and child focused to programs that included an emphasis on families as part of an interdisciplinary team, the coordination of community services and supports, the establishment of parent-professional partnerships, and the increased use of inclusive settings. Prior to the passage of the Education of the Handicapped Act Amendments or PL 99–457 in 1986, "first generation" research efforts focused on whether early intervention for children with disabilities was effective (Guralnick, 1997b). Since then, researchers have called for a shift to answering questions that are more useful in guiding program direction, such as determining the differential effectiveness of program components for specific populations of children and families (Guralnick, 1997b).

From the scientific perspective, the methodological challenges in assessing early intervention effectiveness for children with disabilities have been more numerous than those in assessing its efficacy for economically disadvantaged children. Children with disabilities are a very heterogeneous group, representing a wide range of different disabilities, thus making it difficult to conduct studies with large sample sizes and appropriate control groups. In addition, the severity of children's disabilities has been shown to influence the effectiveness of early intervention (Guralnick, 1997b; Shonkoff & Phillips, 2000). Much of the research reviewed below did not include random assignment to control and intervention groups, and control groups were not identified in many studies, relying instead on demonstrating improvements in children across time.

Effects on Outcomes for Children With Disabilities

General Effectiveness

Numerous studies have concluded that well-designed and well-implemented interventions produce substantial short-term cognitive and social gains in children with disabilities (Castro & Mastroprieri, 1986; Guralnick, 1997a; Shonkoff & Phillips, 2000). The National Research Council report (Shonkoff & Phillips, 2000) asserted that more structured interventions and those that focused on caregiver-child relationships were more effective, although the effects were variable due to the wide range of disabilities and their severity. Research has consistently demonstrated that children with more severe disabilities make less substantial gains than children with mild disabilities (Farran, 2000; Fewell & Glick, 1996; Guralnick, 1991), even though they may receive more services (Farran, 2000). There is also evidence that earlier interventions are associated with more positive changes in children's development (Mastroprieri, 1987; Watkins, 1987).

Long-Term Benefits

No follow-up study of children after they have entered school-age programs has been published (Farran, 2000). However, a longitudinal study of children's placements following preschool early intervention was conducted for the Pennsylvania Department of Education (Zigmond & Kappel, 1998). This investigation revealed that more than half of the children who participated in preschool early intervention were not found on special education rosters by the age of eight, suggesting that early intervention services in Pennsylvania may have reduced the need for special education services at school age. Furthermore, of those children who continued to receive special education, more than 80% were placed in their neighborhood elementary schools (i.e., the schools they would have attended had they not had disabilities) and less than 1% were living in residential placements.

Effects on Outcomes for Families of Children With Disabilities

The effectiveness of early intervention for families of children with disabilities can be categorized into social support, parent-child interaction, and the utilization of services.

Social Support

Social support refers to the provision of resources to the family, such as information or tangible items (Dunst, Trivette, & Deal, 1994). Social support studies conducted after PL 99-457 (Dunst, Trivette, & Jodry, 1997) have found that *social supports rendered or identified by nonprofessionals, such as neighbors, relatives, and friends, had the greatest positive effects especially on behavioral functioning.* Although these informal supports had the biggest impact on the recipient of the support, they also influenced the behavior and development of other family members, including other children. This review further pointed out that professionals who mirror the characteristics of informal help givers can produce similar positive outcomes as their informal counterparts.

Parent-Child Interaction

McCollum & Hemmeter (1997) reviewed 10 studies published since 1980 that focused explicitly on the characteristics or qualities of interaction between parents and their young children with disabilities. These studies ranged from single subject research designs to pre/postdesigns with random group assignments to intervention and control groups. All studies changed parent interaction behaviors, but positive effects such as improved social and language development of the children occurred only when such behaviors were targeted as part of the intervention.

The parenting behaviors that were targeted in these programs included sensitivity and responsiveness to cues provided by the child by following the child's lead, responding contingently, and promoting turn taking (Girolametto, 1988; Mahoney, 1988; Mahoney & Powell, 1988). Marfo (1991) found that parents of children with disabilities often were much more directive and dominant in their interactions than parents of children without disabilities. In addition, warmth in and predictability of parent behavior were consistently encouraged as well as the appropriate level of stimulation from the parent (Clarke-Stewart, 1973). These interventions support the notion that the core issue in parent-child interactions for children with disabilities is readability of cues (Dunst, 1985). Disabilities may disturb the child's ability to read cues from the adult or to provide cues to the adult. Practice by parents is necessary and training is helpful in reading the cues of children with disabilities.

Utilization of Services

A number of studies have indicated that the amount of services that children with disabilities and their families receive appears to be related to family characteristics (Kochanek & Buka, 1998; Mahoney & Filer, 1996; Sontag & Schacht, 1994). These studies have shown that *well-educated families with positive family characteristics and few needs for support received more services than families who were low income, more needy, and less educated.*

Effectiveness of Inclusion for Young Children With Disabilities

Definition

Inclusion refers to the provision of "services and supports to young children with disabilities together with typically developing children" (Guralnick, 2001b).

Several legislative mandates, such as the Education of All Handicapped Children Act (PL 94-142) (1975) and its subsequent amendments now known as the Individuals With Disabilities Education Act (1997), the Americans With Disabilities Act (1990), Section 504 of the Rehabilitation Act (1973), and the Economic Opportunity Act (1964), have promoted the inclusion of children with disabilities into natural settings—that is, those settings in which the children would spend time had they not had disabilities.

> Within the context of children's educational and developmental programs, inclusion is predicated on *planned participation* between children with and without disabilities (Guralnick, 2001b).

Guralnick (2001b) identified four types of inclusive models that have emerged for young children with disabilities: full inclusion model, cluster model, reverse inclusion model, and social inclusion model. The *full inclusion* model refers to placing one child or children with disabilities in a typical early childhood setting under the direction of the usual early childhood staff with supports and services provided by specialized, usually itinerant, personnel (e.g., special educator, occupational therapist) as appropriate. Such settings include community-based day care centers and preschool programs. When a group of children with disabilities is placed in a typical early childhood setting along with one or more specialized, permanently placed personnel, a *cluster* model results. This model is also referred to as a "co-teaching" or "overlay" model; the specialized and general staff members collaborate on an ongoing basis.

A *reverse inclusion* model occurs when typically developing children are placed in special education settings. Personnel in such settings are usually specialized staff. Finally, *social inclusion* refers to situations in which programs for children with and without disabilities are largely independent of each other, but the children from both programs get together for special activities such as picnics, playground sessions, or other recreational activities on a planned or sporadic basis.

General Results

Research on the effectiveness of inclusion has been conducted since the mid-1970s. For children with disabilities, there are no clear mental and educational advantages of inclusive rather than specialized programs, but inclusive settings appear to produce social benefits, such as increased levels of social interaction, when compared to specialized settings (Buysse & Bailey, 1993). While no differences in levels of friendships in inclusive and specialized environments have been discerned, providing additional support to children with and/or without disabilities has been successful in promoting higher interaction rates and more advanced social interaction skills using a range of strategies, such as peer-mediated interventions, direct teaching of social skills, environmental arrangements, and affection activities (Chandler, Lubeck, & Fowler, 1992; McEvoy, Odom, & McConnell, 1992; Odom & Brown, 1993).

Process outcomes for children with disabilities in inclusive settings have been identified. Children with disabilities have

- displayed more cognitively mature forms of play in programs or play groups with typically developing children (Guralnick, Connor, Hammond, Gottman, & Kinnish, 1996; Odom & Bailey, 2001) and
- engaged in more social interaction in play situations that have more rather than less structure (DeKlyen & Odom, 1989).

More adult interactions with children with disabilities are associated with fewer peer interactions between children with and without disabilities (Hundert, Mahoney, & Hopkins, 1993; McWilliam & Bailey, 1995).

Serving Young Children With Disabilities

The most recent version of *Recommended Practices for Early Intervention/Early Childhood Special Education* was developed by the Division for Early Childhood (DEC) of the Council for Exceptional Children and published in 2000 (Sandall, McLean, & Smith, 2000). The DEC is the primary professional organization for individuals who provide early intervention services to children with disabilities under the age of five and their families. The development of the *Recommended Practices* (Smith, McLean, Sandall, Synder, & Ramsey, 2005) involved a stringent three-stage process that included focus groups of scientific experts, other stakeholders, and the identification of the empirical research base from the literature. The practices were republished in 2001 in a program assessment format (Hemmeter, Joseph, Smith, & Sandall, 2001) and again in 2005 with more comprehensive information about implementation (Sandall, Hemmeter, Smith, & McLean, 2005). The strands of the recommended practices are described in Table 2.1, and the specific DEC recommended practices are listed as well.

CONCLUSIONS AND RECOMMENDATIONS

There is a greater emphasis on accountability in the 21st century than ever before. This need has given rise to a federally funded project designed to identify and systematically measure the outcomes of early intervention for young children with disabilities and their families. The Early Childhood Outcomes Center is expected to develop measures of outcomes that can be used in local, state, and national accountability systems. Readers are referred to the ECO Web site to read about the current status of this work (http://www.fpg.unc.edu/~eco/index.cfm). Following are recommendations for practice and policy:

- *Early intervention for children who are at risk due to poverty should include a parent and family component as well as a child component with sufficient individualization that families can address their own goals for themselves and their children.* Evaluations of programs that include individualized parental involvement and family support have demonstrated improved child outcomes.

- *Early intervention should be continued into elementary school for children at risk of delay due to poverty as well as those with disabilities.* Gains made during preschool and earlier will not be sustained if children are placed in elementary schools without such interventions.

- *For English language learners (ELL), the child's native language should be used to assist the child to achieve English-speaking competencies.* Experts in the ELL field agree that positive attitudes among English-speaking classmates and flexibility in a high quality bilingual program with a curriculum that introduces new materials that relate

(Text continued on page 49)

Table 2.1 DEC Strands and Recommended Practices

Strand	Strand Description	Recommended Practices*
Assessment	Assessment is a critical component of early intervention services for children with disabilities. In addition to being used to determine eligibility for services, assessment is essential to planning an individualized, developmentally appropriate program for a child. Collaboration among professionals and families in planning and implementing assessment is an important feature of recommended practices. By including family members in planning a child's assessment, assessment is individualized so that useful information for program planning can result.	1. Professionals and families collaborate in planning and implementing assessment. 2. Assessment is individualized and appropriate for the child and family. 3. Assessment provides useful information for intervention. 4. Professionals share information in respectful and useful ways. 5. Professionals meet legal and procedural requirements and meet recommended practice guidelines.
Child-focused interventions	The cornerstone of early intervention practice is supporting the learning and functioning of young children with disabilities within their natural routines and activities, whether at home, in the community, or in early childhood classrooms. This strand reminds us that young children with disabilities learn best when systematic procedures are used and modified based upon ongoing data collection documenting process.	1. Adults design environments to promote children's safety, active engagement, learning, participation, and membership. 2. Adults use ongoing data to individualize and adapt practices to meet each child's changing needs. 3. Adults use systematic procedures within and across environments, activities, and routines to promote children's learning and participation.

(Continued)

Table 2.1 (Continued)

Strand	Strand Description	Recommended Practices*
	Systematic procedures include making adaptations, embedding learning objectives, and designing intensive interventions within the environments that are frequented by the child and family.	
Family-based practices	Because families are an essential part of the lives of young children, early intervention practices are geared to acknowledge and include families as a central force in their children's services to the extent to which families wish to participate. This strand underscores the need for professionals to work in partnerships with families in designing and, as appropriate, implementing individualized education plans (IEPs). All families are viewed as having strengths and assets, which they bring to the task of raising their children. To accommodate families, early intervention practices are individualized and flexible and they always focus on strengthening family functioning.	1. Families and professionals share responsibilities and work collaboratively. 2. Practices strengthen family functioning. 3. Practices are individualized and flexible. 4. Practices are strengths- and assets-based.
Interdisciplinary models	In addition to education, services to preschool children with disabilities often include speech-language pathology, occupational therapy, and physical therapy. This strand focuses on how professionals interact with each other for the benefit of the children and families being served.	1. Teams including family members make decisions and work together. 2. Professionals cross disciplinary boundaries. 3. Intervention is focused on function, not services.

Strand	Strand Description	Recommended Practices*
	Professionals work collaboratively on teams that include family members in decision making and other aspects of service delivery. Because intervention focuses on children's functioning in natural environments, regular caregivers such as parents and child care providers are often the ones who implement interventions where young children learn best—within their natural routines and activities.	4. Regular caregivers and regular routines provide the most appropriate opportunities for children's learning and receiving most other interventions.
Technology applications	Technology has had and will continue to have a major impact on all of our lives. This strand focuses on how technology should be used in early intervention services, including the use of technology to enhance the functioning of children (i.e., assistive technology) as well as to provide information for families and professionals. It highlights the need for training and technical assistance to support technology applications.	1. Professionals utilize assistive technology in intervention programs for children. 2. Families and professionals collaborate in planning and implementing the use of assistive technology. 3. Families and professionals use technology to access information and support. 4. Training and technical support programs are available to support technology applications.
Policies, procedures, and systems change	Policies and procedures at the program, local, state, and national levels shape early intervention service delivery. This strand reminds us that, as professionals, we have an obligation to include	1. Families and professionals shape policy at the national, state, and local levels. 2. Public policies promote the use of recommended practices.

(Continued)

Table 2.1 (Continued)

Strand	Strand Description	Recommended Practices*
	families in developing policies and practices at all levels, to promote the use of recommended practices, and to strive for better interagency and interdisciplinary collaboration. Finally, it indicates that various forms of program evaluation should inform efforts at all levels to promote systems change.	3. Program policies and administration promote family participation in decision-making. 4. Program policies and administration promote the use of recommended practices. 5. Program policies and administration promote interagency and interdisciplinary collaboration. 6. Program policies, administration, and leadership promote program evaluation and systems change efforts.
Personnel preparation	The final strand provides indicators of quality personnel preparation in early intervention and early childhood special education. This strand recommends several structural aspects of quality training: having qualified faculty and structured, supervised practicum experiences. In addition, it calls for learning experiences in personnel preparation that are systematic, sequenced, and interdisciplinary and that include family members and the study of cultural and linguistic diversity.	1. Families are involved in learning activities. 2. Learning activities are interdisciplinary and interagency. 3. Learning activities are systematically designed and sequenced. 4. Learning activities include study of cultural and linguistic diversity. 5. Learning activities and evaluation procedures are designed to meet the needs of students and staff. 6. Field experiences are systematically designed and supervised. 7. Faculty and other personnel trainers are qualified and well prepared for their role in personnel preparation. 8. Professional development (inservice) activities are systematically designed and implemented.

*NOTE: This column reprinted with the permission of the Division for Early Childhood (DEC) of the Council for Exceptional Children (Sandall, Hemmeter, Smith, & McLean, 2005). This column does not represent the complete DEC Recommended Practices but instead the Guiding Principals from the Practices.

to what is already familiar to the child will produce positive child outcomes.

- *Children with disabilities should be included with typically developing peers in educational and care settings, and personnel staffing these sites should receive adequate training and support.* Research shows inclusion to be beneficial to the social outcomes of children with disabilities. However, community-based staff and early intervention teachers should receive training on how to better collaborate with each other.

- *The early intervention programs for children with disabilities should continue to be supported at the state and national levels.* Studies have shown that early intervention for children with disabilities improves future functioning in developmental gains and reduces the need for increased services.

- *Low-income families who have children with disabilities need more services designed specifically for them and better access to these services.* Research has found that early intervention services for children with disabilities are distributed disproportionately to children from families who are better educated and who come from higher income brackets.

- *Early intervention programs should be monitored and encouraged to practice the elements of recommended practices, which include interdisciplinary personnel, coordinated services, naturalistic and interactive teaching approaches, inclusive environments, family-centered supports, and continuous reflective supervision.* Research supports such practices as producing beneficial outcomes to children.

- *ECE programs should be enhanced to include the better integration of services across service sectors, particularly quality behavioral health interventions using the consultant model in diverse settings, such as Head Start, child care, and the early school years.* The emotional development of children is a predominant influence on their school readiness and success. Those who experience early serious emotional problems are at risk of school failure. Research suggests that emotional and behavioral problems are costly but that they can be identified early, are amenable to change, and can be reduced (Raver, 2002).

REFERENCES

Administration for Children and Families. (1996). *Head Start program performance standards and other regulations.* Washington, DC: U.S. Department of Health and Human Services.

Americans With Disabilities Act of 1990, 42 U.S.C.A. § 12101 *et seq.* (West 1993).

August, D., & Hakuta, K. (1997). *Improving schooling for language-minority children: A research agenda.* Washington, DC: National Academy Press.

Bagnato, S. J., Suen, H. K., Brickley, D., Smith-Jones, J., & Dettore, E. (2002). Child developmental impact of Pittsburgh's Early Childhood Initiative (ECI) in high-risk communities: First-phase authentic evaluation research. *Early Childhood Research Quarterly, 17*(4), 559–580.

Barnett, W. S. (1998). Long-term effects on cognitive development and school success. In W. S. Barnett & S. S. Boocock (Eds.), *Early care and education for children in poverty: Promises, programs, and long-term outcomes* (pp. 11–14). Buffalo, NY: SUNY.

Barrera, I. (2000). Honoring difference: Essential features of appropriate ECSE services for young children from diverse sociocultural environments. *Young Exceptional Children, 3*(4), 17–24.

Bowe, F. G. (1995). Population estimates: Birth-to-5 children with disabilities. *Journal of Special Education, 20,* 461–471.

Bowman, B. T., Donovan, S., & Burns, S. (2000). *Eager to learn: Educating our preschoolers.* Washington, DC: National Academy Press.

Bronfenbrenner, U. (1979). *The ecology of human development.* Cambridge, MA: Harvard University Press.

Brooks-Gunn, J., Berlin, L. J., & Fuligni, A. S. (2000). Early childhood intervention programs: What about the family? In J. P. Shonkoff & S. J. Meisels (Eds.), *Handbook of Early Intervention* (2nd ed., pp. 549–588). New York: Cambridge University Press.

Brooks-Gunn, J., & Duncan, G. J. (1997). The effects of poverty on children and youth. *The Future of Children, 7*(2), 55–71.

Burchinal, M. R., Campbell, F. A., Bryant, D. M., Wasik, B. H., & Ramey, C. T. (1997). Early intervention and mediating processes in cognitive performance of children of low-income African American Families. *Child Development, 68*(5), 935–954.

Buysse, V., & Bailey, D. B. (1993). Behavioral and developmental outcomes in young children with disabilities in integrated and segregated settings: A review of comparative studies. *The Journal of Special Education, 26,* 434–461.

Campbell, F. A., & Ramey, C. T. (1994). Effects of early intervention on intellectual and academic achievement: A follow-up study of children from low-income families. *Child Development, 65,* 684–698.

Campos, M. M., & Rosenberg, F. (1995). *Our day-care settings respect children: Quality criteria for day-care.* Paper presented at the Fifth European Conference on the Quality of Early Childhood Education, Paris, France. (ERIC Document Reproduction Service No. ED 394646)

Castro, G., & Mastroprieri, M. A. (1986). The efficacy of early intervention programs: A meta-analysis. *Exceptional Children, 52*(5), 417–424.

Chandler, L. K., Lubeck, R. C., & Fowler, S. A. (1992). Generalization and maintenance of preschool children's social skills: A critical review and analysis. *Journal of Applied Behavior Analysis, 25,* 415–428.

Children's Defense Fund. (2004). *Defining poverty and why it matters to children.* Retrieved April 13, 2005, from http://www.childrensdefense.org/familyincome/childpoverty/default.asp

Children's Defense Fund. (2005). *Child poverty.* Retrieved April 13, 2005, from http://www.childrensdefense.org/familyincome/childpoverty/default.asp

Clarke-Stewart, K. A. (1973). Interactions between mothers and their young children: Characteristics and consequences. *Monographs of the Society for Research in Child Development, 38*(6–7, Serial No. 153).

Crnic, K., & Stormshak, E. (1997). The effectiveness of providing social support for families of children at risk. In M. J. Guralnick (Ed.), *The effectiveness of early intervention* (pp. 209–225). Baltimore: Brookes.

DeKlyen, M., & Odom, S. L. (1989). Activity structure and social interaction with peers in developmentally integrated play groups. *Journal of Early Intervention, 13,* 342–351.

Dunst, C. J. (1985). Communicative competence and deficits: Effects on early social interactions. In E. T. McDonald & D. L. Gallagher (Eds.), *Facilitating social-emotional development in multiply handicapped children* (pp. 93–140). Philadelphia: Michael C. Prestegord.

Dunst, C. J., Trivette, C. M., & Deal, A. G. (1994). *Supporting and strengthening families: Vol. 1. Methods, strategies and practices.* Cambridge, MA: Brookline Books.

Dunst, C. J., Trivette, C. M., & Jodry, W. (1997). Influences of social support on children with disabilities and their families. In M. J. Guralnick (Ed.), *The effectiveness of early intervention* (pp. 499–522). Baltimore: Brookes.

Economic Opportunity Act of 1964, 42 U.S.C. § 2701 *et seq.*

Education of All Handicapped Children Act of 1975, Pub. L. No. 94-142, 20 U.S.C. § 1400 *et seq.*

Farran, D. C. (2000). Another decade of intervention for children who are low income or disabled. In J. P. Shonkoff & S. J. Meisels (Eds.), *Handbook of early intervention* (2nd ed., pp. 510–548). New York: Cambridge University Press.

Fewell, R, & Glick, M. (1996). Program evaluation findings of an intensive early intervention program. *American Journal of Mental Retardation, 101,* 233–243.

Frede, E. C. (1998). Preschool program quality in programs for children in poverty. In W. S. Barnett & S. S. Boocock (Eds.), *Early care and education for children in poverty: Promises, programs, and long-term outcomes* (pp. 77–98). Buffalo, NY: SUNY.

Garcia, E. (2001). *Hispanic education in the United States: Raices y alas.* Lanham, MD: Rowman & Littlefield.

Garcia, E. (2005). *Teaching and learning in two languages: Bilingualism & schooling in the United States.* New York: Teachers College Press.

Girolametto, L. (1988). Improving the social-conversational skills of developmentally delayed children: An intervention study. *Journal of Speech and Hearing Disorders, 53,* 146–167.

Glennen, S., & Masters, M. (2002). Typical and atypical language development in infants and toddlers adopted form Eastern Europe. *American Journal of Speech-Language Pathology, 11*(4), 417–433.

Groza, V., & Ileana, D. (1996). A follow-up study of adopted children from Romania. *Child and Adolescent Social Work Journal, 13*(6), 541–565.

Gunnar, M. (2001). Effects of early deprivation; Findings from orphanage-reared infants and children. In C. A. Nelson & M. Luciana (Eds.), *Handbook of developmental cognitive neuroscience* (pp. 617–629). Cambridge, MA: MIT Press.

Guralnick, M. J. (1991). The next decade of research on the effectiveness of early intervention. *Exceptional Children, 58,* 174–183.

Guralnick, M. J. (1997a). *The effectiveness of early intervention.* Baltimore: Brookes.

Guralnick, M. J. (1997b). Second generation research in the field of early intervention. In M. J. Guralnick (Ed.), *The effectiveness of early intervention* (pp. 3–20). Baltimore: Brookes.

Guralnick, M. J. (2001a). *Early childhood inclusion: Focus on change.* Baltimore: Brookes.

Guralnick, M. J. (2001b). A framework for change in early childhood inclusion. In M. J. Guralnick (Ed.), *Early childhood inclusion: Focus on change.* (pp. 3–35). Baltimore: Brookes.

Guralnick, M. J., Connor, R., Hammond, M., Gottman, J. M., & Kinnish, K. (1996). Immediate effects of mainstreamed settings on the social interaction and social integration of preschool children. *American Journal on Mental Retardation, 100,* 359–377.

Hakuta, K. (1986). *Mirror of language: The debate on bilingualism.* New York: Basic Books.

Halpern, R. (2000). Early intervention for low-income children and families. In J. P. Shonkoff & S. J. Meisels (Eds.), *Handbook of early intervention* (2nd ed., pp. 361–386). New York: Cambridge University Press.

Hanson, M. J. (2002). Cultural and linguistic diversity: Influences on preschool inclusion. In S. L. Odom (Ed.), *Widening the circle: Including children with disabilities in preschool programs* (pp. 137–153). New York: Teachers College Press.

Hemmeter, M. L., Joseph, G. E., Smith, B. J., & Sandall, S. (2001). *DEC recommended practices program assessment: Improving practices for young children with special needs and their families.* Longmont, CO: Sopris West.

Hough, S. (2005). *Language outcomes in school-aged children adopted from eastern European orphanages.* Pittsburgh, PA: Unpublished doctoral dissertation, University of Pittsburgh.

Hundert, J., Mahoney, B., & Hopkins, B. (1993). The relationship between the peer interaction of children with disabilities in inclusive preschools and resource and classroom teacher behaviors. *Topics in Early Childhood Special Education, 13,* 328–343.

Individuals With Disabilities Education Act of 1997, 20 U.S.C. § 1400 *et seq.*

Karoly, L. A., Greenwood, P. W., Everingham, S. S., Hoube, J., Kilburn, M. R., Rydell, C. P., Sanders, M., & Chiesa, J. (1998). *Investing in our children: What we know and don't know about the costs and benefits of early childhood interventions.* Santa Monica, CA: RAND.

Kochanek, T., & Buka, S. (1998). Patterns of service utilization: Child, maternal, and service provider factors. *Journal of Early Intervention, 21,* 217–231.

Lamb, M. E. (1998). Nonparental child care: Context, quality, correlates. In W. Damon, I. E. Sigel, & K. A. Renninger (Eds.), *Handbook of child psychology: Vol. 4. Child psychology in practice* (5th ed., pp. 73–134). New York: John Wiley & Sons, Inc.

Lazar, I., Darlington, R., Murray, H., Royce, J., & Snipper, A. (1982). Lasting effects of early education: A report from the Consortium for Longitudinal Studies. *Monographs of the Society for Research in Child Development, 47*(2–3, Serial No. 195).

MacLean, K. (2003). The impact of institutionalization on child development. *Development and Psychopathology, 15,* 853–884.

Mahoney, G. (1988). Enhancing the developmental competence of handicapped infants. In K. Marfo (Ed.), *Parent-child interaction and developmental disabilities: Theory, research, and intervention* (pp. 145–162). New York: Praeger.

Mahoney, G., & Filer, J. (1996). How responsive is early intervention to the priorities and needs of families? *Topics in Early Childhood Special Education, 16,* 437–457.

Mahoney, G., & Powell, A. (1988). Modifying parent-infant interaction: Enhancing the development of handicapped children. *Journal of Special Education, 22,* 82–96.

Marfo, K. (1991). The maternal directiveness theme in mother-child interaction research: Implications for early intervention. In K. Marfo (Ed.), *Early intervention in transition: Current perspectives on programs for handicapped children* (pp. 177–203). New York: Praeger.

Mastroprieri, M. A. (1987). Age at start as a correlate of intervention effectiveness. *Psychology in the Schools, 24,* 59–62.

McCollum, J. A., & Hemmeter, M. L. (1997). Parent-child interaction intervention when children have disabilities. In M. J. Guralnick (Ed.), *The effectiveness of early intervention* (pp. 549–576). Baltimore: Brookes.

McEvoy, M. A., Odom, S. L., & McConnell, S. R. (1992). Peer social competence interventions for young children with disabilities. In S. L. Odom, S. R. McConnell, &

M. A. McEvoy (Eds.), *Social competence of young children with disabilities: Issues and strategies for intervention* (pp. 113–133). Baltimore: Brookes.

McLean, M. (2001). Conducting culturally sensitive child assessments. In Council for Exceptional Children, *Serving the underserved: A review of the research and practice in child find, assessment, and the IFSP/IEP process for culturally and linguistically diverse young children* (pp. 11–16). Arlington, VA: Council for Exceptional Children. (ERIC Document Reproduction Service No. ED 454640)

McWilliam, R. A., & Bailey, D. B. (1995). Effects of classroom social structure and disability on engagement. *Topics in Early Childhood Special Education, 15,* 123–147.

National Association for the Education of Young Children (NAEYC) & National Association of Early Childhood Specialists in State Departments of Education (NAECS/SDE). (2003). *Early childhood curriculum, assessment, and program evaluation: Building an effective, accountable system in programs for children birth through age 8* [Joint position statement]. Washington, DC: NAEYC.

National Association for the Education of Young Children (NAEYC) & National Association of Early Childhood Specialists in State Departments of Education (NAECS/SDE). (2005). *Screening and assessment of young English-language learners* [Draft NAEYC recommendations]. Washington, DC: NAEYC.

Odom, S. L., & Bailey, D. B. (2001). Inclusive preschool programs: Classroom ecology and child outcomes. In M. J. Guralnick (Ed.), *Early childhood inclusion: Focus on change,* (pp. 253–291). Baltimore: Brookes.

Odom, S. L., & Brown, W. H. (1993). Social interaction skills interventions for young children with disabilities in integrated settings. In C. A. Peck, S. L. Odom, & D. D. Bricker (Eds.), *Integrating young children with disabilities into community programs: Ecological perspectives on research and implementation* (pp. 39–64). Baltimore: Brookes.

Olds, D. L., Henderson, Jr., C. R., Kitzman, H., Eckenrode, J. J., Cole, R. E., & Tatelbaum, R. C. (1999). Prenatal and infancy home visitation by nurses: Recent findings. *The Future of Children, 9*(1), 44–65.

Peisner-Feinberg, E. S., Burchinal, M. R., Clifford, R. M., Culkin, M. L., Howes, C., Kagan, S. L., & Yazejian, N. (2001). The relation of preschool child care quality to children's cognitive and social developmental trajectories through second grade. *Child Development, 72*(5), 1534–1553.

Pennsylvania Partnerships for Children. (2002, June). *From building blocks to books: Learning from birth through 8 in Pennsylvania,* Harrisburg, PA: Author. (Available from http://www.papartnerships.org/pdfs/birth-8.pdf)

Peters, B. R., Atkins, M. S., & McKay, M. M. (1999). Adopted children's behavior problems: A review of five explanatory models. *Clinical Psychology Review, 19,* 297–328.

Phillips, D. A., McCartney, K., Scarr, S., & Howes, C. (1987). Selective review of infant day care research: A cause for concern? *Zero to Three, 7*(3), 18–21.

Ramey, C. T., & Campbell, F. A. (1984). Preventive education for high-risk children: Cognitive consequences of the Carolina Abecedarian Project. *American Journal of Mental Deficiency, 88,* 515–523.

Raver, C. C. (2002). Emotions matter: Making the case for the role of young children's emotional development for early school readiness. *SRCD Social Policy Report, 16*(3).

Rehabilitation Act of 1973, 29 U.S.C. § 794 *et seq.*

Reynolds, A., & Temple, J. (1998). Extended early childhood intervention and school achievement: Age thirteen findings from the Chicago Longitudinal Study. *Child Development, 69,* 231–246.

Rice, M. L., & Wilcox, K. A. (1995). *Building a language-focused curriculum for the preschool classrooms: Vol. 1. A foundation for lifelong communication.* Baltimore, MD: Brookes.

Rutter, M., & English-Romanian Adoption Study Team. (1998). Developmental catch-up, and deficit, following adoption after severe global early deprivation. *Journal of Child Psychology & Psychiatry, 39*(4), 465–476.

Sameroff, A. J., & Fiese, B. H. (2000). Transactional regulation: The development ecology of early intervention. In J. P. Shonkoff & S. J. Meisels (Eds.), *Handbook of early intervention* (2nd ed., pp. 135–159). New York: Cambridge University Press.

Sandall, S., Hemmeter, M., Smith, B., & McLean, M. (Eds.). (2005). *DEC recommended practices: A comprehensive guide for practical application in early intervention/early childhood special education* (p. 170). Longmont, CO: Sopris West.

Sandall, S., Hemmeter, M. L., Smith, B. J., & McLean, M. (Eds.). (2005). *DEC recommended practices: A comprehensive guide for practical application in early intervention/early childhood special education* (p. 77). Longmont, CO: Sopris West.

Sandall, S., McLean, M. E., & Smith, B. J. (2000). *DEC recommended practices in early intervention/early childhood special education* (p. 132). Longmont, CO: Sopris West.

Schweinhart, L., Barnes, H., Weikart, D., Barnett, W. S., & Epstein, A. S. (1993). Significant benefits: The High/Scope Perry Preschool study through age 27. *Monographs of the High/Scope Educational Research Foundation, 10.* Ypsilanti, MI: The High/Scope Press.

Shaw, E., Goode, S., Ringwalt, S., & Ayankoya, B. (2005). *Minibibliography: Early identification of culturally and linguistically diverse children (aged 0–5).* Chapel Hill, NC: NECTAC Clearinghouse on Early Intervention & Early Childhood Special Education.

Shonkoff, J. P., & Meisels, S. J. (2000). *The handbook of early childhood intervention* (2nd ed.). New York: Cambridge University.

Shonkoff, J. P., & Phillips, D. A. (Eds.). (2000). *From neurons to neighborhoods: The science of early childhood development.* Washington, DC: National Academy Press.

Smith, B. J., McLean, M. E., Sandall, S., Synder, P., & Ramsey, A. B. (2005). DEC recommended practices: The procedures and evidence base used to establish them. In S. Sandall, M. L. Hemmeter, B. J. Smith, & M. E. McLean (Eds.), *DEC recommended practices: A comprehensive guide for practical application in early intervention/early childhood special education* (p. 77). Longmont, CO: Sopris West.

Smolensky, R., & Gootman, J. A. (2003). *Working families and growing kids: Caring for children and adolescents.* Washington, DC: National Academies Press.

Sontag, J. C., & Schacht R. (1994). An ethnic comparison of parent participation and information needs in early intervention. *Exceptional Children, 60,* 422–433.

Stechuk, R. A., & Burns, M. S. (2005). *Making a difference: A framework for supporting first and second language development in preschool children of migrant farm workers.* Washington, DC: Academy for Educational Development.

Stipek, D., Ryan, R., & Alarcon, R. (2001). Bridging research and practice to develop a two-way bilingual program. *Early Childhood Research Quarterly, 16,* 133–149.

Tabors, P. O. (1997). *One child, two languages: A guide for preschool educators of children learning English as a second language.* Baltimore, MD: Brookes.

Tabors, P. O. (2003). What early childhood educators need to know: Developing effective programs for linguistically and culturally diverse children and families. In C. Copple (Ed.), *A world of difference: Readings on teaching young children in a diverse society* (pp. 17–23). Washington, DC: National Association for the Education of Young Children (NAEYC).

Thomas, W. P., & Collier, V. P. (1995). *A longitudinal analysis of programs serving language minority students.* Washington, DC: National Clearinghouse on Bilingual Education.

U.S. Census Bureau. (2000). *Projected population of the United States, by race and Hispanic origin: 2000–2050* (Table 1a). Retrieved January 21, 2006, from www.census.gov/ipc/www/usinterimproj/natprojtab01a.pdf

U.S. Department of Education, National Center for Education Statistics. (2005), *The condition of education 2005* (NCES Publication No. 2005094). Washington, DC: U.S. Government Printing Office.

Vandall, D. (2004). Early child care: The known and the unknown. *Merrill-Palmer Quarterly, 50,* 387–414.

Watkins, S. (1987). Long term effects of home intervention with hearing-impaired children. *American Annals of the Deaf, 132,* 267–271.

Winsler, A., Días, R. M., Espinosa, L., & Rodríguez, J. (1999). When learning a second language does not mean losing the first: Bilingual language development in low-income, Spanish-speaking children attending bilingual preschool. *Child Development, 70,* 349–362.

Yoshikawa, H. (1995). Long-term effects of early childhood programs on social outcomes and delinquency. *The Future of Children,* 5(3), 51–75.

Zigmond, N., & Kappel, A. (1998). *Final report: A longitudinal study of the placements of children with disabilities served in preschool special education once they reach school age.* Harrisburg, PA: Pennsylvania Department of Education.

Best Practices for Transitions Into Kindergarten

3

Kelly E. Mehaffie and Mary Wolfson

While all change is potentially stressful for adults and children alike, early shifts in services and environments are critical because they represent changes in physical environments, in role expectations for children, in staff training and philosophy, and in parental involvement that can positively or adversely affect children's development. The potential stress that these changes hold for young children and the ways in which they are handled by adults can influence children's success in school. Although transitions of infants and toddlers into care and transitions from early care into preschool services are of crucial importance, this chapter focuses on transitions into kindergarten.

There has been little research examining the effectiveness of transition programs (or their absence) in which students are randomized to receive different forms of transition services. Two exceptions are the Abecedarian K–2 Transition Program (See Box 3.1) and the Head Start Transition Study, which was developed using the results of the Abecedarian K–2 Transition Program (Ramey & Ramey, 1999; see Box 3.2).[1] Longitudinal, nonexperimental studies indicate that students who experience effective transitions before school and into school generally possess a positive attitude towards school and subsequently display a steady growth in academic skills (Hamre & Pianta, 2001; Ramey & Ramey, 1994). Conversely, students who experience ineffective transitions are

Box 3.1   The Abecedarian K–2 Transition Program

The *Abecedarian K–2 Transition Program* was a program for high-risk children in kindergarten through second grade. The randomized design included cohorts who received the transition program and had experience in an intensive (health, education, family support) birth-to-five early intervention program, those who received the transition program and who had experience in a quality early childhood program without the early intervention, those who received the early intervention but not the transition program, and those who received none of the mentioned programs. This study was conducted despite the fact that each group was comprised of a small number of children.

The project set to have an impact on both the school and home environment under the notion that parent involvement was crucial to a child's success in school. The transition project relied on the teacher to choose the academic tasks each child needed assistance mastering. Home-school resource teachers conducted the intervention and provided the services administered at home and at school through coordinated supports for families, children, and teachers. These activities and supports were above and beyond the regular education program provided by the school. In addition, children attended an educational summer camp. Child and family outcomes were assessed in eight domains including measures of basic skills. The program had a positive effect on reading and math achievement and reduced grade retention. The effects were even more pronounced for those who had also been in the early intervention program before the transition project.

Box 3.2   The National Head Start/Early Childhood Transition Demonstration

The *National Head Start/Early Childhood Transition Demonstration* was a national longitudinal study of two groups of former Head Start families; one group was assigned to transition schools, which provided Head Start–like family services to promote academic achievement and family involvement in school, and the other to control schools. Results from this study found that former Head Start students continued to show progress in standardized assessments of reading and math through the first four years of school (Ramey et al., 2000).

This study is the first to demonstrate continued academic growth in the elementary grades for children in Head Start. However, the extent to which the transition services provided by the program were in part responsible for children's success could not be determined. Difficulty with the maintenance of treatment fidelity and with the integrity of the design in which transition-like services were provided in comparison schools precluded a rigorous experimental evaluation of the program, which involved approximately 12,000 children and families in 31 states.

more likely to struggle academically and socially in school (Hamre & Pianta, 2001; Kagan & Newman, 1998; Ramey & Ramey, 1999).

TRANSITIONS IN CONTEXT

Traditionally, the student who has academic problems has been viewed and treated by direct attempts to improve the deficient skills. However, it has been reported that child cognitive skills and other child factors account for less than 25% of the variance in academic outcomes (Pianta & Kraft-Sayre, 1999). Consequently, student academic difficulty or referral for special education is now also being viewed as a contextual phenomenon, in which child factors and the child's current and early environments combine to influence the child's academic outcome (Docket & Perry, 2001; Early, Pianta, & Cox, 1999; Love, Logue, Trudeau, & Thayer, 1992; Pianta & Cox, 1999; Ramey et al., 2000).

According to Rimm-Kaufman and Pianta (2001), there are four views on transition to school: (1) a skills only model which focuses on the abilities and maturation that the child possesses upon entering school; (2) an environmental input model in which a child's skill level is considered to be influenced by experiences in the different environments of home (e.g., parent reading to child), school (e.g., class size, peer relationships), and other community settings (e.g., church, play groups); (3) a linked environments model in which, at a given point in time, the relations between home and school environments are considered influential as well as the skills and experiences of the child; and (4) a developmental model in which all of the above models are included as well as a focus on maintaining relationships over time and on changing the model to fit the changing needs of the child.

Parent Views on Transition to School

A survey by Kraft-Sayre and Pianta (1999) identified common themes within parents' views on transition to school. The major theme was that parents were excited about their child starting school. Parents also felt that the type of contact made between schools and families was important for their child's transition experience. Parents expressed a desire to have the schools understand their child's individual personality and needs, thus necessitating the need to start planning for transitions early.

The School Transition Study analyzes Comprehensive Child Development Program (CCDP) data to find that parents have strong feelings about the transition process. The study found that when teachers reached out to parents about their child's development as well as family issues and built a relationship with the children's parents, parents became more involved in school readiness activities and education at home as well as at school (Kreider, 2002). The Even Start program also found that assisting parents in the home environment regarding family and child needs had a positive influence on children's transition experience and the level of family involvement (Reidinger, 1997).

> These survey results emphasize the contextual/developmental model approach in that communication between parents, schools, and early childhood programs is vital to the transition process (Pianta & Kraft-Sayre, 2003).

Increasing Diversity of Children Entering Kindergarten

Discussion and research on transitions in early childhood is particularly important today in light of the increasing diversity among the backgrounds of students entering kindergarten. The Early Childhood Longitudinal Study, conducted by the U.S. Department of Education, identified three factors that are associated with this increasing diversity among today's students—high divorce rates, different types of prekindergarten care, and increasing racial and ethnic diversity (U.S. Department of Education, 2000). In addition, children's transitional experiences vary from child to child, even when children from very similar backgrounds are entering the same classroom and can influence academic outcomes (Peters, 2000).

> Transition practices should be considered for all children, not just for those students traditionally identified as being "at risk" (Kagan & Newman, 1998).

BEST PRACTICES FOR TRANSITIONS

Unfortunately, few schools and communities engage in effective transition practices, and many that do only engage in what they call "transition" practices after school starts in the form of phone calls, flyers, or open houses for parents (Pianta, Cox, Taylor, & Early, 1999). Therefore, randomized experimental research on the effects of transition practices on children is minimal. What we do know about best practices in transitions is based on demonstration projects and professional consensus (e.g., NAEYC, Head Start Association, etc.). There is ample professional consensus in terms of what constitutes best transition practices.

Effective transitions involve and characteristics of good programs include

- program continuity,
- ongoing communication and cooperation between teachers and administrators at different programs,
- preparation of children for the transition,
- preparation of the individual child for entering environments, and
- parent/guardian involvement in the transition (Bredenkamp & Copple, 1997; Dockett & Perry, 2001; Mangione & Speth, 1998; Ramey & Ramey, 1999).

Further, good transition practices involve other people in the child's life, such as service providers and other community members (Wesley, 2001). One of the national regional educational laboratories, SERVE, developed a toolkit encompassing these best practices, titled *Planning for Terrific Transitions: A Guide for Transition-to-School Teams*, which includes information on how to involve communities in working on transition issues (SERVE, 2004). This toolkit contains a step-by-step trainers' guide, a CD of reproducible material, trainer support materials, a participants' guide, and references and resources. The toolkit is available free of charge at www.serve.org. In addition, SERVE and the National Head Start Association developed a transition Web site to provide information on transition to families, professionals, and community partnerships (www.terrifictransitions.org). Although effective transition practices do have common characteristics, the specific developmental needs of children differ and must be accounted for in transitions to school.

Aligning Preschool and Kindergarten Pedagogy

Evidence and professional consensus suggest that there should be some consistency between early care and education settings and kindergarten. There has been controversy in the field as to how (or whether) to teach preschool children preacademic skills that may assist them in the transition to school. Some educators promote the direct instruction of letters and prereading skills as well as numeracy and premath skills, while others suggest that a primary focus on socioemotional development and play is most appropriate. Abrupt transitions between these distinct pedagogical approaches could make the transition to kindergarten difficult for some children. Such a scenario reinforces the idea that consistency in programming and communication between early childhood educators and schools is paramount (Education Commission of the States, 2000). Further, adopting a contextual-based framework demonstrates that children's skills, as well as the abilities of schools and communities, are important in the transition to school (Bohan-Baker & Little, 2004).

Positive, Caring Relationships With Kindergarten Teachers

Transition practices to promote success in kindergarten should emphasize the establishment of a caring positive relationship with the kindergarten teacher and should work to help the child to adjust socially to the classroom. Correlational evidence from three studies shows the importance of these goals:

- Children having more positive relationships with their kindergarten teacher appear more able to make the most of learning opportunities available in the classroom (Howes, Phillipsen, & Peisner-Feinberg, 2000).
- Kindergarten students for whom academic failure or special education had been predicted but who were not actually retained or referred had more positive relationships with their teacher (Hamre & Pianta, 2001).
- Teacher-reported negativity in student-teacher relationships in kindergarten continued to predict unique variance in standardized test scores through upper elementary school above and beyond other covariates, such as grades, achievement, work habits, and disciplinary records (Hamre & Pianta, 2001).
- Students who are socially adjusted are capable of accessing the academic environment more readily than those students who are struggling socially (Meisels, 1998).

Kindergarten teachers believe that the skills least important for success in kindergarten are alphabet knowledge, ability to count, problem solving skills, and knowledge of shapes and colors. The characteristics kindergarten teachers believe to be most important for success in kindergarten are ability to communicate needs, thoughts, and wants plus enthusiasm for activities (Meisels, 1998). It should not be concluded that teachers consider the more academic skills unimportant for success in kindergarten. Rather, it is their experience that students who adjust socially to school can readily be taught the skills that they need for success over the course of the first two years of school (Dockett & Perry, 2001).

CONCLUSIONS AND RECOMMENDATIONS

Although there seems to be a professional consensus that all children are in need of transition programming, the research has generally focused on at-risk populations (Bredenkamp & Copple, 1997; Kagan & Newman, 1998; Pianta, 1999; Ramey & Ramey, 1999; Ramey et al., 2000). However, the limited evidence we have does point to better outcomes, both socially and academically, for children who have experienced well-planned, collaborative transitions. Future research should strive for a more rigorous scientific examination of the contribution of specific transition practices and of the specific outcomes associated with those practices (Innes, Denton, & West, 2001; Kagan & Newman, 1998). The following statements recommend further practices for meeting the needs of children with and at risk for delays:

- *Education regarding transitions and transition practices in early childhood, including the importance of both social experiences and academics, should be an essential component of a quality professional development program.* Unfortunately, the Transition Practices Survey conducted by NCEDL found that only 22.7% of the 3,595 kindergarten teachers surveyed indicated that they had received any training or information on transitions (Early, Pianta, & Cox, 1999).
- *Public education, especially of parents, is an important component of effective transitions and should be promoted as part of a good awareness campaign.* All stakeholders (e.g., parents, teachers, caregivers, other service providers) should be informed regarding transition practices to ensure effective implementation of transition practices and programs (Bredenkamp & Copple, 1997; Kagan & Newman, 1998). Family involvement is a must for transition to work effectively (Bohan-Baker & Little, 2004).
- *Communities should be encouraged to develop transition teams consisting of parents, early childhood professionals, elementary school teachers and principals, and other community leaders to devise transition strategies that are individualized to their community, families, and children.* These transition teams should include a transition coordinator who is primarily responsible for the activities and functions of the team (Kraft-Sayre & Pianta, 2000).

REFERENCES

Bohan-Baker, M., & Little, P. (2004). *The transition to kindergarten: A review of current research and promising practices to involve families.* Cambridge, MA: Harvard Family Research Project, Harvard Graduate School of Education.

Bredenkamp, S., & Copple, C. (Eds.). (1997). *Developmentally appropriate practice in early childhood programs.* Washington, DC: National Association for the Education of Young Children.

Dockett, S., & Perry, B. (2001). Starting school: Effective transitions. *Early Childhood Research and Practice, 3*(2), 35–51.

Early, D. M., Pianta, R. C., & Cox, M. J. (1999). Kindergarten teachers and classrooms: A transition context. *Early Education and Development, 10*(1), 25–46.

Education Commission of the States. (2000). *Easing the transition to kindergarten.* Denver, CO: Author.

Hamre, B. K., & Pianta, R. C. (2001). Early teacher-child relationships and the trajectory of children's school outcomes through eighth grade. *Child Development, 72*(2), 625–638.

Howes, C., Phillipsen, L. C., & Peisner-Feinberg, E. (2000). The consistency of perceived teacher-child relationships between preschool and kindergarten. *Journal of School Psychology, 38*(2), 113–132.

Innes, F. K., Denton, K. L., & West, J. (2001). *Child care factors and kindergarten outcomes: Findings from a national study of children.* Minneapolis, MN: Society for Research in Child Development.

Kagan, S. L., & Newman, M. J. (1998). Lessons from three decades of transition research. *The Elementary School Journal, 98*(4), 365–379.

Kraft-Sayre, M. E., & Pianta, R. C. (1999). *Kindergarten Transition Project parent interviews.* Charlottesville: University of Virginia, National Center for Early Development & Learning.

Kraft-Sayre, M. E., & Pianta, R. C. (2000). *Enhancing the transition to kindergarten: Linking children, families, and schools.* Charlottesville: University of Virginia, National Center for Early Development & Learning.

Kreider, H. (2002). *Getting parents "ready" for kindergarten: The role of early childhood education.* Cambridge, MA: Harvard Family Research Project, Family Involvement Network of Educators (FINE).

Love, J. N., Logue, M. E., Trudeau, J. V., & Thayer, K. (1992). *Transitions to kindergarten in American schools: Final report of the National Transition Study.* Washington, DC: U.S. Department of Education.

Mangione, P. L., & Speth, T. (1998). The transition to elementary school: A framework for creating early childhood continuity through home, school, and community partnerships. *The Elementary School Journal 98*(4), 381–397.

Meisels, S. J. (1998). Assessing readiness. *NCEDL Spotlights, 3,* 3–7. (Available from the National Center for Early Development & Learning Web site, http://www.fpg.unc.edu/~ncedl/index.cfm)

Peters, S. (2000). *Multiple perspectives on continuity in learning and the transition to school.* Paper presented at the European Early Childhood Education Association Conference, University of London, London.

Pianta, R. C. (1999). *Enhancing relationships between children and teachers.* Washington, DC: American Psychological Association.

Pianta, R. C., & Cox, M. J. (Eds.). (1999). *The transition to kindergarten.* Baltimore, MD: Paul H. Brooks Publishing Co.

Pianta, R. C., Cox, M. J., Taylor, L., & Early, D. (1999). Kindergarten teachers' practices related to the transition to school: Results of a national survey. *The Elementary School Journal, 100*(1), 71–86.

Pianta, R. C., & Kraft-Sayre, M. (1999). Parents' observations about their children's transitions to kindergarten. *Young Children, 54*(3), 47–52.

Pianta, R. C. & Kraft-Sayre, M. (2003). *Successful kindergarten transition: Your guide to connecting children, families, and schools.* Baltimore: Brookes.

Ramey, C. T., & Ramey, S. L. (1999). Beginning school for children at risk. In R. C. Pianta & M. J. Cox (Eds.), *The transition to kindergarten* (pp. 217–251). Baltimore: Brookes.

Ramey, S. L., & Ramey, C. T. (1994). The transition to school. *Phi Delta Kappan, 76*(3), 194–199.

Ramey, S. L., Ramey, C. T., Phillips, M. M., Lanzi, R. G., Brezausek, C., Katholi, C. R., Snyder, S., & Lawrence, F. (2000). Head Start children's entry into public school: A report on the National Head Start/Public Early Childhood Transition Demonstration Study. Washington, DC: U.S. Department of Health and Human Services.

Reidinger, S. A. (1997). *Even Start: Facilitating transitions to kindergarten.* Plainsboro, NJ: Mathematica Policy Research.

Rimm-Kaufman, S., & Pianta, R. C. (2001). An ecological perspective on the transition to kindergarten: A theoretical framework to guide empirical research. *Journal of Applied Developmental Psychology, 21*(5), 491–511.

SERVE. (2004). *Planning for terrific transitions: A guide for transition-to-school teams.* Tallahassee, FL: Author.

U.S. Department of Education. (2000). *Early Childhood Longitudinal Study: Kindergarten class of 1998–1999.* Washington, DC: Author.

Wesley, P. W. (2001). *Smooth moves to kindergarten.* Chapel Hill, NC: Chapel Hill Training-Outreach Project.

NOTE

1. For more information on the Abecedarian Transition Program and the Head Start Transition Study, see Chapter 7: School-Age Services: Programs That Extend the Benefits of Early Care and Education Services.

PART II

Evidence-Based Programs

4

Publicly Funded Programs and Their Benefits for Children

Wendy M. Barnard

In France, nearly 100% of all three- and four-year-olds are in state-sponsored preschool programs, and most European countries have similar numbers. By contrast, less than half of all children the same age attend an early education program in the United States (U.S. Department of Education, 2005). Further, U.S. children from economically and educationally disadvantaged families, who are most in need of the early education, are even less likely to attend a preschool program.

In addition, 69.5% of children with a mother who has a college degree compared to only 38% of children with a mother without a high school degree attend preschool (Karoly & Bigelow, 2005). The number of economically disadvantaged children enrolled in preschool remains low even with the increase in both federal and state agencies providing more public preschool programs for children.

While 78% of children ages three to five living in families with household incomes over $100,000 attend some type of educational program, only 44% of similar children whose families have household incomes of $10,000 or less are enrolled in some type of prekindergarten program (National Institute for Early Education Research, 2004).

Thirty-eight states provide at least one type of prekindergarten for low-income children, but only two states (Georgia and Oklahoma) provide prekindergarten for all children regardless of income eligibility. However, even with income restrictions, many states still serve only a small proportion of eligible children. For example, 20 states serve less than 10% of the eligible four-year-olds, and Alabama and Nevada serve only 1% of eligible children (National Institute for Early Education Research, 2004).

There is a large body of research documenting the importance of early childhood education. Children who participate in early educational programs have both immediate and lasting benefits throughout school. Using all of the studies described on the following pages, children who attend publicly funded early childhood programs have

- Increased kindergarten readiness skills (e.g., increased knowledge of colors, shapes, numbers, and vocabulary or words and higher teacher reports of "readiness");
- Increased cognitive skills (e.g., higher school achievement through elementary school, decreased rates of grade retention and special education placement, and increased likelihood of graduating from high school);
- Increased social and emotional development (e.g., increased social skills in kindergarten, higher scores on a life skills competency test, and lower rates of juvenile delinquency and arrests); and
- Better health care (e.g., more preventive health care, a higher number of health screenings, and a higher number of dental examinations).

The following pages look at specific programs for early childhood education whose effectiveness has been documented.

FEDERAL PROGRAMS

Federal and state programs that address early childhood care and education vary in a number of important ways, including approach, scale, and reported effectiveness. Profiles of several of these programs are included in this section.

Head Start

Goal and Background

The U.S. Health and Human Services' Administration on Children, Youth and Families (ACYF) states that "Head Start's mission is to help children from low-income families start school ready to learn. Head Start's comprehensive programs and services incorporate all components of child development: (1) early learning and literacy, (2) health, (3) disabilities services, and (4) family and community partnerships" (Administration on Children, Youth and Families, 2004). Since Head Start's inception in 1965, over 22 million children have been provided preschool services.

Early Evaluations

A 1985 report synthesizing findings from the first 15 years of Head Start determined that children who attended Head Start made significant short-term gains on cognitive tests, socioemotional development, and health. However, these benefits tended to fade over time. This report also concluded, based on smaller studies of Head Start children, that participants were less likely to be retained in grade and to be placed in special education (McKey et at., 1985).

Two decades after the inception of Head Start, there were only a handful of studies that empirically documented the impact of the program, because Congress preferred to fund more slots for children than evaluations of program effectiveness. Not surprisingly, a 1997 U.S. General Accounting Office (GAO) report concluded that very little was actually known about the outcome of Head Start, identifying only 22 out of 200 studies that utilized some type of comparison group, and results were often mixed or contradictory.

Recent Evaluations

A recent follow-up study of Head Start participants and a comparison group at age 22 found that the women who attended Head Start as children were significantly more likely to graduate from high school or get a GED (95% vs. 81%), and significantly fewer of these women had been arrested (5% vs. 15%). Further, both boys and girls who were in a child-directed Head Start classroom (as opposed to a more traditional teacher-directed classroom) had higher grade point averages in elementary school and fewer criminal convictions (Oden, Schweinhart, & Weikart, 2000).

Currently, Head Start is examining a randomly selected sample of participating families (3,200 families) who entered 43 representative Head Start programs (FACES Project). Although the study does not have a no-program group for comparison, results show that Head Start children improved their vocabulary, writing skills, and social skills more than expected on these measures for children their age, and they continued to have better vocabulary, early mathematics, and writing skills during their kindergarten year (Administration on Children, Youth and Families, 2003). However, performance, while improved, was still below national averages, and the report also found that Head Start teachers had lower teaching credentials when compared to public school prekindergarten teachers. Nonetheless, Head Start classrooms received high quality ratings by trained outside observers, and more teachers had graduate degrees than in past years.

Currie and Thomas (1999) examined the effects of Head Start in the representative National Longitudinal Survey of Youth by comparing Head Start children to their siblings who did not attend Head Start by interviewing the children's mothers. Focusing on 750 Latino children, they found that relative to their non-Head Start siblings, Head Start children had higher vocabulary and mathematics test scores and were less likely to repeat a grade. Applying the same method to the nationally representative Panel Study of Income Dynamics data, Garces, Thomas, and Currie (2000) found long-term benefits of Head Start experience in a sample of 255 young adults: higher high school completion and college attendance rates for whites and lower crime conviction rates for African Americans.

The most current data released from the National Head Start Impact Study, a $23.8 million longitudinal study mandated by the U.S. Congress in 1998 to examine approximately 5,000 children randomized to Head Start or non-Head Start programs, showed mixed results (U.S. Department of Health and Human Services, 2005). Children, ages three and four, who attended Head Start had significantly higher scores than non-Head Start children in prereading, prewriting, vocabulary, and parent reports of literacy skills; however, no significant changes were found in oral comprehension or early mathematics skills. Further, no significant changes were detected between the groups on social-emotional constructs, such as problem behaviors, social skills, or social competencies.

Program Characteristics

Who Is Eligible: Head Start regulations require that at least 90% of families attending Head Start are low income and that at least 10% have special needs.

Who Is Served: In 2004, approximately 905,851 children were served in Head Start per year in over 20,000 centers. The majority of children were three- and four-year-olds (34% were three years old and 53% were four years old). In addition, 12.7% of those served were children with special needs (Administration on Children, Youth and Families, 2005).

Educational Program: Curriculum is based on child development principles and performance standards defined by Head Start that include "goals for children's development and learning; experiences through which they will achieve the goals; roles for staff and parents to help children to achieve these goals; and materials needed to support the implementation of a curriculum" (Administration on Children, Youth and Families, 2001). Programs are encouraged to modify and enhance curriculum to best meet the needs of the children in their program.

> Parent involvement is a critical component of Head Start.

Parents are encouraged to serve on the policy council and to be involved in administrative decisions. Further, home visits and parent workshops emphasize that parents are the best teachers for their children.

Funding	Federal funding
Teacher Qualifications	At least 50% of all teachers in Head Start must have at least a bachelor's or associate's degree in early education, or a bachelor's or associate's degree in a related field with preschool classroom experience. All other teachers must have a CDA or state equivalent within 180 days of being hired. As of 2002, 51.7% of teachers had degrees (U.S. GAO, 2003b).
Teacher/Child Ratios	1:10
Maximum Class Size	17 for 3-year-olds and 20 for 4- and 5-year-olds
Hours of Operation	Classes at least 4 days per week (half or full day)
Cost	In 2004, the cost was $7,222 a year per child.

Even Start Family Literacy Program

Goal and Background

Started in 1988 as a U.S. Department of Education federal demonstration project, the Even Start Family Literacy Program is currently reauthorized by the Literacy Involves Families Together (LIFT) Act of 2000 and the No Child Left Behind Act of 2001.

> Even Start integrates early childhood education, adult education, parent education, and interactive literacy activities for the parents and children together.

Even Start staff coordinates available services for families, provides services to children and parents together, and conducts home visits to parents to increase both their knowledge of child development and their ability to assist in their child's educational success. Families are eligible for services if the parent is eligible for adult education (under the Adult Education Act) and at least one child in the household is under the age of eight. Ninety percent of families participating in Even Start have incomes below the federal poverty level.

Evaluation Findings

A randomized trial of the effects of Even Start was conducted by ABT Associates (St. Pierre, Swartz, Murray, & Deck, 1996) and included an examination of child and family outcomes at five program sites. Even Start children outperformed similar children not in the program on school readiness skills at the end of the program; but after kindergarten, Even Start and comparison children scored similarly on the Peabody Picture Vocabulary Test and on the Preschool Inventory, which involves measuring knowledge of colors, shapes, and sizes (U.S. Department of Education, 1998). There were no effects on the children's receptive vocabulary, on parent-child reading interactions, or on any other aspects of parenting.

In the most recent evaluation of Even Start (U.S. Department of Education, 2003), benefits for children participating in the program were small. While children made literacy gains during the program, the gains were similar to those made by children in the control group, and children remained below average when compared to national norms.

Program Characteristics

Who Is Eligible: Low-income families with children age eight and younger are eligible to participate. Parents must qualify under the Adult Education Act: Parents must be at least 16 years old without a high school degree or equivalent, must not be enrolled in another school program, and must lack basic educational skills or be unable to read, write, or speak English.

Who Is Served: Approximately 50,000 families at 1,300 sites are served (Even Start, 2004). Forty percent of the children served were two years old or younger, 28% were three or four, 11% were five years of age, and 21% were six or older. Families served were extremely disadvantaged:

Only 15% of Even Start parents had a high school diploma or equivalent and 41% of families had incomes under $6,000.

Educational Program: There are three components to the program: adult education, parenting education, and early childhood education. Adult literacy and instruction for non-English-speaking adults are incorporated into the main components of the program. Programs have flexibility in how they offer the components to the participants. While child and adult programs are offered independently, child-adult interaction is a key component of the program, and activities that encourage parent involvement are emphasized.

Funding	Federal funding
Teacher Qualifications	All instructional staff must have a bachelor's degree, and administrators must have family literacy training.
Teacher/Child Ratios	Varies by coordinating program
Maximum Class Size	Varies by coordinating program
Hours of Operation	Varies by coordinating program
Cost	Approximately $3,137 per family per year (1998 data)

STATE PROGRAMS

In 2002–2003, 738,000 children attended a state-funded prekindergarten program (National Institute for Early Education Research, 2004). However, that number only reflects approximately 10% of children three to four years old in the United States. Further, only two states (Georgia and Oklahoma) have prekindergarten programs available to all children, and approximately 10 states have no state-supported prekindergarten programs at all. In addition, states vary in the design of their programs and their quality benchmarks. For example, only 13 state prekindergarten programs currently require a teacher to have a Bachelor's degree in addition to early childhood education training.

However, over three-quarters of the 33 state-supported prekindergarten programs met or exceeded Head Start's teacher-child ratio of 1:10

and had no more than 20 children per classroom as recommended by the National Association for the Education of Young Children (NAEYC). In fact, 50% of the 33 prekindergarten programs adhere to either NAEYC or Head Start guidelines for quality (U. S. Department of Health and Human Services, 2003).

Across separate state studies (Gilliam & Zigler, 2000; U. S. Department of Health and Human Services, 2003), children who attended state-sponsored preschools had increased scores on cognitive assessments and language ability assessments (nine out of ten states), significantly higher scores on standardized reading and mathematics tests in elementary school (six out of seven states), better attendance (one state), and lower rates of grade retention than comparison children during at least one year of elementary school. While these findings are promising, not all states had follow-up data, and some of the results were mixed. Therefore, it is crucial to continue to verify the benefits of state programs in general as well as the components of programs that are associated with increased quality and child outcomes. Some specific state programs are described below.

Georgia's Prekindergarten Program

Goal and Background

Launched in 1993 and fully funded with state lottery proceeds, this program established Georgia as the first state to provide preschool services to all four-year-old children. The prekindergarten program is provided in both public schools and private preschools. The goal of the program is to provide developmentally appropriate education to young children in an effort to increase school readiness (Office of School Readiness, 2003).

Evaluation Findings

Currently, a longitudinal study is following approximately 4,000 children to ascertain the effects of prekindergarten on their development.

Overall, 64% of children who participated in prekindergarten were rated by the kindergarten teacher as being prepared "well" to "extraordinarily well" for kindergarten (Henderson, Basile, & Henry, 1999).

So far, 26% of kindergarten teachers reported that the skills gained in prekindergarten would help them teach more prereading skills, and 23% said those skills would help them teach more premath skills.

At the beginning of second grade, 79% of teachers reported that children in their classrooms who attended the prekindergarten were average or better in their readiness skills for entering the second grade compared with all children. At the end of second grade, 82% of teachers reported that the prekindergarten children were average or better in their readiness for entering third grade compared with their peers (Henry, Gordon, Mashburn, & Ponder, 2001).

While there is no comparison group for this evaluation and the results reflect teacher perceptions rather than assessments made directly on the children, the researchers did find apparent benefits among the children who attended the prekindergarten program. Children who turned four years old before June outperformed children who turned four years old after June in elementary school, indicating that slightly older children may benefit more from a prekindergarten program. Further, children who attended a program with an increased number of disruptive students preformed worse than children who did not. Last, children who were in a program with child-centered teaching methods performed better than children in teacher-directed classrooms (Henry, Gordon, Mashburn, & Ponder, 2001).

In addition, the most recent evaluation (Henry et al., 2003) found that children who were in the Georgia prekindergarten program "caught up" with children attending private prekindergarten programs in the state on kindergarten readiness skills (premath, letter-word recognition, vocabulary, story/print comprehension, and basic skills mastery). Moreover, children in the state prekindergarten program outperformed children in Georgia's Head Start program on letter-word recognition, vocabulary, and story/print recognition.

Program Characteristics

Who Is Eligible: All four-year-olds in the state are eligible.

Who Is Served: Approximately 68,119 children participated during 2003–2004 (56% of all four-year-olds in the state) in 100% of the school districts.

Educational Program: While local school districts have flexibility, the following curricula are listed as approved by the state: Bank Street, Creative Curriculum, High Reach, High/Scope, Montessori, and Scholastic Workshop. Parent involvement is encouraged in the program; there must be at least two parent-teacher conferences per year in addition to parent volunteering and parent participation in activities and workshops.

Funding	Funding for the program is provided through state lottery dollars. Prekindergarten providers are awarded contracts through a competitive process.
Teacher Qualifications	Associate's degree or Montessori diploma; however, reimbursement for the program is based on teacher's qualification level
Teacher/Child Ratios	1:10
Maximum Class Size	20 Children
Hours of Operation	6.5 hours per day, 5 days per week during the school year
Cost	For 2003–2004, the cost was $3,830 per year per child (rate of reimbursement varies depending on teacher's certification).

Oklahoma's Prekindergarten

Goal and Background

Like Georgia, Oklahoma provides prekindergarten without eligibility restrictions. The program started as a pilot program in 1980 and is currently available in 91% of the school districts. A developmentally appropriate, comprehensive curriculum is used that is consistent with the curriculum provided in kindergarten.

Evaluation Findings

A significant association was found between enrollment in prekindergarten and scores in language arts, cognitive skills and knowledge, and motor skills. Participation in the Tulsa, Oklahoma prekindergarten program was associated with a 17.2 % increase in cognitive/knowledge score, a 16.5% increase in language arts score, and an 8.4% increase in motor skills score (Gormley & Gayer, 2003).

Program Characteristics

Who Is Eligible: All four-year-olds are eligible on a first-come, first-served basis.

Who Is Served: 28,060 four-year-olds participated (59% of the eligible children).

Educational Program: Standards are set by the Oklahoma Department of Education. While school districts are allowed flexibility, the curriculum must be developmentally appropriate, and continuity between the pre-kindergarten and kindergarten must be apparent. Programs must encourage parent involvement to complement the educational experiences of children in the program.

Funding	State formula funding to schools based on part-day and full-day programming
Teacher Qualifications	Early Childhood Education Certification or a Special Early Childhood Certification (a bachelor's degree in addition to passing an early childhood competency test)
Teacher/Child Ratios	1:10
Maximum Class Size	20 children per class
Hours of Operation	2.5 to 6 hours per day, 5 days a week for the 9-month school year (hours are determined locally)
Cost	For 2003–2004, the cost was $2,049 per child.

New Jersey's Prekindergarten

Goal and Background

New Jersey has two types of prekindergarten. The Abbott Preschool was mandated by the New Jersey court system to provide high quality preschool programs in the 30 highest poverty school districts. The Non-Abbott Early Childhood Program Aid (ECPA) is available in school districts in which 20% to 40% of children are eligible for free or reduced lunch (approximately 128 districts). Both programs are comprehensive in scope with strict guidelines for quality to provide school readiness to children at risk for school failure.

Evaluation Findings

A report by the Early Learning Improvement Consortium (2004) indicated that children in the prekindergarten programs had increased oral language skills at the time of kindergarten entry, although they still scored below the national averages. Further, the majority of children who participated in the prekindergarten program entered kindergarten with letter knowledge and linguistic awareness skills (as measured by the state kindergarten screening tool). When some of the quality components were examined, less experienced teachers, larger school districts, and the most economically disadvantaged districts were associated with lower performance measures.

Program Characteristics

Who Is Eligible: In Abbott districts, all three- and four-year-olds are eligible. In non-Abbott districts, all four-year-olds who are residents are eligible on a first-come, first-served basis. Non-Abbott districts are allowed to set additional limits on participation.

Who Is Served: 43,678 children are served (25% of four-year-olds in New Jersey), 36,465 in the Abbott Preschool Program, and 7,213 in the Non-Abbott Early Childhood Program.

Educational Program: Abbott districts are encouraged to form a collaborative relationship with local child care centers. Programming "must be comprehensive, providing supplementary health, nutrition, and social services" (Education Commission of the States, 2000). For Abbott district programs, there must be a strong parent involvement component. For non-Abbott districts, curriculum is determined by local district, and no parent involvement component is required.

Funding	For the Abbott districts, there is no predetermined formula; state money is granted by the state based on the needs of the district. For non-Abbott districts, a state formula determines reimbursement.
Teacher Qualifications	Bachelor's degree and an early childhood certificate
Teacher/Child Ratios	2:15
Maximum Class Size	15 children per class
Hours of Operation	For the Abbott Preschool Program, 5 full days per week during the school year; for the Non-Abbott Early Childhood Program, a minimum of a half day, 5 days per week during the school year
Cost	For 2003–2004, the cost was $8,725 per child.

Michigan's Prekindergarten

Goal and Background

Started in 1985 as a pilot program, the Michigan School Readiness Program (MSRP) serves four-year-olds who are considered to be at risk for school failure. The prekindergarten program is funded by the state and provides children with developmentally appropriate education in an attempt to increase school readiness.

Evaluation Findings

An evaluation compared 338 participating kindergarten children with 258 kindergarten children of similar socioeconomic background who did not participate in the preK program. Kindergarten teachers rated children who attended the state prekindergarten program better in language, literacy, logic, math, music, movement, creativity, social relations, and initiative. Teachers from kindergarten through fourth grade also rated participants as being more interested in school, taking more initiative, having better school attendance, and being better able to work with others than the comparison group. Students who participated in the prekindergarten were also significantly more likely to pass the fourth-grade Michigan Educational Assessment Program reading and math sections than students not in the preschool program.

> Taking into account background characteristics, retention rates were 35% lower for students in the program versus those not in the program, which saves the state an estimated $11 million annually.

Further, parents of children who attended the MSRP were more likely to be involved in their children's school and to communicate with their children's teacher (Xiang & Schweinhart, 2002).

Program Characteristics

Who Is Eligible: Four-year-olds not enrolled in Head Start are eligible. Fifty percent of participants must be considered low income. Children must also have at least 2 risk factors out of 24 associated with school failure (Mitchell, Ripple, & Chanana, 1998).

Who Is Served: 25,712 children participate a year in 85% of the school districts (19% of children in the state). The program is available to four-year-old children at risk for school failure, who are not eligible for or enrolled in Head Start. Fifty percent of the children must be identified as low income.

Educational Program: The programs must follow the *Michigan Standards of Quality and Curriculum Guidelines* (Michigan State Board of Education, 1987). One of the curriculum standards focuses on the socioemotional well-being of the child; for example, "the program is structured to enhance children's feelings of comfort and security" (pg. 26). Further, activities should be developmentally appropriate for children; children should learn through play, manipulation, and various other modes; children should experience challenges and successes when engaged in an activity; instruction should be individualized; and rich language experiences should be incorporated to encourage problem solving. A parent involvement component is required. At least two home visits and two conferences must occur each year in addition to classroom volunteering and other activities determined by the school. For every 18 children in the program, one parent must serve on the advisory council.

Funding	State funding for school districts is based on a formula determined by local needs. For nonschool programs, competitive grants are available from the state.
Teacher Qualifications	Bachelor's degree in public school districts and an associate's degree plus CDA in nonpublic school districts
Teacher/Child Ratios	1:8 (4-year-olds)
Maximum Class Size	18 children per class (4-year-olds)
Hours of Operation	Half day for 4 days or 2 full days (if additional days are offered, tuition may be charged) for the 9-month school year
Cost	For 2003–2004, the cost was $3,300 per child (approximately $6.60 per hour).

Chicago Child-Parent Center Program

Goal and Background

The Child-Parent Center (CPC) Program has been in the Chicago public school system since 1967. The program was started using federal Title I funding to provide preschool services to children living in the most economically disadvantaged communities in Chicago. In 1977, State of Illinois Chapter 1 funding allowed for the expansion of the program through the third grade. To be eligible for services, families must live in a Title I neighborhood, children may not be enrolled in any other type of intervention, and parents must also agree to participate in the Center.

In addition to offering early educational services to children, the CPCs encourage parent involvement in all aspects of the program. Each site has a parent room and a full-time parent-community representative who provides both educational services to parents and resources and referrals to families.

> Children can participate for up to six years of comprehensive language-based intervention: one to two years of preschool, one year of kindergarten, and up to three years of extended services in elementary school.

Evaluation Findings

A quasi-experimental study compared children participating in the CPCs with children participating in alternative early childhood programs. Children who participated in the CPC preschool program had significantly better kindergarten-tested readiness skills (language, listening, word analysis, vocabulary, and math) than children in alternative programs. Participants also had higher achievement in both reading and math from 6 to 15 years of age. Youth who had participated had lower rates of grade retention, lower rates of special education placement, less time spent in special education if placed in special education, higher scores on a life skills competency test at age 14, were less likely to drop out of school, and were less likely to be involved in the juvenile justice system than the comparison group. Further, parents of children who attended the CPC had higher rates of parent involvement than parents of children in the comparison group (Reynolds, Miedel, & Mann, 2000; Reynolds, Temple, Robertson, & Mann, 2001). Taking into account savings to society and schools, the program is estimated to save $47,759 per participant, a nearly $7:$1 benefit-to-cost ratio.

Program Characteristics

Who Is Eligible: Children ages three and up who live in the neighborhoods where the program is available can participate.

Who Is Served: Approximately 5,600 children, ages three to nine, are served in 24 centers.

Educational Program: Teachers have flexibility in selecting their curriculum, though there must be an emphasis on basic language and math skills through varied learning opportunities (small group, field trips, individualized activities, etc.). Parent involvement is required. Parents are encouraged to volunteer in the classroom, go on field trips, and serve on an advisory board.

Funding	Title I, state funding, and local funding
Teacher Qualifications	Teacher certification
Teacher/Child Ratios	1:8
Maximum Class Size	17
Hours of Operation	Half day (2.5 to 3 hours) or full day (6 hours) for a 9-month school year
Cost	$6,692 yearly for children in the preschool program and in the half-day kindergarten program. For children receiving follow-on services, the cost is $2,981 per year above the cost of the regular school program (1998 costs).

TRENDS IN PUBLICLY FUNDED EARLY CHILDHOOD PROGRAMS

The following pages note and explore trends in publicly funded early childhood programming (Mitchell, 2001):

Growth

More states are now funding or supplementing federal funding for prekindergarten programs. Because of the consistent evidence that early childhood education increases children's ability to do well in kindergarten and beyond, many states are taking the initiative to provide prekindergarten to children. While only two states fund universal enrollment, 36 states are providing preschool programs to children living in poverty.

Funding

Both federal and state funding levels for early childhood programs are increasing. In 1988, state spending on prekindergarten was close to $190 million; as of 2002–2003, states were spending $2.54 billion on prekindergarten, a greater than fivefold increase in 12 years (National Institute for Early Education Research, 2004).

Prekindergarten Sites

States are using both traditional and nontraditional sites for their prekindergarten programs. The use of existing sites, such as public schools, private child care, and Head Start facilities, increases the availability of prekindergarten classrooms without investing in totally new facilities and increases the availability and convenience of such services to many families. However, relationships must be formed so that there is more collaboration and partnering to provide children services wherever families are located and so early childhood programming is consistent with kindergarten and primary school curricula.

Universal PreK

States are slowly decreasing eligibility restrictions so that more children receive free or reduced-cost early education services. Only Georgia and Oklahoma currently offer universal prekindergarten. However, New York, Connecticut, and New Jersey are moving toward offering services to all four-year-olds.

Family Needs

The related needs of families are increasingly being considered. Given the large proportion of working families involved, programs must be more flexible in meeting the needs of diverse families. Additional "wraparound" services are being considered by both Head Start and many states so that children can attend a full-day program. This increases the continuity of care for the child and decreases parental anxiety. The government has required all families, including single-parent families, to work essentially full time for the full year, but the vast majority of government-funded or supported early childhood services are available (or reimbursed) for only part of the day and year. This disparity may partly explain why many low-income parents do not or cannot use the higher quality services provided especially for them by the government—because they must make additional care and transportation arrangements to cover the remaining hours of work per day and days per year.

Quality

Both federal and state programs are increasing the quality of programs. Higher quality teachers for preschool programs and higher standards for the classrooms are being enacted by Head Start and many of the state prekindergarten programs. Increased accreditation requirements and increased staff qualifications are now becoming more commonplace.

CONCLUSIONS AND RECOMMENDATIONS

While more research is needed, existing data indicate that early education programs are beneficial, and the long-term benefits include less school failure, higher rates of employment, and less crime. These advances have the potential benefit of improving the quality of life of the participants and providing more qualified people for the workforce of the future. Federal and state funding has clearly helped support programs that are making a difference in children's lives and the future of our society, though increasing program quality, staff development, and parent involvement remain critical issues. To address these areas, recommendations are listed below:

- *Parent involvement is necessary to make programs more successful.* The most successful early childhood programs, described previously, are able to incorporate the entire family. Because parents play such a pivotal role in their children's school success, programs that involve parents as partners in their children's development tend to produce better child outcomes. By involving parents in the educational process, children learn through their parents the importance of school, and parents will also have opportunities to bring education taught at school into the home.

- *Enrollments in quality early childhood programs should be increased.* The United States lags behind other industrial nations when it comes to the number of children attending some type of preschool. While there has been an increase in prekindergarten programs for children living in poverty, there are still too many children who are not attending, whether it is because of the location and availability of the program or because of financial constraints.

- *Early education programs must strive to meet the needs of all families.* With so many working families, it is critical that early education remains adaptable to the various needs of families. By providing wrap-around services, parents are able to send their children to regulated educational programs, enabling children to remain in one setting.

- *Early education programs must be of high quality to achieve the benefits research shows are possible.* Children deserve to attend early education programs that are of the highest quality possible. Federal and state education standards need to be set at rigorous levels so that the highest quality of staff and the highest educational standards are met. Small child-teacher ratios, developmentally appropriate practice, and highly trained teachers must be a part of every classroom.

- *Evaluation of prekindergarten programs needs to be continued and expanded.* As evidenced by the relative lack of data, not all programs have extensive evaluations. However, it is critical that researchers look beyond the question "Does early education work?" and start asking, "What components of early education work best and for whom?" By focusing on *for whom* early education works and *what about* early education works, we'll be better able to determine best practices for prekindergarten that are individualized to meet the needs of children, and, ultimately, implement these practices in other programs.

REFERENCES

Administration on Children, Youth and Families, Head Start Bureau. (2001). Education and early childhood development curriculum. In *Head Start program performance standards and other regulations* (subpart 1304.21). Retrieved January 25, 2006, from http://www.acf.hhs.gov/programs/hsb/performanc/1304b2_curiculum.htm

Administration on Children, Youth and Families, Head Start Bureau. (2005). *Head Start program fact sheet. Fiscal year 2004.* Retrieved January 25, 2006, from http://www.acf.hhs.gov/programs/hsb/research/2005.htm

Administration on Children, Youth and Families, Office of Planning, Research and Evaluation. (2003, May). *Head Start FACES 2000: A whole-child perspective on program performance.* Washington, DC: U.S. Department of Health and Human Services. Retrieved January 25, 2006, from http://www.acf.hhs.gov/programs/opre/hs/faces/reports/faces00_4thprogress/faces00_title.html

Administration on Children, Youth and Families, Office of Public Affairs (OPA). (2004, August). *Head Start Bureau (HSB)* [Fact sheet]. Retrieved January 25, 2006, from http://www.acf.hhs.gov/opa/fact_sheets/headstart_factsheet.html

Currie, J., & Thomas, D. (1999). Does Head Start help Hispanic children? *Journal of Public Economics, 74*(2), 235–262.

Early Learning Improvement Consortium. (2004). *Inch by inch, row by row gonna' make this garden grow: Classroom quality and language skills in the Abbott Preschool Program.* Trenton, NJ: New Jersey Department of Education. Retrieved January 25, 2006, from http://www.state.nj.us/njded/ece/app.pdf

Education Commission of the States. (2000). *Pre-kindergarten database.* Retrieved January 25, 2006, from http://www.ecs.org/clearinghouse/27/24/2724.htm

Even Start. (2004, November 30). [Personal communication].

Garces, E., Thomas, D., & Currie, J. (2000, December). *Longer-term effects of Head Start* (Working Paper No. 8054). Cambridge, MA: National Bureau of Economic Research. Retrieved January 24, 2006, from http://www.nber.org/papers/w8054

Gilliam, W. S., & Zigler, E. F. (2000). A critical meta-analysis of all evaluations of state-funded preschool from 1977 to 1998: Implications for policy, service delivery, and program implementation. *Early Childhood Research Quarterly, 15,* 441–473.

Gormley, W. T., & Gayer, T. (2003, October). *Promoting school readiness in Oklahoma: An evaluation of Tulsa's Pre-K program* (Crocus Working Paper No.1). Washington, DC: Center for Research on Children in the U.S. Retrieved January 24, 2006, from http://www.crocus.georgetown.edu/reports/working.paper.1.pdf

Henderson, L. W., Basile, K. C., & Henry, G. T. (1999). *Prekindergarten longitudinal study 1997–1998 school year annual report.* Atlanta: Georgia State University Applied Research Center School of Policy Studies. Retrieved January 25, 2006, from http://www.arc.gsu.edu/prek/report/prek9798Long.pdf

Henry, G. T., Gordon, C. S., Mashburn, A., & Ponder, B. D. (2001). *Pre-K longitudinal study: Findings from the 1999–2000 school year.* Atlanta: Georgia State University Applied Research Center School of Policy Studies. Retrieved January 25, 2006, from http://www.arc.gsu.edu/prek/report/PrekAR9900.pdf

Henry, G. T., Henderson, L. W., Ponder, B. D., Gordon, C. S., Mashburn, A. J., Rickman, D. K. (2003). *Report of the findings from the Early Childhood Study: 2001–02.* Atlanta: Georgia State University Andrew Young School of Policy Studies. Retrieved January 25, 2006, from http://aysps.gsu.edu/publications/2003/earlychildhood.pdf

Karoly, L. A., & Bigelow, J. H. (2005). *The economics of investing in universal preschool education in California* (Monograph Series No. MG-349). Santa Monica, CA: RAND.

McKey, R. H., Condelli, L., Ganson, H., Barrett, B. J., McConkey, C., & Plantz, M. C. (1985). *The impact of Head Start on children, families, and communities* (DHHS Publication No. OHDS 85–31193). Washington, DC: U. S. Government Printing Office.

Michigan State Board of Education. (1987). *Standards of quality and curriculum guidelines for preschool programs for four-year-olds.* Lansing, MI: Author.

Mitchell, A. (2001). *Prekindergarten programs in the states: Trends and issues.* Climax, NY: Early Childhood Policy Research.

Mitchell, A., Ripple, C., & Chanana, N. (1998). *Prekindergarten programs funded by the states, essential elements for policy makers.* New York: Families and Work Institute. Retrieved January 24, 2006, from http://www.familiesandwork.org/summary/prek.pdf

National Institute for Early Education Research. (2004). *The state of preschool: 2004 state preschool yearbook.* New Brunswick, NJ: Rutgers University.

Oden, S., Schweinhart, L. J., & Weikart, D. P. (2000). *Into adulthood: A study of the effects of Head Start.* Ypsilanti, MI: High/Scope Press.

Office of School Readiness. (2003). State summary. *The 2002–2003 annual report card on the State of Georgia.* Retrieved June 16, 2005, from http://reportcard.gaosa.org/yr2003/osr/CenterReport.aspx

Reynolds, A. J., Miedel, W. T., & Mann, E. A. (2000, March). Innovation in early intervention for children in families with low incomes: Lessons from the Chicago Child-Parent Centers. *Young Children, 55,* 84–88.

Reynolds, A. J., Temple, J. A., Robertson, D. L., & Mann, E. A. (2001). Long-term effects of an early childhood intervention on educational achievement and juvenile arrest: A 15-year follow-up of low-income children in public schools. *Journal of the American Medical Association, 285,* 2339–2346.

St. Pierre, R. G., Swartz, J. P., Murray, S., & Deck, C. (1996). *Improving family literacy: Findings from the national evaluation of Even Start.* Cambridge, MA: ABT Associates, Inc. Retrieved January 24, 2006, from http://www.abtassociates.com/reports/ paper5.pdf

U. S. Department of Education. (1998). *Even Start: Evidence from the past and a look to the future.* Washington, DC: Author.

U. S. Department of Education. (2003). *Third national Even Start evaluation: Program impacts for implications for improvement.* Washington, DC: Author.

U. S. Department of Education (2005). *Comparative indicators of education in the United States and other G8 countries: 2004.* Washington, DC: Author.

U. S. Department of Health and Human Services. (2003). *State-funded pre-kindergarten: What the evidence shows.* Washington, DC: Author.

U. S. Department of Health and Human Services. (2005). *Head Start Impact Study: First year findings.* Washington, DC: Author.

U. S. General Accounting Office. (1997). *Head Start: Research provides little information on impact of current program* (Publication No. GAO/HEHS-97–59). Washington, DC: Author.

U. S. General Accounting Office. (2003a). *Education and care: Head Start key among array of early childhood programs, but national research on effectiveness not completed* (Publication No. GAO-03–840T). Washington, DC: Author.

U. S. General Accounting Office. (2003b). *Head Start: Increased percentage of teachers nation-wide have required degrees, but better information on classroom teachers' qualifications needed* (Publication No. GAO-04–05). Washington, DC: Author.

Xiang, Z., & Schweinhart, L. (2002). *Effects five years later: The Michigan School Readiness Program Evaluation through age 10.* Ypsilanti, MI: High/Scope Educational Research Foundation. Retrieved January 24, 2006, from http://www.highscope.org/Research/msrpEvaluation/msrp-Age10-2.pdf

Demonstration Programs and Successful Outcomes

5

Wendy M. Barnard and Christina J. Groark

Early childhood education demonstration programs are programs that have been designed "at least in part for the purpose of generating practical knowledge"; that is, they have been created not only to serve children but also with the goal of establishing measurable and potentially replicable environments to inform stakeholders and policymakers of the programs' effectiveness with regard to current and future practices (Travers & Light, 1982). These programs—which children typically begin at three to four years of age, but some earlier—have been shown to have several benefits for low-income children relative to comparable children who do not experience the program. This chapter focuses only on long-term studies of programs with academic outcome data. These programs served children at risk for school failure. Included in this chapter are only the model programs that have been determined to have both quality of design and length of follow-up sufficient enough to draw conclusions about the program.

As discussed in earlier chapters, the purpose of early childhood education is to provide children with the skills necessary to succeed in school and, in the long run, to become productive citizens. Those skills include, but are certainly not limited to, cognitive skills, school readiness skills, and social and emotional development skills (Currie, 2001).

However, with only about half of all American children of preschool age attending a preschool program, kindergarten teachers report that 46% of children are not prepared for kindergarten. (Rimm-Kaufman, Pianta, & Cox, 2000). Further, for those who do attend a preschool program, there has been a rise in behavior problems resulting in a prekindergarten expulsion rate of 3.2 times the rate for grade school (K–12) students (Gilliam, 2005).

Follow-up studies on programs for children living in poverty indicate that, when compared to control or comparison groups, children who attend preschool programs not only came to school ready to learn but also had

- Increased cognitive skills
  - Better school achievement
  - Lower retention rates
  - Lower rates of special education placement
  - Higher educational levels

- Increased social and emotional development
  - Lower rates of juvenile delinquency
  - Fewer lifetime adult arrests

RANDOMIZED EXPERIMENTS

The following programs randomly selected children either to receive educational services or to be part of a control group (no educational services). Using this type of comparison, group differences that appear after the program are attributed to the program itself.

The Perry Preschool Program

One of the most widely cited studies of early intervention research, the Perry Preschool Program in Ypsilanti, Michigan, was designed to examine the influence of a high quality preschool program for children living in poverty. The project, which ran from 1962 until 1967, included African American children, aged three and four, with IQs lower than 90 who were randomly assigned either to educational intervention services or to a comparison group that received no services. Children participated in a half-day preschool program for two years. The program emphasized child-directed learning, and there was a low teacher-child ratio. In addition to school activities, teachers conducted home visits to all of the families in the program. Since the 1960s, 123 of these children have been tracked to gauge the short- and long-term effects of the early intervention on their development (Barnett, 1996; Berrueta-Clement, et al., 1984; Schweinhart, Barnes, & Weikert, 1993; Schweinhart, et al., 2005).

Cognitive Skills

Children who participated in preschool were less likely to have been enrolled in special education classes and had higher school achievement test scores through age 14. Further, the participants were less likely to have dropped out of high school, had better attitudes about school than the control group, and as youth, had significantly more years of education than the comparison group.

Social-Emotional Development

Students who were enrolled in the Perry Preschool Program had fewer teenage pregnancies and had decreased rates of juvenile delinquency. Interestingly, at age 19, youth who had attended preschool were also more likely than the comparison group to take an active role in caring for themselves and their families (measured by home repairs, house cleaning, caring for family members, etc.). At age 27, participants were also less likely to be receiving social services or to have been arrested. At age 40, when compared with the control group, those adults who attended the Perry Preschool had higher levels of education, were more likely to be employed, had higher annual salaries, were more likely to own a home, and were more likely to have a savings account (Schweinhart et al., 2005).

Cost-Benefit Analysis

While this program was relatively expensive to implement, the savings to society far exceed the investment. Overall, there was a total net benefit of almost $38,000 per participant (Karoly, Kilburn, Bigelow, Caulkins, & Cannon, 2001) or, in 2000 dollars, about $17 per each $1 spent (Schweinhart et al., 2005).

Funding	Local and federal
Teacher Child Ratios	5 to 6 children per teacher
Curriculum	High/Scope
Hours of Operation	2.5 hours a day, 5 days a week
Cost	$15,166 per child a year, in 2000 dollars

Abecedarian Project

The Abecedarian Project was a comprehensive education program in North Carolina conducted from 1972 through 1985 and focusing on mothers with low IQs and living in poverty (98% were African American). While all families received social services, only one group received educational services. Educational services included parent groups for mothers and education for children birth through kindergarten or second grade. At infancy, children were randomly assigned to a control group or treatment group, and, at age five, the treatment group was randomly assigned to additional school educational services (thus making a three-group comparison: no intervention, early educational intervention only, and early educational intervention plus school intervention). Education was language based with emphasis on cognitive development, motor development, and social and adaptive skills. From infancy through age five, children received educational services from a child care center, and, after age five, children received education resources through the school system.

Cognitive Skills

At age 15, when compared to the control group, children who had received both early childhood education and preschool services had higher scores on achievement tests, were less likely to have been retained, and had lower rates of special education placement (Campbell & Ramey, 1995; Ramey & Ramey, 1992). At age 21, these participants also scored higher on IQ, reading, and math tests; had more years of education; and were significantly more likely to be enrolled in some type of postsecondary education.

Social-Emotional Development

At age 21, those who had participated in the program were more likely to have delayed parenthood and to be gainfully employed. Participants were also less likely to have become adolescent parents, to have used marijuana, and to smoke cigarettes (Campbell, Ramey, Pungello, Sparling, & Miller-Johnson, 2002).

Cost-Benefit Analysis

For every $1 spent, $4 were saved when taking into consideration future earnings (related to less special education and school retention, better academic achievement, and less teen pregnancy) and health costs (Masse & Barnett, 2002).

Funding	Federal funding
Teacher Child Ratios	3 children per teacher for infants
	6 children per teacher at preschool
Curriculum	For younger children, the curriculum focused on language, motor, social, and cognitive skill development. At 3 years of age, a standardized curriculum was used (for example, the Peabody Early Experiences Kit, Bridge-to-Reading, GOAL math program, My Friends and Me social skills program, and a prephonics reading program). For preschool children, communication skills and literacy skills were the focus.
Hours of Operation	5 days a week, 50 weeks per year from 7:45 AM to 5:30 PM
Cost	$13,900 per child a year, in 2002 dollars

QUASI-EXPERIMENTAL STUDIES

The following pages look at quasi-experimental programs, which include some type of comparison group but in which children were not randomly selected to be in a participation group or a control group. This methodology leaves open the possibility that the factors associated with those self-selecting into a program may also have contributed to the outcomes.

The Consortium for Longitudinal Studies examined 11 early studies (experimental and quasi-experimental) and pooled the results to ascertain what, if any, long-term effects early intervention programs had on economically disadvantaged children (Lazar & Darlington, 1982; Royce, Darlington, & Murray, 1983). The Consortium examined whether children who participated in an educational early intervention program would have higher school competency (defined as lower grade retention rates and special education placement) than children who did not participate in such a program (Lazar & Darlington, 1982). Results indicated that children receiving intervention services were less likely to be placed in special education or to be retained. Even when background characteristics, such as the child's IQ entering the program, gender, ethnicity and other family variables, were statistically controlled, participation in early intervention still had a positive impact on school competency.

Syracuse University Family Development Research Program (FDRP)

Comprehensive family services were offered to 108 low-income families living in Syracuse, New York, beginning with prenatal care for the mother and ending when the child reached elementary school (Lally, Mangione, & Honig, 1988). The FDRP was offered from 1969 through 1976 with the goal of the program being to help the entire family by offering supportive services to mothers with the intention of enhancing the children's development. Services included educational services for children in addition to nutrition, health and safety, and human services resources for the family. Families were recruited into the program when the mother was in her third trimester of pregnancy. Families were African American, living in poverty, and the mother had less than a high school education.

Cognitive Skills

At kindergarten entrance, significantly more children in the participation group had IQ scores of 89 or higher. In eighth grade, females were less likely to have failing grades, and they had higher grade point averages than comparison youth (Lally et al., 1988).

Social-Emotional Development

At kindergarten entrance, participants in the program were observed to have significantly higher social-emotional functioning than the comparison youth. However, by first grade, this finding receded. Girls in the participation group also had better attendance rates than the comparison group. Last, participants were significantly less likely to have committed violent crimes (Lally et al., 1988).

Cost-Benefit Analysis

Using crime rates only, a savings of $7,795 was obtained, bringing the cost of the program down to just over $10,000 per family (Aos, Phipps, Barnoski, & Lieb, 2001). However, this analysis only incorporates crime benefits, so it is incomplete (see table on next page).

The Brookline Early Education Project (BEEP)

Begun in 1972, the Brookline Early Education Project provided family-oriented services to families with children birth through kindergarten; it

Funding	Federal
Teacher/Child Ratios	Not available
Curriculum	Mother-focused home visitation sessions were offered in which "Child Development Trainers" helped mothers learn developmentally appropriate ways to interact with their children.
	While children were at the Children's Center, a variety of motor and literacy activities were used to match the individual needs of the child.
Hours of Operation	Child Development Trainers met with families weekly. Children could have been in child care various amounts of time.
Cost	$18,037 annually per family (1997 dollars)

offered health and developmental screenings, play groups for toddlers, and preschool services. Additional services included home visits with families, parenting groups, a lending library with toys and books, and a drop-in center for child care needs or other issues. Any family residing in the Brookline area of Boston was eligible for these services (The Brookline Early Education Project, 2002; Tivnan, 1988). Families were randomly assigned to varying levels of program intensity (Palfrey et al., 2005).

Cognitive Skills

In the second grade, children who had participated in the more intensive BEEP services showed greater skill mastery and higher reading comprehension skills than those with less intense services and a comparison group. Further, the follow-up study found that young adults who had participated in the program reported more years of education than the comparison group (The Brookline Early Education Project, 2002; Palfrey et al., 2005).

Social-Emotional Development

In kindergarten, children who participated in BEEP were more cooperative and spent more time on task than children in the comparison group. At follow-up, the longer participants had attended the program, the more likely they were to be engaged in more "intellectually challenging employment." Further, youth who had attended the program in an urban setting reported higher incomes, less depression, and fewer risk-taking behaviors than the comparison group (The Brookline Early Education Project, 2002). Participants were also less likely to report earning less than $20,000 as young adults and were more likely to report better health behaviors (Palfrey et al., 2005).

Cost-Benefit Analysis

No cost-benefit analysis is available.

Funding	Foundation funding
Teacher/Child Ratios	Not available
Curriculum	The preschool and prekindergarten component was based on Piagetian constructivist developmental theory and High/Scope.
Hours of Operation	5 days a week during the school year
Cost	Not available

Allegheny County's Early Childhood Initiative

Located in Allegheny County (Pittsburgh), Pennsylvania, the Early Childhood Initiative (ECI) provided quality early child care to families living in high-risk neighborhoods from 1997 to 2003. Working together, ECI teachers and families provided children, from infancy to preschool, with developmentally appropriate experiences to promote early learning and school readiness. ECI programs emphasized ongoing mentoring intended to increase program quality leading to National Association for the Education of Young Children (NAEYC) accreditation, creative solutions to involve parents, curriculum development based on individual child assessments, and collaborative relationships with other agencies and the public schools (Bagnato, Suen, Brickley, Smith-Jones, & Dettore, 2002).

Cognitive Skills

Whereas 14% of children who entered the program were eligible for special education and 18% were eligible for mental health diagnosis, after three years in the program, all these children improved enough to fall into the "normal range of development." Further, once in kindergarten, children who had attended ECI programs were less likely to be retained and were less likely to be placed into special education than their schoolmates who had not attended an ECI program. In addition, children who had participated in an ECI program gained scholastic skills faster than children who did not attend an ECI program (Bagnato et al., 2002).

Social-Emotional Development

Children in the program gained social skills, such as cooperation in groups, turn taking, sharing, following directions, making friends, and showing respect towards adults (Bagnato et al., 2002).

Cost-Benefit Analysis

No cost-benefit analysis is yet available.

Funding	Foundation funding
Teacher/Child Ratios	NAEYC Standards
Curriculum	Developmentally appropriate curriculum
Hours of Operation	Typical child care operating hours (varied by location)
Cost	$13,129 annually per child, in 2002 dollars

CHARACTERISTICS OF SUCCESSFUL PROGRAMS

While early education programs for children living in poverty cannot ameliorate all of the challenges these children will face, it is certain that providing quality preschool programs has a positive influence on children's development. Characteristics of successful programs include timing, intensity, breadth, and quality programming (McCall, Larsen, & Ingram, 2003).

Timing

Education should start early and last as long as possible. Starting early is important, not so much because earlier is better for the children but because it is better for the parents. Programs provided early might then offer comprehensive services to deal with parents' basic needs, which typically interfere with parenting. It is also important to get the parent involved with the child and in the child's development early because parents likely produce many of the longer-term benefits for their children in such programs.

Intensity

Programs should be intense in hours and days per week. The more intense and the longer lasting the program, the better the outcomes. The more home visits per month, the more hours of early childhood programming per day (i.e., full- versus half-day), and the more years in the program, the greater and more permanent the benefits for parents and children. "Lite" programs in terms of intensity and extent often do not produce even "lite" benefits (Ramey & Ramey, 1992).

Breadth

Services should be comprehensive. The effective program provides, coordinates, and refers clients to a comprehensive, integrated set of adult- and child-focused services. The more risk factors and problems facing a family, the worse the outcome for parents and children. The program needs to be able to arrange for appropriate services to meet any major need identified by a family. Also, parents have difficulty finding time or motivation to focus on parenting and child goals if major adult needs are present, unmet, and producing stress. It is important, then, to address major parent needs such as food, clothing, shelter, medical care, drug and alcohol rehabilitation, mental health services, education and job training, employment, child care or early education, and transportation.

Quality Programming

The better the quality of the program, the better the outcomes. Quality of program is reflected in several characteristics:

Staff should have high levels of general education and more education and training specifically in the focal areas emphasized by the program. An early childhood center program, for example, should be directed by a professional with a graduate degree in child development and early childhood programming, and primary staff should have as much previous and continuing education and training as possible. Community staff can bring valuable social-cultural knowledge to the service, and they also should be trained in child development and early education (Vandell & Pierce, 2003).

Staff should be closely supported, monitored, and supervised by a trained professional. Staff knowledge and training produce a quality program only if they put that knowledge to work in their behavior and practices, which well-trained, attentive, and supportive supervisors encourage (Vandell & Pierce, 2003).

Fewer children per staff member and smaller groups are associated with better outcomes. Staff need time beyond routine caregiving responsibilities to listen to, teach, and encourage individuals and to accommodate the individual needs and interests of children and families in order to promote their development (Boocock, 2003; Vandell & Pierce, 2003).

Early childhood programming that emphasizes developmentally appropriate practices and direct tuition of cognitive, social, and emotional skills and behaviors is more likely to produce benefits in each area of emphasis than strictly adult-centered programming.

> Primary school curricula and methods are not appropriate for preschool-age children, who benefit most from a good balance of child-centered, child-initiated, and teacher-child mutual activities as opposed to the more traditional teacher-directed activities.

Early childhood programming also needs to be more balanced in topic, with more emphasis on social and emotional development and behavior and less on cognitive and academic skills than in primary school. Balance among these general developmentally appropriate emphases is more important for positive outcomes than which specific curriculum strategy (e.g., didactic versus direct instruction, open versus traditional classroom, interactive versus cognitive-developmental) is employed (McCall et al., 2003).

The greater the involvement of the parents in the direct programming of the early childhood service, the better the short-term and long-term outcomes for children. Involvement must go beyond attending open houses or driving on field trips. Parents need to be involved with, and support at home, the lessons the early childhood program is attempting to promote and teach the children (McCall et al., 2003).

CONCLUSIONS AND RECOMMENDATIONS

Several recommendations emerge from these studies:

- *Programs should be funded at a level sufficient to pay for the extent, duration, and quality of services needed to produce benefits for both parents and children.* Because "lite" programs often do not produce even "lite" results, they are a waste of money, at least in terms of achieving the specific child and family results discussed here. Service programs are often funded at only a fraction of the cost of the model program that was demonstrated to be effective, and funders sometimes prefer to enroll more children rather than to ensure program extent, duration, and quality sufficient to produce benefits.

- *Services could be targeted at children and families with the most social, demographic, and economic risk factors, because these people are likely to have the worst outcomes without services, and they also will benefit most from early childhood and family services.* When resources are limited, income should be the primary eligibility criterion used in targeting services.

- *While targeting programs to children at the greatest risk may be most efficient, there may be benefits to universal early childhood programming, or at least programs that mix risk and non-risk children.* Children from diverse backgrounds can learn from each other. Greater public, parental, policy, and financial attention and support might be paid to the quality of such programs if they are provided for all segments of society.

- *The public schools represent a potentially cost-effective vehicle for administering and housing early childhood services and should be considered as a primary provider of early childhood services.* The public schools are well distributed geographically, they have (or could be renovated at less cost to have) the required physical facilities, they have a financial and administrative infrastructure in place, and use of their physical facilities would eliminate transportation problems and the frequent cobbling together of diverse service arrangements that families now often make. Early childhood, extended day, and vacation day program services may be best "out-sourced" by the schools to independent agencies but operated on school premises to deal with the need for specialized training, hours, and salaries of early childhood staff.

- *Continuous monitoring and evaluation are needed to improve the quality of services.* Policymakers should not expect the first one or two cohorts to demonstrate benefits until the program has been developed, implemented, and improved over several cohorts. Also, some program benefits for children may not be realized until years after they have left the program, and then those benefits may be in terms of preventing costly disasters in a few participants (e.g., grade failure, unemployment, criminality) rather than in improving the average performance of the entire group of participants (e.g., grade averages or test scores).

- *A combination of family support and early childhood education plus extensions of similar specialized services into the first three years of primary school should be considered because the combination can increase the magnitude and permanence of the benefits of early childhood services.*

- *Deliberate attempts should be made to improve the persistence of early programming.* This can be done in several ways:
  - Improving the quality of the schools that low-income children will attend after the early childhood program.
  - Providing extended services in the primary schools that are similar to those of successful early childhood programs.

REFERENCES

Aos, S., Phipps, P., Barnoski, R., & Lieb, R. (2001). *The Comparative Costs and Benefits of Programs to Reduce Crime: Version 4.0.* Olympia, Washington: Washington State Institute for Public Policy. http://www.promisingpractices.net/

Bagnato, S. J., Suen, H. K., Brickley, D., Smith-Jones, J., Dettore, E. (2002). Child development impact of Pittsburgh's Early Childhood Initiative (ECI) in high-risk communities: First phase authentic evaluation research. *Early Childhood Research Quarterly, 17,* 559–580.

Barnett, W. S. (1996). Lives in the balance: Benefit-cost analysis of the Perry Preschool Program through age 27. *Monographs of the High/Scope Educational Research Foundation, 11.* Ypsilanti, MI: High/Scope Press.

Belsky, J. (1988). The effects of infant day care reconsidered. *Early Childhood Research Quarterly, 3,* 235–272.

Berrueta-Clement, J. R., Schweinhart, L. J., Barnett, W. S., Epstein, A. S., & Weikart, D. P. (1984). *Changed Lives.* Ypsilanti, MI: High/Scope.

Boocock, S. S. (2003). Lessons from Europe: European preschools revisited in a global age. In A. J. Reynolds, M. C. Wang, & H. J. Walberg (Eds.), *Early childhood programs for a new century* (pp. 299–328). Washington, DC: CWLA Press.

The Brookline Early Education Project. (2002). *Follow-up study.* Retrieved June 10, 2005, from http://www.bc.edu/bc_org/avp/soe/beep/

Campbell, F., & Ramey, C. T. (1995). Cognitive and school outcomes for high-risk African-American students at middle adolescence: Positive effects of early intervention. *American Educational Research Journal, 32*(4), pp. 743–772.

Campbell, F., Ramey, C., Pungello, E., Sparling, J. & Miller-Johnson, S. (2002). Early childhood education: Young adult outcomes from the Abecedarian Project. *Applied Developmental Science, 6*(1), 42–57.

Clarke-Stewart, A. K., & Fein, G. G. (1983). Early childhood programs. In P. H. Mussen (Series Ed.), M. M. Haith, & J. J. Campos (Vol. Eds.), *Handbook of Child Psychology: Vol. 2. Infancy and developmental psychology* (pp. 917–999). New York: Wiley.

Currie, J. (2001). Early childhood education programs. *Journal of Economic Perspectives, 15*(2), 213–238.

Gamble, T. J., & Zigler, E. (1986). Effects of infant day care: Another look at the evidence. *American Journal of Orthopsychiatry, 56,* 26–42.

Gilliam, W. S. (2005). *Prekindergarteners left behind: Expulsion rates in state prekindergarten systems.* New Haven, CT: Yale University Child Study Center.

Karoly, L., Kilburn, R., Bigelow, J. H., Caulkins, J. P., & Cannon, J. S. (2001). *Assessing costs and benefits of early childhood intervention programs: Overview and applications to the Starting Early Starting Smart program.* Seattle: Casey Family Programs; Santa Monica: RAND.

Lally, J. R., Mangione, P., & Honig, A. (1988). The Syracuse University Family Development Program: Long-range impact of an early intervention with low-income children and their families. In *Parent education as early childhood intervention: Emerging directions, theory, research, and practice.* Norwood, NJ: Ablex.

Lazar, I., & Darlington, R. (1982). Lasting effects of early education: A report from the Consortium for Longitudinal Studies. *Monographs of the Society for Research in Child Development, 47*(2–3, Serial No. 195).

Masse, L. N., & Barnett, W. S. (2002). *A benefit-cost analysis of the Abecedarian early childhood intervention.* New Brunswick, NJ: National Institute for Early Education Research.

McCall, R. B., Larsen, L., & Ingram, A. (2003). The science and policies of early childhood education and family services. In A. J. Reynolds, M. C. Wang, & H. J. Walberg (Eds.), *Early childhood programs for a new century: Issues in children's and families' lives* (pp. 255–298). The University of Illinois at Chicago Series on Children and Youth. Washington, DC: CWLA Press.

National Institute of Child Health and Human Development (NICHD), Early Child Care Research Network (2003). Does amount of time spent in child care predict socioemotional adjustment during the transition to kindergarten? *Child Development, 74*(4), 976.

Palfrey, J. S., Hauser-Cram, P., Bronson, M. B., Warfield, M. E., Sirin, S., & Chan, E. (2005). The Brookline Early Education Project: A 25-year follow-up study of a family-centered early health and development intervention. *Pediatrics, 116,* 144–152.

Ramey, S. L., & Ramey, C. T. (1992). Early educational intervention with disadvantaged children: To what effect? *Applied & Preventive Psychology, 1,* 131–140.

Rimm-Kaufman, S. E., Pianta, R. C., & Cox, M. J. (2000). Teachers' judgments of problems in the transition to kindergarten. *Early Childhood Research Quarterly, 15,* 147–166.

Royce, J., Darlington, R., & Murray, H. (1983). Pooled analyses: Findings across studies. In Consortium for Longitudinal Studies (Ed.), *As the twig is bent: Lasting effects of preschool programs* (pp. 411–459). Hillsdale, NJ: Erlbaum.

Schweinhart, L. J., Barnes, H. V., & Weikert, D. P. (1993). Significant benefits: The High/Scope Perry Preschool study through age 27. *Monographs of the High/Scope Educational Research Foundation, 10.* Ypsilanti, MI: High/Scope Press.

Schweinhart, L. J., Montie, J., Xiang, Z., Barnett, W. S., Belfield, C. R., & Nores M. (2005). Lifetime effects: The High/Scope Perry Preschool Study through age 40. *Monographs of the High/Scope Educational Research Foundation, 14.* Ypsilanti, MI: High/Scope Press.

Tivnan, T. (1988). Lessons from the evaluation of the Brookline Early Education Project. In H. B. Weiss & F. H. Jacobs, (Eds.), *Evaluating Family Programs* (pp. 221–238). Hawthorne, NY: Aldine De Gruyter.

Travers, J. R., & Light, R.J. (Eds.). (1982). *Learning from experience: Evaluating early childhood demonstration programs.* Washington, DC: National Academies Press.

Vandell, D. L., & Pierce, K. M. (2003). Child care quality and children's success at school. In A. J. Reynolds, M. C. Wang, and H. J. Walberg (Eds.), *Early childhood programs for a new century* (pp. 115–140). Washington, DC: CWLA Press.

Home-Based and Family Child Care: Characteristics and Quality Issues

6

Richard Fiene and Martha Woodward Isler

The importance of regulating home-based and family child care and improving the quality of these services is clear. The National Child Care Survey (Hofferth, Brayfield, Deitch, & Holcomb, 1991) suggests that the majority of children under five years of age whose mothers work full time are cared for in the homes of a neighbor, friend, family child care provider, or relative. Thirty-eight percent of children are cared for in home-based care verses thirty-five percent in center-based care.

CATEGORIES OF HOME-BASED FACILITIES

There are three basic categories of home-based providers who care for young children: regulated, legally unregulated, and illegally operating.

Regulated Providers

Regulated providers follow state laws, which determine a threshold of children allowed to be served at any one time and the standards child care providers must meet. These providers are licensed, registered, or certified, depending on the state, and include family child care home providers (one adult cares for six or fewer children) and group child care home providers (two adults care for 7–13 children).

Legally Unregulated

These providers serve a number of children less than the threshold required for licensing or registration, or they are relatives of the child and exempt from regulation. Family child care homes usually have additional standards that caring for children in one's home does not. A relative or neighbor can take in one, two, or possibly three children and not be regulated by a state. These providers are considered legally unregulated.

Illegally Operating

Illegally operating providers are not licensed or registered even though they serve the threshold number of children. This category also includes providers serving more children than allowed, even if they are licensed, registered, or certified.

Most home-based caregivers are unregistered and unregulated (Hayes, Palmer, & Zaslow, 1990; Kahn & Kamerman, 1995). In one study, 81% of the nonregulated providers were illegally caring for more than the number of children their state allowed (Kontos, Howes, Shinn, & Galinsky, 1995).

CURRENT QUALITY OF HOME-BASED FACILITIES

Little is known about the quality of these arrangements. Some studies report that families who are the least well educated, have less income from the mothers' jobs, and have higher levels of stress tend to have lower quality child care (Goelman & Pence, 1987a, 1987b). Family child care has been under-researched (Kontos et al., 1995). A number of recent studies have sought to characterize family child care quality, focusing on regulated providers and using observations as primary data sources. Approaches to studying quality include examining regulated characteristics (ratios and group size) and more process-oriented approaches that examine factors such as provider behavior and type of children's experiences (Kontos et al., 1995).

Studies have also compared home-based child care to center-based child care (Fiene et al., 2002; Fiene & Melnick, 1991; Melnick & Fiene, 1990). In each, the overall quality of homes as measured by the Family Day Care Environmental Rating Scale (FDCRS; Harms & Clifford, 1990)

Figure 6.1   ECERS-R Mean Scores by Type of Center-Based Facility

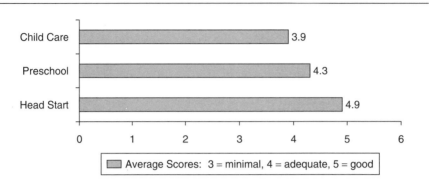

Figure 6.2 FDCRS Mean Scores by Type of Facility

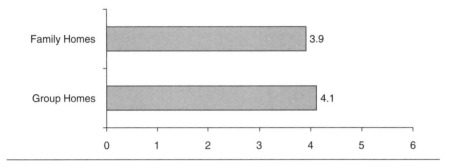

scored at or lower than center-based care when compared to the Early Childhood Environment Rating Scale (ECERS), which are similar scales for two different early childhood environments (Harms & Clifford, 1980). For more information on these rating scales, see Appendix 1 at the end of this chapter. In a recent study (Fiene et al., 2002), centers and homes scored about the same (see Figures 6.1 and 6.2), but lower than Head Start and nursery school programs.

Family Child Care (FCC) is generally perceived as "informal," implying a less structured environment lacking in curriculum, a less educated provider, and a lower quality program. However, quality varies widely among family child care homes. Melnick and Fiene (1990), Fiene and Melnick (1991), and Fiene and colleagues (2002) found that the variation in the FDCRS scores of homes was much greater than it was in the ECERS scores of center-based facilities. Home-based facilities offered some of the best child care, but also some of the worst.

The primary incentives that lead family child care homes to become licensed include public subsidies, the possibility for referrals from resource and referral agencies, access to the professional development and training provided by states, and the ability to obtain liability insurance. Providers who see their services as a business or career are often more eager to gain the visibility that licensing and registration offers. However, many others do not approach home-based care as a business or career and tend to care for children only while their own children are of preschool age (Hayes et al., 1990).

OBSTACLES TO IMPROVING THE QUALITY OF FAMILY CHILD CARE

It is far more difficult to study quality in family day care (home-based facilities) than in centers. The definition of quality varies across communities and among researchers, parents, and providers. Many providers do not want to be evaluated and are not accessible to researchers (Fiene et al., 2002). These and other factors suggest the few studies available may depict family child care as better than it is. This is a concern considering that legally exempt care homes serve the most children, but offer the lowest quality (Fiene et al., 2002).

Fiene and colleagues (2002) found the quality of regulated homes to be roughly comparable to that of child care centers, but not to the quality of Head Start or nursery schools. Poor quality was common in nonregulated homes (see Figure 6.3 on the next page). Children in informal settings are much less likely to engage in activities promoting literacy and learning than children in centers and regulated FCC homes (Zinsser, 1991).

The following section discusses research that may help to improve the overall quality of care in home-based child care.

CHARACTERISTICS OF IMPROVED HOME-BASED AND FAMILY CHILD CARE PROGRAMS

Several characteristics of homes have been found to be related to quality. They include the intentionality of the caregiver to view the care as a professional business and the caregiver having more education, utilizing a curriculum, and taking advantage of training and mentoring programs. Some characteristics are regulated, such as educational level, utilizing a curriculum, and the amount of training or mentoring. Others are not amenable to regulation, such as viewing a program as a business, but can be encouraged through training and mentoring.

Figure 6.3   Percentage of Facilities With Minimal, Adequate, and Good
Scores on Environmental Quality

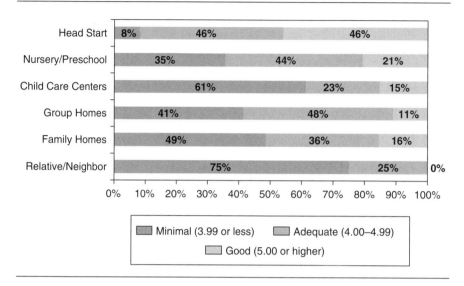

Intentionality

Intentionality is an important factor in determining quality (Brandon, Maher, Joesch, & Doyle, 2002) and is defined as being committed to caring for children, seeking out child development learning opportunities and other professionals, and creating environments where children can be nurtured and learn. Intentional providers offer the high quality, warm, and more attentive care associated with better growth and development. These providers are found more frequently in family child care than in relative care.

> The issue of intentionality is critical to the overall quality of care provided by a caregiver.

Fiene and colleagues (2002) found a significant relationship between the education of the home-based provider and the overall quality of the home as measured by the FDCRS. Family child care homes, which cared for 4–6 children, and group child care homes, which cared for 7–11 children, were observed. The more education that the primary caregiver had, the greater the quality scores were. Having a college degree made a distinct difference in quality. These caregivers viewed themselves as professionals, had more administrative safeguards in place for parents, and more programmatic items in place, such as a curriculum for the children. The majority of those without a college degree saw themselves in the child care business short term, while their children were of preschool age.

Curriculum

Another way to improve the quality of home-based child care is to have family child care home providers utilize a curriculum (see Figure 6.4). Substantially higher quality scores were earned by family child care homes that utilized a curriculum, but a curriculum earned only slightly higher scores among group child care homes. In this study, the variation in educational levels was not as great in group child care homes as in family child care homes because the group child care homes were licensed and the educational requirements were more stringent than in family child care homes, which operated under a registration system.

> Caregivers with a college degree provided care on an average of seven to eight years, while those without a degree had tenures of two to three years (Fiene et al., 2002).

Training and Mentoring Programs

A few experimental studies have examined ways to improve family child care. A quasi-experimental study (Galinsky, Howes, & Kontos, 1995) of a short-term training program, "Family to Family," indicated that the training increased global quality but not process quality (e.g., interactions between caregiver and children). The Quality Early Learning Evaluation (Bagnato & SPECS Program Evaluating Team, 2002) identified key elements that enable low-income children to enter school prepared, learn early, and begin to succeed.

Figure 6.4 Curriculum Use in Type of Home Setting and FDCRS Scores

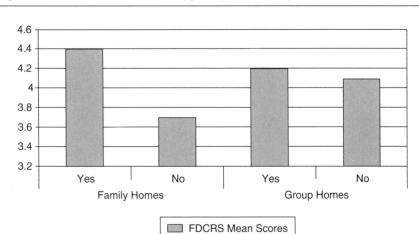

> Findings suggest that when quality standards are met in family child care homes, children achieve at the same rate as those in center-based care (Bagnato et al., 2002).

High quality standards, ongoing mentoring (quality assurance), and the expectation that quality standards will be maintained were essential to achieving and sustaining high quality. The study also reported that mentoring ensures program quality, community leadership breeds program success, and parents learn to help their children succeed.

The findings are consistent with an Infant Caregiver Mentoring Study (Fiene, 2002), which found that mentoring of infant caregivers produced positive behavioral change. Caregivers who received the mentoring intervention (see Box 6.1) were more sensitive and responsive to infant cues. The study is one of the few randomized control trials of a mentoring intervention. In the fall, 20 caregivers received mentoring, and 20 were assigned to a control group, which received the usual workshop training offered by the state. In the spring, the control group received mentoring, and the intervention group became the control. In each semester, those who received mentoring scored significantly higher on all quality measures, and the gains lasted at least through the following summer.

The National Association for Education of Young Children (NAEYC, 1987) has identified common program features related to quality:

- weekly mentoring to improve quality based on NAEYC and the National Association for Family Child Care (NAFCC) standards and practices;
- parent participation;
- ongoing child assessment and feedback to guide instruction and care; and
- community leadership and interagency partnerships, especially with schools.

Box 6.1   Capital Area Early Childhood Training Institute's Caregiver Mentoring Program

This program offers intensive onsite technical assistance and mentoring to directors and caregivers. The program has been effective in making caregivers more sensitive and responsive to children's cues. It is supported by Commonwealth of Pennsylvania and foundation funds, and the unit cost is about $40.00/hour. Mentors visit weekly with protégés in their individual programs. The ratio of protégés to mentor is 10:1. Protégés receive 70–80 hours of mentoring and technical assistance during an academic year.

NAFCC has set quality standards for accreditation in six domains: relationships, environment, activities, developmental learning goals, safety and health, and professional and business practices.

In one study of health and safety, regulated family child care providers had higher levels of compliance than unregulated family child care and relative providers (Galinsky, Howes, Kontos, & Shinn, 1994). It also reported that home caregivers provided higher quality care when they cared for relatively more children–three to six children–instead of one to two children. This result is related to intentionality. The caregivers saw themselves as professionals, planned more effectively, and utilized a curriculum.

RELATIVE AND NEIGHBOR CARE

In the United States, many employed parents depend on relatives to care for their children during work hours. The National Survey of America's Families (NSAF) found that, in 2002, 33% of children under age three and nearly a third of preschool children were cared for by a relative while their parents worked. Over 25% of children under age three were in relative care only as opposed to a combination of care arrangements (Snyder, Dore, & Adelman, 2005). However, there is little research on care provided by relatives and friends. One study (Kontos et al., 1995) found a pattern of behavior among relative providers that suggested less interaction with the relative's children than with unrelated children. Relative care was characterized as less structured, less formal, and less focused on the children. In another study (Brandon, Maher, Joesch, & Doyle, 2002), a majority of relatives and friends who provided child care reported at least some problems in providing care, and two-thirds said they would welcome training or support. However, no wide-scale training programs are available for this group of providers.

CONCLUSIONS AND RECOMMENDATIONS

Family child care or relative care is widely used by families with young children. Unfortunately, the quality of care in family child care and relative care is generally lower than the quality of center-based care. However, several recommendations to improve the quality of home–based care can be drawn from research. They include the following:

- *Attending an orientation session before the registration application is approved should be required.* Such a session should, at a minimum, explain that family child care is a business, review regulations and the "how to" of operating a business, explain administrative requirements, and define financial arrangements.

- *Require "registration" for all home-based care receiving public subsidies.* Research shows that unregulated care is much lower in quality than regulated care.
- *High quality preservice training initiatives specific to family child care should be funded.*
- *Mentoring models that involve intensive in-home training for caregivers should be implemented.*
- *A public education campaign should be implemented to inform parents and communities about what registration means and that "intentional" caregivers generally provide higher quality care than those who "watch" children.*
- *All home-based family child care providers should be brought into the regulatory system, which must provide technical assistance that helps providers improve the quality of care they offer.*

APPENDIX 1: OVERVIEWS AND DESCRIPTIONS OF THE EARLY CHILDHOOD ENVIRONMENT RATING SCALE (ECERS) AND THE FAMILY DAY CARE RATING SCALE (FDCRS)

This section provides examples of what constitutes high and low quality by outlining key indicators of several ECERS-R and FDCRS items. These scales have been used in several major child care and early childhood studies over the past 20 years (Cryer, 1999; Galinsky et al., 1994; Helburn & Howes, 1996; Iutcovich, Fiene, Johnson, Koppel, & Langan, 1997; Jaeger & Funk, 2001) and are among the most reliable program quality instruments available.

Overviews

ECERS-R is designed to assess center-based programs for children in preschool through kindergarten (ages two and a half through five). The scale consists of 43 items organized into 7 scales: Space and furnishings, personal care routines, language reasoning, activities, interactions, program structure, parents and staff.

The FDCRS is designed to assess family child care programs. The scale consists of 40 items, including 8 supplementary items for programs serving children with disabilities. The descriptors cover the needs of a range of ages from infancy through kindergarten. The items are organized into

7 subscales: Space and furnishings for care and learning, basic care, language and reasoning, learning activities, social development, adult needs, provisions for exceptional children.

Each is described in four levels of quality: inadequate, minimal, good, and excellent. Inadequate and minimal ratings focus on the provision of basic materials and on health and safety precautions. The good and excellent ratings require positive interaction, planning, and personalized care, as well as good materials.

ECERS-R Description

A minimal score (3.00–3.99 on the ECERS-R), for example, on the language-reasoning subscale under books and pictures translates into a setting that has some books for children and at least one staff-initiated receptive language activity time (e.g., reading books to children or storytelling). A good or excellent score (above a 5.00 on the ECERS-R) requires more: (e.g., a wide selection of books are accessible for a substantial portion of the day, books are organized in a reading center, staff read books to children informally [e.g., during free play or at naptime], some books relate to current classroom activities or themes [e.g., books borrowed from the library on a seasonal theme], and books and language materials are rotated to maintain interest).

A minimal score on the furnishings for relaxation item indicates some soft furnishings and toys are accessible. However, other indicators would not be observed, such as a cozy area for children for a large part of the day and keeping most soft furnishings clean and in good repair. A minimal score on child-related display means some children's work is displayed, and there are appropriate materials for the predominant age group. But other indicators would not be observed, such as having displays that relate closely to current activities and children in the group or allowing children to do most of the work on the display.

A minimal score on activity items (e.g., fine motor, art, music/movement, dramatic play, nature/science, math/number) means that some developmentally appropriate materials were accessible and in good repair, but the caregiver fell short in other areas, such as not having the materials well organized or available at different levels of difficulty for the children or not providing opportunities to use materials for individual or creative expression.

FDCRS Description

A minimal score (3.99 or less on the FDCRS) for the child-related display category means that no child related pictures, mobiles, or children's artwork are put up for children to look at. A minimal score on the active physical play item means that, in some homes, there is little or no safe outdoor or indoor space for physical play. A minimal score on the activity items—art or sand and water play, for example—means that some materials were accessible, but the materials were not organized to encourage self help, the caregiver did not help children develop skills, and the materials were not well organized for independent use.

REFERENCES

Bagnato, S, & SPECS Program Evaluating Team. (2002). *Quality early learning–Key to school success: A first phase program evaluation research report for Pittsburgh's early childhood initiative (ECI)*. Pittsburgh, PA: Children's Hospital of Pittsburgh.

Brandon, R. N., Maher, E. J., Joesch, J. M., & Doyle, S. (2002) *Understanding family, friend, and neighborhood care in Washington state: Developing appropriate training and support*. Seattle, WA: University of Washington, Human Services Policy Center. Retrieved January 27, 2006, from http://hspc.org/publications/pdf/FFN_report_2002.pdf

Cryer, D. (1999). Defining and assessing early childhood program quality. In Suzanne Helburn (Ed.), The silent crisis in U.S. child care [Special issue]. *Annals of the American Academy of Political and Social Science, 563*, 39–55.

Fiene, R. (2002). Improving child care quality through an infant caregiver mentoring project. *Child and Youth Care Forum, 31*(2), 75–83.

Fiene, R., Greenberg, M., Bergsten, M., Carl, B., Fegley, C., & Gibbons, L. (2002). *The Pennsylvania early childhood quality settings study*. Harrisburg, PA: Governor's Task Force on Early Care and Education.

Fiene, R., & Melnick, S. (1991). *Quality assessment of early childhood programs: A multidimensional approach*. Paper presented at the annual meeting of the American Educational Research Association, Chicago, IL. (ERIC Document Reproduction Service No. ED 334225)

Galinsky, E., Howes, C., & Kontos, S. (1995). *The family child care training study: Highlights and findings*. New York: Families and Work Institute.

Galinsky, E., Howes, C., Kontos, S., & Shinn, M. (1994). *The study of family child care and relative care*. New York: Families and Work Institute.

Goelman, H., & Pence, A. (1987a). Some aspects of the relationship between family structure and child language in three types of day care. In D. Peters & S. Kontos (Eds.), *Annual advances in applied developmental psychology* (Vol. 2, pp. 129–146). Norwood, NJ: Ablex.

Goelman, H., & Pence, A. (1987b). Effects of childcare, family, and individual characteristics on children's language development: The Victoria Day Care Research Project. In D. Phillips (Ed.), *Quality in childcare: What does research tell us?* (pp. 43–56). Washington, DC: National Association for the Education of Young Children.

Harms, T., & Clifford, R. (1980). *Early Childhood Environmental Rating Scale*. New York: Teachers College Press.

Harms, T., & Clifford, R. (1990). *Family Day Care Environmental Rating Scale*. New York: Teachers College Press.

Hayes, C., Palmer, J., & Zaslow, M. (1990). *Who cares for America's children? Child care policy in the 1990s*. Washington, DC: National Academy Press.

Helburn, S. W., & Howes, C. (1996). Child care cost and quality. *Future of Children, 6*(2), 62–82.

Hofferth, S. L., Brayfield, A., Deitch, S., & Holcomb, P. (1991). *National child care survey.* Washington, DC: The Urban Institute.

Iutcovich, J., Fiene, R., Johnson, J., Koppel, R., & Langan, F. (1997). *Investing in our children's future.* Erie, PA: Keystone University Research Corporation.

Jaeger, E., & Funk, S. (2001). *The Philadelphia child care quality study: An examination of quality in selected early care and education settings.* Philadelphia, PA: St Joseph's University.

Kahn, A., & Kamerman, S. (1995). *Starting right: How America neglects its youngest children and what we can do about it.* New York: Oxford University Press.

Kontos, S., Howes, C., Shinn, M., & Galinsky, E. (1995). *Quality in family child care and relative care.* New York: Teachers College Press. (ERIC Document Reproduction Service No. ED390536)

Melnick, S., & Fiene, R. (1990). *Licensure and program quality in early childhood and child care programs.* Paper presented at the annual meeting of the American Educational Research Association, Boston, MA. (ERIC Document Reproduction Service No. ED312270)

National Association for the Education of Young Children. (1987). *Accreditation standards.* Washington, DC: Author.

Snyder, K., Dore, T., & Adelman, S. (2005). Use of relative care by working parents. *Snapshots III of America's Families, 23.* Retrieved January 27, 2006, from the Urban Institute and Social Policy Research Organization Web site: http://www.urban.org/url.cfm?ID=311161

Zinsser, C. (1991). *Raised in East Urban: Child care in a working class community.* New York: Teachers College Press.

School-Age Services: Programs That Extend the Benefits of Early Care and Education Services

7

Suh-Ruu Ou and Arthur J. Reynolds

Participation in early childhood programs is consistently associated with many developmental outcomes, such as higher levels of school readiness, achievement, and social adjustment and lower rates of special education and grade retention. However, some findings indicate that program effects on cognitive development and school achievement fade over time (Barnett, 1995; Guralnick, 1997). Evidence suggests that the "fade-out" phenomenon is associated, in part, with the low quality elementary schools that children attended after they left early childhood programs (Currie & Thomas, 2000; Lee & Loeb, 1995). Effects of early childhood programs are more likely to last if children continue attending high quality schools, because interventions need supports and a stable environment to maintain gains and facilitate ongoing development (Entwisle, 1995).

WHY EXTEND EARLY CHILDHOOD PROGRAMS?

Participation in extended early childhood programs may lead to greater and longer-lasting effects than less extensive interventions for several reasons, which are explored below.

> A major justification for extended early childhood intervention is that elementary schools play an important role in sustaining the benefits of early childhood programs, and a continuation of programs into the primary grades will promote successful transitions and help prevent the fading effects following preschool intervention.

1. *Longer periods of implementation may be necessary to promote greater and longer-lasting changes in child outcomes.* Early interventions are often comprehensive, and they provide many services to children that require significant coordination. They may be more effective if they have more time to work. A common element of successful prevention programs is the provision of services for more than one year (Weissberg & Greenberg, 1998). Another factor that reinforces the need for longer lasting interventions is that children in many urban settings are at higher risk of school failure than in the past; thus, early interventions must be more extensive than before to be equally effective.

2. Extended early childhood programs are designed to encourage more stable and predictable learning environments, which are consensus features of child development theories. Participation in extended interventions, for example, may promote higher rates of school and home stability than would otherwise be expected. Certainly, environmental forces continue to operate after preschool and kindergarten. One assumption of early interventions that continue into the primary grades is that the postprogram learning environment at home and in school can reinforce, limit, or neutralize earlier gains in learning, and thus should not be left to chance.

3. Extended programs provide opportunities for better coordination of instructional and teaching practices from preschool to third grade. In addition to more frequent communication among staff from preschool to kindergarten and into the primary grades, extended interventions have a built-in capacity for curriculum alignment across ages, for the implementation of classroom practices and family-school partnerships that are consistently reinforced over time, and for joint planning on staff development and out-of-classroom learning experiences. These attributes can help create a strong culture of learning.

4. Extended childhood interventions occur at a time increasingly viewed as a sensitive if not "critical" period in children's scholastic development (Entwisle, 1995). It is expected that the provision of additional educational and social support services to children and families during this key transition would promote greater success and would help prevent major learning problems by third grade. In the past decade, many studies provided empirical validation for the strong link between early school adjustment and later educational success (Alexander, Entwisle, & Kabbani, 2001; Ou & Reynolds, 2005; Reynolds, Ou, & Topitzes, 2004).

As a result of these features, extended early childhood programs may not only promote children's learning more strongly than less extensive interventions but help prevent the dissipating effects of earlier interventions in preschool and kindergarten, a pattern found in many previous studies.

The purpose of this chapter is to review the evidence about programs that extend the benefits of early care and education services. Other chapters in this book address the effects of early childhood programs in preschool, so we do not discuss this research in detail.

EXISTING EXTENDED EARLY CHILDHOOD PROGRAMS

Extended early childhood programs are intervention programs that begin before a child enters kindergarten and continue through at least second grade. Several extended programs have provided preschool and school-age services to children and families at risk due to economic disadvantage and other socioenvironmental conditions. Four well-known continuation programs are described below: The Carolina Abecedarian Project, Head Start/Follow Through, the Chicago Child-Parent Center and Expansion Program, and the National Head Start Early Childhood Transition Demonstration Project. Although the Chicago Child-Parent Center and Expansion Program and the Carolina Abecedarian Project are described in Chapters 3 and 4 as examples of public programs and successful demonstration programs, they are also included here because these programs shed light on the efficacy of continuation interventions.

Table 7.1 provides key characteristics of these programs, and Table 7.2 (p. 118) summarizes findings from selected evaluations. In reporting the findings of these programs, the benefits of both (1) participation in the school-age components of the program and (2) the added value of this participation above and beyond participation in earlier preschool intervention are considered.

Table 7.1   Major Characteristics of Four Extended Early Childhood Programs for Low-Income Families

Early intervention programs	Age of entry / Length	Organization	Program description	Classroom environment	Parent component	Other services
Carolina Abecedarian Project (1972–1985)	6 weeks–5 or 8 years/ 5 to 8 years	Elementary school Home-school resource teacher	Full-day child care for preschoolers; Parent program for those with school-age children	Limited to activities of home-school teacher	Home visits, school support, outreach	Outreach and referrals
Head Start/Follow Through (1968–1996)	5 years/ 5 years	Elementary school Program coordinator	Kindergarten to third-grade program	Distinct curriculum model Curricular resources Staff inservices	Class volunteers Home visitors Advisory council	Examinations Referrals
Chicago Child-Parent Centers (1967–present)	3 or 4 years/ 1 to 6 years	One administrative system	Half-day preschool program; Half-day or full-day kindergarten program	Individual instruction in language and math Curricular resources Staff inservices	Parent room at each site Coordinator school and home support activities Advisory council	Services of school community representative Outreach and Referrals
Head Start Early Childhood Transition Demonstration (1991–1998)	5 years/ 5 years	Elementary school Family service coordinator	Kindergarten to third grade program	Developmental curricula Inservice training and workshops	Parent resources at each site Home visits School involvement Transition governing board	Nutrition services Family outreach Dental care

117

118

Table 7.2 Selected effect sizes on school competence for studies of extended early childhood programs

Program and studies	Program sample and experiences/ Control sample and experiences	Ages of effects	Effects[1]				
			Reading	Math	Retention	Special education	HS com.
Carolina Abecedarian Project							
Campbell & Ramey, 1995;	25 in child care (0 to age 5) +	8	.27	.33	–	–	
Ramey et al., 2000; Campbell	K–grade 2	15	.20	.00	.02	.24	
et al., 2002 (up to age 21)	24 in child care from birth	21[2]	.23	–.20			
	to age 5 only						
Head Start/Follow Through							
Abelson, Zigler, & DeBlasi, 1974;	35 in Bank Street FT in K–3	8–9					
Seit, Apfel, Rosenbaum,	91% had HS	12–15	.00	.51	–	–	
& Zigler, 1983 (up to age 14)	26 other-school controls		.00	.13	–	–	
	28% had HS	8–9		>boys			
Becker & Gersten, 1982 (up to	1,097 in Direct Inst. FT in 1–3	12–15	>.50	>.50	–	–	
age 12)	907 in non-FT classrooms in same		.19	.26	–	–	
Schweinhart & Wallgren, 1993	schools	8–9					
(up to age 9)	281 in High/Scope FT in K–3		.39	.29	–	–	
	528 same-school controls; 1% had HS						
Chicago Child-Parent Centers							
Fuerst & Fuerst, 1993	419 with 4 or more years CPC	12–15	.33	.20		–	–
(up to age 14)	503 in feeder-school controls; no CPC						
Reynolds, 1994 (up to age 11)	462 in CPC PreK and K plus grades 1–3	8–9	.55	.48	–.13	–.03	–
	207 in CPC PreK and K only						
Reynolds & Temple, 1998	426 in CPC PreK and K plus	8–9	.48	.35	–		
(up to age 13)	grades 1–3	12–13	.43	.28	–.15	–.06	–
	133 in CPC PreK and K only						

Study	Sample			
Reynolds et al., 2002 (up to age 21)	599 in CPC PreK and K plus grades 1-3 242 in CPC PreK and K only	15–18 21	−.32	−.29	.06[3]
Reynolds et al., 2005 (up to age 24)	522 in CPC PreK and K plus grades 1–3 510 in CPC PreK and K only 336 had no participation	23			.24[3]
Head Start Early Childhood Transition Demonstration Ramey et al., (2000)	30 sites across the country 3,411 had Head Start and Transition 3,137 had Head Start only	9	−.10	−.07	.18 any −.13 mental retardation −.12 emotional disturbance
Redden et al., (2001)	3,221 had Head Start and Transition 2,941 had Head Start only				

NOTES: 1. Values for reading and math achievement are proportions of standard deviations. Values for grade retention, special education, and high school completion (HS com.) were derived from probit transformation of proportions. In Abelson et al., the effect sizes for the cross-sectional sample were .34 and .51, respectively for third grade reading and math achievement. In Schweinhart and Wallgren, average effect across Grades 1 to 3 was .63.
2. Effect sizes of the Abecedarian Project were obtained for extended intervention compared to preschool only. The effect sizes for extended intervention compared to no intervention at age 21 were .79 for reading and .42 for math.
3. Effect sizes of the Chicago Child-Parent Centers from Reynolds et al. (2002) were obtained for extended intervention compared to less extended intervention. Participants who had no participation were excluded. Effect sizes from Reynolds et al. (2005) were obtained through comparing extended intervention (4–6 year) with less than 4 years (0–3 years).

SOURCE: Adapted from Reynolds (2003). The added value of continuing early intervention into the primary grades. In A. J. Reynolds, M. C. Wang, & H. J. Walberg (Eds.), *Early childhood programs for a new century* (pp. 173–174). Washington, DC: Child Welfare League of America Press.

Carolina Abecedarian Project (ABC)

The Carolina Abecedarian Project began in rural North Carolina in 1972 with the aim of improving development and school performance of low-income children. The goal was to examine whether "continual, consistent enrichment of the early environment might alter this negative trend toward developmental retardation and also reduce academic failure in such children [in poverty]" (Campbell & Ramey, 1995, p. 746).

Program Description

The Abecedarian Project served children that met a certain level of sociodemographic risk of cognitive delays or academic problems. ABC employed an experimental design, with random assignment of families to either a program group or a limited program control group (Campbell & Ramey, 1995). Children in the program group received five years of enriched educational child care from age four months to five years (prior to kindergarten). A systematic curriculum, including learning activities in cognitive, language, and social-emotional development, was used. This program occurred at a single site for yearly cohorts through 1977, followed by a school-age intervention for three years starting in kindergarten and continuing to second grade (age eight).

The school-age program was designed with the aim of supporting children's academic development through increasing and enhancing parent involvement in the educational process (Campbell & Ramey, 1995).

While the child care program emphasized language and literacy skills with very small child-to-teacher ratios, the school-age intervention followed a family-support model of intervention.

The three-year school-age program provided families a home school resource teacher who offered learning activities and provided materials for mothers to use at home with their children (Campbell, Helms, Sparling, & Ramey, 1998). Teachers served as a home-school liaison on behalf of the student, and worked on community outreach. In addition, the school-age program included a six-week summer transition program prior to kindergarten entry.

After completing the early intervention, participants were randomly assigned to either a new program group or a new control group, forming four types of groups. The new program group received intervention through age eight, and the new control group did not receive further intervention. The original sample was 111 children, 57 randomly assigned to the preschool group, and 54 to the control group. Of the total of four groups at age five, 25 children participated in extended early childhood intervention for eight years, and 24 children participated during only preschool for five years. Ninety-eight percent of the sample was African American.

Research Findings

Evaluations have consistently shown that the five-year preschool program produced greater intellectual and academic outcomes than the three-year school-age program. Nevertheless, an additional dosage-response effect has been found for children who participate in both preschool and school-age programs. These children have the highest levels of intellectual and scholastic performance at the end of the program at age eight; and the extended intervention group surpassed the performance of the preschool-only group by one-third of a standard deviation (Campbell & Ramey, 1995).

At the age 15 follow-up, the extended surpassed the nonextended group only for reading achievement (Ramey, Campbell, Burchinal, Skinner, Gardner, & Ramey, 2000). No differences between groups were found for math achievement, intelligence test scores, and cumulative rates of grade retention and special education placement. At the age 21 follow-up, although the extended group had higher scores on reading than the nonextended group, the difference was not significant (C. T. Campbell, Ramey, Pungello, Sparling, & Miller-Johnson, 2002). While participation in the preschool program was associated with greater intellectual and academic outcomes, participation in the school-age program alone did not show long-term effects.

Cost-Benefit Analysis

The average cost and benefit of the Abecedarian Project were $35,864 and $135,546 respectively per child in 2002 dollars. The costs were estimated to be about $13,400 a child per year in 2002 dollars. The estimated cost-benefit ratio is $3.78 in benefits for every $1 invested; these benefits accrue by increasing future earning and tax revenues and by reducing public expenditures for special education, other K–12 education costs, and smoking-related and other health care costs (Masse & Barnett, 2002).

Head Start/Follow Through (FT)

Originated in 1967, Head Start/Follow Through (FT) offered Head Start–like services in the public schools in an effort to enhance children's transition from preschool to the early elementary grades for low-income children, thereby strengthening long-term success in school.

Program Description

Although the original plan was to serve 200,000 children in the fall of 1968, due to cutbacks in funding plus the observed incompatibilities between the social service orientation of Head Start centers and the more regimented educational establishment of public schools, FT never achieved its original goal as a coordinated continuum of early childhood intervention (Kennedy, 1993).

The Head Start/Follow Through programs tested the effects of alternative instructional methods on children's educational development in kindergarten to third-grade classrooms. It was implemented as a series of "planned variations" of five instructional models and mixtures including (a) Parent Education Model, (b) Direct Instruction Model, (c) Behavioral Analysis Model, (d) High/Scope Cognitively Oriented Curriculum Model, and (e) the Bank Street Model of Developmental-Interaction. Like Head Start, FT programs included health and social service components, home visits from paraprofessionals that encouraged parents' participation in their child's education, and participation in school advisory councils. Moreover, most classrooms had teacher aides. FT programs were sponsored by entire schools, and were then implemented at the classroom level. Although 50% or more of the students in a FT classroom were required to be graduates of Head Start, participation was not limited to Head Start graduates. The intervention schools were matched with comparison schools.

Research Findings

A national evaluation showed that substantial modifications in the classroom learning environment in kindergarten and the early primary grades could enhance children's early educational success and social and emotional development, thus improving the transition to school. However, the instructional models were not equally associated with student academic achievement. The Direct Instruction and Behavioral Analysis models were most consistently associated with higher achievement test scores across location and time. As shown in Table 7.2 (p. 118), studies based on the High Scope, Bank Street, and Direct Instruction models found that Head Start with FT was associated with higher school achievement in the short term, but these effects were reduced over time (Abelson, Zigler, & DeBlasi, 1974; Becker & Gersten, 1982; Schweinhart & Wallgren, 1993; Seitz, Apfel, Rosenbaum, & Zigler, 1983).

There were not sufficient samples of Head Start graduates who had not participated in FT programs to separate the effects of the FT interventions from those of Head Start. Therefore, FT does not provide an optimal test of the added value of extended early childhood programs. Although it is difficult to know precisely the added value of FT, this research does generally indicate that enhancements in the quality of schools in the early grades promote children's educational success with or without earlier intervention.

Cost-Benefit Analysis

The average cost of one year of Head Start was $6,091 per child in 1999 dollars. The short- and medium-term benefits offset 40 to 60 percent of the costs by improving health and nutrition and reducing public expenditures for special education and grade retention (Currie, 2001). Other possible long-term benefits were not estimated. Although the cost-effectiveness of the Follow Through programs has not been estimated, the demonstrated effects on school achievement would be expected to lead, at a minimum, to reduced need for remedial education.

Chicago Child-Parent Center and Expansion Program (CPC)

The Chicago Child-Parent Center and Expansion Program was developed to promote academic success among low-income children and to encourage parents to become involved in their children's education.

Program Description

The CPC program was established in 1967 through funding from Title I of the landmark Elementary and Secondary Education Act of 1965. It is the second oldest (after Head Start) federally funded preschool program in the United States, and it is the oldest extended early childhood intervention. Today, 24 centers operate in the Chicago schools, and, since 1977, the primary grade component has been integrated with regular elementary school programs.

Three features distinguish the CPC program from Head Start/Follow Through. First, the CPC program is implemented within one administrative system, the Chicago Public Schools.

Second, the CPC program operates in early childhood centers that are physically

Advantages of a single administrative system include enhanced continuity between preschool and school-age programs through centralized oversight with each school's principal, and having geographic proximity between preschool/kindergarten and school-age components.

separate from the elementary schools. Finally, there is substantial variation in the number of years that children participate. By administrative
design, six centers provide services up to third grade for a total of six
years; the remaining centers provide services up to second grade for a
total of five years.

The components of this program include a structured half-day
preschool program for three- and four-year-olds, a half-day or an all-
day kindergarten program for five-year olds, with a child-centered
focus on the development of reading/language skills, literacy skills,
and other family support services. The center operates on the regular
nine-month school-year calendar; an eight-week summer program is
also provided.

The program is offered in different sites, and has no uniform curriculum. Each site tailors its program to children's needs through a unified philosophy of literacy learning and a common core of activities that
include individualized instruction, small group activities, and field trips.
Parents are required to be involved in the center at least one half-day per
week. Involvement may include a wide variety of activities, such as
volunteering as classroom aides, interacting with other parents in the
center's parent resource room, participating in educational workshops
and courses, attending school events, accompanying classes on field
trips, and attending parent-teacher meetings on behalf of the child
(Reynolds, 2000; Reynolds, Mavrogenes, Bezruczko, & Hagemann,
1996).

The comprehensive services include (a) attending to children's nutritional and health needs (i.e., free breakfasts and lunches and health
screening); (b) coordinated adult supervision, including a CPC head teacher,
parent resource teacher, school-community representative, and a teacher
aide for each class; (c) funds for centralized inservice teacher training in
child development as well as instructional supplies; and (d) emphasis on
reading readiness through reduced class size, reading and writing activities in the learning center, and reinforcement and feedback (Reynolds
et al. 1996).

The expansion program continued to provide parents with a parent
resource room and a community representative, and it encouraged parent
involvement. The program was designed to enrich the primary grade
classroom experience. In each grade, class sizes were reduced to a maximum of 25 children, and each teacher was provided with a teacher aide.
Like the Head Teacher, the Curriculum Parent Resource Teacher provides
inservice training to classroom teachers and aides in the expansion
classrooms.

Research Findings

Participation in the CPC Program has been found to be significantly associated with higher levels of academic achievement and parent involvement in children's education (Reynolds, 2000). Children participating in the preschool plus follow-on services were found to have higher academic achievement when compared with children receiving only the preschool or follow-on programs (Conrad & Eash, 1983). Children with four or more years of services (which included follow-on services) had higher reading and math achievement in the eighth grade and better high school graduation rates than children who did not participate in the program (Fuerst & Fuerst, 1993).

> CPC participation through second grade was associated with a seven-month advantage in reading and math achievement, lower rates of grade retention, and lower rates of special education placement (Reynolds, 1994).

Students participating through the third grade fared even better, and the benefits persisted up to age 15. Extended program participation to third grade (four to six years of CPC) was associated with significantly lower rates of school remedial services (grade retention by age 15 and special education placement by age 18) and with lower rates of delinquency infractions as reported by schools (Reynolds, Temple, Robertson, & Mann, 2002). Further, relative to no participation, the maximum participation in CPC of six years was associated with an over 50% reduction in school remedial services (Reynolds, 2000).

At the age 24 follow-up, extended program participation was associated with higher rates of high school completion and full-time employment and lower rates of receiving one year or more of Medicaid services and lower rates of violent arrest (Reynolds et al., 2005).

Cost-Benefit Analysis

The average cost and benefit of the CPC preschool program were $6,692 and $47,759 respectively per child in 1998 dollars (Reynolds et al., 2002). This cost is based on an average length of participation of 1.5 years. The average cost and benefit of the CPC school-age program were $2,981 and $4,944 respectively per child in 1998 dollars. The preschool program provided a return to society of $7.14 per dollar invested by increasing economic well-being and tax revenues and by reducing public expenditures for remedial education, criminal justice treatment, and crime victims. The extended intervention program (4 to 6 years of participation) provided a return to society of $6.11 per dollar invested while the school-age program yielded a return of $1.66 per dollar invested.

National Head Start Early Childhood Transition Demonstration Project

In 1991, the U.S. Department of Health and Human Services sponsored the National Head Start Early Childhood Transition Demonstration Project (HST) in school districts around the country, which revamped the concept behind Head Start/Follow Through (see HST also described in this chapter as an example of a public transition program to kindergarten). Approximately 12,000 children and families in 31 sites participated in the demonstration program. The study design involved random assignment of schools to a Transition Demonstration group, which received additional supports and staff funded by the project, or to a comparison group. There were some differences across the 31 sites in whether schools or school districts were randomly assigned, and some local decision making was involved.

Program Description

HST was launched to test the value of extending comprehensive, Head Start–like supports through the first four years of elementary school. This program provides a range of Head Start–like family services to assist in the transition from Head Start to public schools, help families with health issues, and improve children's school performance.

A total of 7,515 former Head Start children and families were recruited at 31 sites to participate in the National Study in 1992–1993 and 1993–1994. Thousands of other children and families, however, participated in the Transition Demonstration Program; supports and educational enhancements were offered to all children and families in the classrooms.

There are four key features of the HST program: parent involvement, educational enhancement, family social support services, and health and nutrition services (S. L. Ramey, C. T. Ramey, Phillips et al., 2000).

1. *Parent involvement.* Families participating in the HST were encouraged to participate in their children's schooling and were provided with a number of educational resources.

2. *Educational enhancement.* This component was provided especially to promote the use of developmentally appropriate curricula and practices and continuity in children's educational experiences. In addition, parent education programs were provided to promote

strong parenting skills and educational growth for adult family members to strengthen and stabilize family functioning.

3. *Family social support services.* Participating schools provided supportive social services to help facilitate positive family-school interactions and to assist in securing and coordinating services across agencies.

4. *Health and nutrition services.* Participating schools provided health and nutrition services and activities to ensure the physical and mental health of the entire family.

In addition to these features, most local sites had plans for promoting the inclusion of children with disabilities in regular classrooms, addressing cultural and linguistic diversity and appreciation, and developing individualized transition plans for each child.

Research Findings

To date, evaluations of HST indicated no overall treatment effect (Bryant, Campbell, Taylor, & Burchinal, 1998; Hegland & Colbert, 1998; S. L. Ramey, C. T. Ramey, & Lanzi, 2002, 2004; S. L. Ramey, C. T. Ramey, Zigler, & Webb, 2000; Seefeldt, Galper, & Younoszai, 1998). There is no difference in academic achievement or social development scores between children in the HST schools and children in the control groups. There are four major findings that informed these results (S. L. Ramey, C. T. Ramey, Phillips et al., 2000). First, many obstacles and barriers were encountered by all sites in their efforts to provide comprehensive supports to children, families, and schools. Second, the strength and implementation of a local program was influenced by leadership. Third, the implementation of programs varied. Only about 20% of the sites implemented very strong programs, while about 26% of the sites implemented weak programs. The majority of local programs showed a mixed implementation in their programs.

Despite results that did not conclusively show improvement for children in HST, schools and families valued many features of the Transition Demonstration Programs, leading to plans for continuation after program funding ended. Moreover, many comparison schools adopted these features, which were supported through reallocation of resources or external funding.

Features of Successful and Unsuccessful HST Programs

The most successful HST programs had several features in common. They had a strong relationship with both the public school and the local

Head Start program, and the leaders in the programs were highly respected in the community and had a history of implementing and evaluating large-scale programs. Programs that were not successful were unable to build strong collaborations between the public school and the local Head Start program, had both personality and agency conflicts, had poor and inexperienced leadership, and were unable to develop appropriate program plans (S. L. Ramey, C. T. Ramey, Phillips et al., 2000). As a result, it could be judged that the lack of support for and quality of some services may have made this study a weak assessment of the effects of follow-on services. However, it notes the need for close coordination between Head Start programs and elementary schools to provide additional services in a coordinated manner when children enter kindergarten. These findings highlight that a wide range of factors were associated with HST implementation and that large-scale demonstration programs of this type are not easily implemented or evaluated using traditional methods.

> HST participants showed significant gains in reading and math in early elementary school and quickly rose to perform close to national averages by third grade.

While the HST findings indicate that these former Head Start children entered school below other children nationally, HST participants demonstrated typical levels of growth in social skills and were rated by their teachers and parents as socially and behaviorally well adjusted to school.

The majority of HST children also reported that they liked school, tried hard, got along well with teachers and peers, and learned a lot at school (S. L. Ramey, C. T. Ramey, Phillips et al., 2000).

Although no significant differences were found between the transition group and the comparison group, a recent study found that participation in the HST was associated with lower rates of certain types of special education identification. Only 0.89% of children in the transition group were identified in the mental retardation category compared to 1.26% in the nontransition group. For emotional disturbance, these figures were 1.21% and 1.65%, respectively. Both differences were statistically significant, but an opposite effect was found in the category of speech or language impairment (Redden et al., 2001).

Collectively, these schools, Head Start programs, and communities strongly endorsed the value of outreach efforts to families and the necessity of addressing the needs of young children during their early years of transition to school.

Cost-Benefit Analysis

Cost-benefit analysis results are not available for the National Head Start/Public School Early Childhood Transition Demonstration Project (HST).

CHARACTERISTICS OF SUCCESSFUL PROGRAMS

The evidence described in this chapter shows that extended early childhood programs can promote more successful transitions to school than preschool interventions alone. Although more longitudinal data from various settings are needed, several characteristics of successful programs can be drawn from this review of the evidence.

1. *A system of intervention is in place beginning at age three and continuing to the early school grades.* This single administrative system promotes stability in children's learning environment that can provide smooth transitions from preschool to kindergarten and from kindergarten to the early grades. This is a "first decade" strategy for promoting children's learning (Reynolds, Wang, & Walberg, 2003). Today, most preschool programs are not integrated within public schools, and children usually change schools more than once by the early grades. In the movement to universal access to early education, schools could take a leadership role in partnership with community agencies. More generally, programs that provide coordinated or "wrap-around" services may be more effective under a centralized leadership structure rather than under a case-management framework.

2. *Teachers have bachelor's degrees and certification in early childhood education.* Teachers with degrees and certification tend to be better compensated and have lower turnover. It is no coincidence that the Chicago program and other successful early interventions such as the High/Scope Perry Preschool were run by staff with at least bachelor's degrees and certification in their specialties. In most early childhood programs, staff members do not have this level of education, training, and compensation, and turnover is high. In contemporary education programs, greater commitment to preservice and ongoing professional training is needed.

3. *Educational content is responsive to all of children's learning needs but special emphasis is given to literacy and school readiness through a structured but diverse set of learning activities.* From its inception, the CPC program has emphasized the development of literacy skills necessary for successful progress. It does this with a blend of instructional activities that include phonics training, field trips, and individualized learning activities (Reynolds, 2000; Sullivan, 1971). Extrapolating these findings to other educational and child welfare programs, one can conclude that programs are more likely to have enduring effects if they provide services that are intensive and are dedicated to the enhancement of specific behavioral skills (Heckman, 2000).

4. *Comprehensive family services that provide many opportunities for positive learning experiences in school and at home.* Most of the extended early childhood programs allocated significant resources to parent involvement, and levels of parental engagement in children's education tended to be higher than would otherwise be expected. This was most extensive in the CPC program as each center has a staffed parent resource room and provides school-community outreach. Therefore, parental involvement is more intensive than in other programs. Health services are provided also, along with referrals to community clinics and agencies for job training and other social services. Those with special needs or who are most at risk benefit from intensive and comprehensive services.

CONCLUSIONS AND RECOMMENDATIONS

Based on the review of the preceding programs, research suggests that it is important to extend interventions into the early years of elementary school. We now know that academic achievement can be enhanced by early intervention plus school-age services, and these services can be provided at reasonable cost. Extended childhood programs have two practical advantages over programs from birth to age three. First, educational systems are already in place to support extended childhood intervention in the primary grades. It is not necessary to develop new early childhood systems. Second, upward expansion of programs into the primary grades may cost less than other alternatives, and they are certainly more cost-effective than continuing the current system of providing little or no extra support for children's transition to school. In Chicago's Child-Parent Center Program, for example, the expenditure for one year of school-age services is about $1,500 per child.

Studies have indicated that the quality and duration of developmentally appropriate early childhood experiences are strongly linked to later school performance and performance in society (Barnett, 1995; Campbell et al., 2002; Reynolds, 2004; Reynolds, Temple, Robertson, & Mann, 2001). While research supports the efficacy of early intervention, the "fade-out" phenomenon has been linked to insufficient school support after early intervention (Currie & Thomas, 2000; Lee & Loeb, 1995).

Because transition into full-time schooling (entry into first grade) is an important period for children's academic development, the following recommendations are offered:

- It is critical to emphasize extended early interventions that provide services beyond kindergarten, services that help in the transition from kindergarten to elementary school, that provide a stable school environment, and that ensure continuity in the lives of children.
- Programs should be tailored to the needs of children across the entire first decade of life. Currently, many children are entering schools at a higher risk than students entering ten years ago; continuous service across the first decade of children's lives provides the optimal level of support for learning and development and does not presume that intervention at any stage of development (infancy, preschool, school-age) alone can prevent children from future underachievement.

REFERENCES

Abelson, W. B., Zigler, E., & DeBlasi, C. L. (1974). Effects of a four-year follow through program on economically disadvantaged children. *Journal of Educational Psychology, 66*, 756–771.

Alexander, K. L., Entwisle, D. S., & Kabbani, N. (2001). The dropout process in life course perspective: Early risk factors at home and school. *Teachers College Record, 103*(5), 760–822.

Barnett, W. S. (1995). Long-term effects of early childhood programs on cognitive and school outcomes. *The Future of Children, 5*(3), 25–50.

Becker, W. C., & Gersten, R. (1982). A follow-up of Follow Through: The later effects of the Direct Instruction model on children in fifth and sixth grades. *American Educational Research Journal, 19*, 75–92.

Bryant, D. M., Campbell, F. A., Taylor, K. B., & Burchinal, M. R. (1998, July). What is 'participation' in North Carolina's Head Start Transition Demonstration? *Summary of Conference Proceedings of the Fourth Head Start National Research Conference.* Washington, DC: Administration on Children, Youth and Families, U.S. Department of Health and Human Services.

Campbell, F. A., Helms, R., Sparling, J .J., & Ramey, C. T. (1998). Early-childhood programs and success in school: The Abecedarian study. In W. S. Barnett & S. S. Boocook (Eds.),

Early care and education for children in poverty: Promises, programs, and long-term results (pp. 145–166). Albany, NY: State University of New York Press.

Campbell, F. A., & Ramey, C. T. (1995). Cognitive and school outcomes for high risk African-American students at middle adolescence: Positive effects of early intervention. *American Educational Research Journal, 32,* 743–772.

Campbell, F. A., Ramey, C. T., Pungello, E., Sparling, J., & Miller-Johnson, S. (2002). Early childhood education: Young adult outcomes from the Abecedarian project. *Applied Developmental Science, 6*(1), 42–57.

Conrad, K. J., & Eash, M. J. (1983). Measuring implementation and multiple outcomes in a Child Parent Center compensatory education program. *American Educational Research Journal, 20,* 221–236.

Currie, J. (2001). Early childhood education programs. *Journal of Economic Perspectives, 15*(2), 213–238.

Currie, J., & Thomas, D. (2000). School quality and the longer-term effects of Head Start. *The Journal of Human Resources, 35*(4), 755–774.

Entwisle, D. R. (1995). The role of schools in sustaining early childhood program benefits. *The Future of Children, 5*(3), 133–144.

Fuerst, J. S., & Fuerst, D. (1993). Chicago experience with an early childhood program: The special case of the Child Parent Center program. *Urban Education, 28,* 69–96.

Guralnick, M. J. (Ed.). (1997). *The effectiveness of early intervention.* Baltimore: Brookes.

Heckman, J. J. (2000). Policies to foster human capital. *Research in Economics, 54,* 3–56.

Hegland, S. M., & Colbert, K. (1998, July). Head Start transition outcomes: Families and children. *Summary of Conference Proceedings of the Fourth Head Start National Research Conference.* Washington, DC: Administration on Children, Youth and Families, U.S. Department of Health and Human Services.

Kennedy, E. M. (1993). The Head Start Transition Project: Head Start goes to elementary school. In E. Zigler & S. J. Styfco (Eds.), *Head Start and beyond: A national plan for extended childhood intervention* (pp. 97–109). New Haven, CT: Yale University Press.

Lee, V. E., & Loeb, S. (1995). Where do Head Start attendees end up? One reason why preschool effects fade out. *Educational Evaluation and Policy Analysis, 17,* 62–82.

Masse, L. N., & Barnett, W. S. (2002). *A benefit cost analysis of the Abecedarian early childhood intervention.* New Brunswick, NJ: National Institute for Early Education Research.

Ou, S., & Reynolds, A. J. (2005). *Predictors of higher educational attainment: Evidence from the Chicago Longitudinal Study.* Manuscript under review.

Ramey, C. T., Campbell, F. A., Burchinal, M., Skinner, M. L., Gardner, D. M., & Ramey, S. L. (2000). Persistent effects of early childhood education on high-risk children and their mothers. *Applied Developmental Science, 4,* 2–14.

Ramey, S. L., Ramey, C. T., Lanzi, R. G. (2002). Successful transitions to school: Factors that dramatically increase the success of former Head Start children in kindergarten through third grade. In *Proceedings of the Sixth Head Start National Research Conference: The First Eight Years Pathways to the Future* (pp. 657–663). Alexandria, VA: Head Start Information and Publication Center. (ERIC Document Reproduction Service No. ED474955)

Ramey, C. T., Ramey, S. L., Zigler, E., & Webb, M. B. (2000). Results from the National Evaluation of the Head Start Transition Demonstration. In *Proceedings of the fifth Head Start National Research Conference: Developmental and Contextual Transitions of Children and Families* (pp. 180–187). Washington, DC: Administration on Children, Youth and Families, U.S. Department of Health and Human Services. (ERIC Document Reproduction Service No. ED450890)

Ramey, S. L., Ramey, C. T., Lanzi, R. G. (2004). The transition to school: Building on preschool foundations and preparing for lifelong learning. In E. Zigler & S. J. Styfco (Eds.), *The Head Start debates* (pp.397–413). Baltimore: Brookes.

Ramey, S. L., Ramey, C. T., Phillips, M. M., Lanzi, R.G., Brezausek, C., Katholi, C. R., Snyder, S., & Lawrence, F. (2000). *Head Start children's entry into public school: A report on the National Head Start/Public School Early Childhood Transition Demonstration Study.* Washington, DC: Administration for Children and Families, U. S. Department of Health and Human Services.

Redden, S. C., Forness, S. R., Ramey, S. L., Ramey, C. T., Brezausek, C. M. & Kavale, K.A. (2001). Children at risk: Effects of a four-year Head Start Transition Program on special education identification. *Journal of Child and Family Studies, 10*(2), 255–270.

Reynolds, A. J. (1994). Effects of a preschool plus follow-on intervention for children at risk. *Developmental Psychology, 30,* 787–804.

Reynolds, A. J. (2000). *Success in early intervention: The Chicago Child-Parent Centers.* Lincoln, NE: University of Nebraska Press.

Reynolds, A. J. (2003). The added value of continuing early intervention into the primary grades. In A. J. Reynolds, M. C. Wang, & H. J. Walberg (Eds.), *Early childhood programs for a new century* (pp. 173–174). Washington, DC: Child Welfare League of America Press.

Reynolds, A. J. (2004). Dosage-response effects and mechanisms of change in public and model programs. In E. Zigler & S. J. Styfco (Eds.), *The Head Start debates* (pp.379–396). Baltimore: Brookes.

Reynolds, A. J., Mavrogenes, N. A., Bezruczko, N., & Hagemann, M. (1996). Cognitive and family support mediators of preschool effectiveness: A confirmatory analysis. *Child Development, 67,* 1119–1140.

Reynolds, A. J., Ou, S., & Topitzes, J. D. (2004). Paths of effects of early childhood intervention on educational attainment and delinquency: A confirmatory analysis of the Chicago Child-Parent Centers. *Child Development, 75*(5), 1299–1238.

Reynolds, A. J., & Temple, J. A. (1998). Extended early childhood intervention and school achievement: Age 13 findings from the Chicago Longitudinal Study. *Child Development, 69,* 231–246.

Reynolds, A. J., Temple, J.A., Ou, S., Robertson, D. L., Mersky, J. P., & Topitzes, J. (2005, May 25–27). *Effects of a school-based early childhood intervention on adult health and well-being: A 20-year follow up of low-income children and families.* Paper presented at the annual meeting of the Society for Prevention Research, Washington, DC.

Reynolds, A. J., Temple, J. A., Robertson, D. L., & Mann, E. A. (2001). Long-term effects of an early childhood intervention on educational achievement and juvenile arrest: A 15-year follow-up of low-income children in public schools. *Journal of American Medical Association, 285,* 2339–2346.

Reynolds, A. J., Temple, J. A., Robertson, D. L., & Mann, E. A. (2002). Age 21 cost-benefit analysis of the Title I Chicago Child-Parent Centers. *Educational Evaluation and Policy Analysis, 24*(4), 267–303.

Reynolds, A. J., Wang, M. C., & Walberg, H. J. (Eds.). (2003). *Early childhood programs for a new century.* Washington, DC: Child Welfare League of America Press.

Schweinhart, L. J., & Wallgren, C. R. (1993). Effects of a follow through program on achievement. *Journal of Research in Childhood Education, 8,* 43–56.

Seefeldt, C., Galper, A. R., & Younoszai, T. M. (1998, July). Transition activities and their effectiveness. In *Summary of Conference Proceedings of the fourth Head Start National*

Research Conference. Washington, DC: Administration on Children, Youth and Families, U.S. Department of Health and Human Services.

Seitz, V., Apfel, N. H., Rosenbaum, L. K., & Zigler, E. (1983). Long-term effects of projects Head Start and Follow Through: The New Haven Project. In Consortium for Longitudinal Studies (Ed.), *As the twig is bent: Lasting effects of preschool programs* (pp. 299–332). Hillsdale, NJ: Earlbaum.

Sullivan, L. M. (1971). *Report on child-parent education centers*. Chicago: Chicago Foresman.

Weissberg, R. P., & Greenberg, M. T. (1998). School and community competence-enhancement and prevention programs. In W. Damon (Ed.), *Handbook of child psychology: Vol. 4. Child psychology in practice* (pp. 877–954). New York: Wiley.

8

Out-of-School-Time Programs That Promote Academic and Behavioral Achievement for Children Ages Six to Eight

Anne E. Farber

A s a result of the higher percentage of mothers in the labor force, an increasing number of children between six and eight years of age require care while their parent works. As of 1997, the mothers of 62% of grade school children were employed (Smith, 2002). Most of these were employed full time, and even part-time maternal employment often does not fall completely within the hours of the day that children are in school. Consequently, there is a great need for before- and afterschool programs that will care for children while parents are at work and, in the process, complement the child's learning and social experience.

In 2001, approximately 20% of kindergarten through second grade children attended center or school-based programs during out-of-school-time (U.S. Department of Education, 2004). These programs can vary on several dimensions. First, different types of organizations provide these programs, including schools, nonprofit community organizations, and nonprofit and for-profit child care businesses. Second, some programs are classified as child care providers and are regulated or licensed by state or local governments. However, most out-of-school-time programs offered by community organizations or schools are not licensed. Third, regardless of who offers these programs, they may be located in schools, community-based organizations, or private businesses (Fashola, 1998). Finally, the purposes of these programs vary and often overlap. In some cases, children attend because they need a safe environment when they are not at school and their parents are at work. Children may also attend to supplement their educational experiences at school and to improve their level of academic achievement. In addition, they may attend to engage in a variety of enrichment activities such as arts, technology, and sports.

OUTCOMES AND EVALUATIONS OF OUT-OF-SCHOOL-TIME PROGRAMS

During childhood, children must master several key developmental tasks, which out-of-school-time programs can assist children in achieving. Mahoney, Larson, Eccles, and Lord (2005) describe these as tasks in the social and emotional realm of development: "(a) acquiring habits of physical and psychological health, (b) forming a positive orientation toward school and achievement, (c) getting along with others including peers and adults, and (d) acquiring appropriate value systems about rules and conduct across different contexts" (p. 6).

These developmental tasks are similar to the assets outlined by the Search Institute (a nonprofit research and training group that promotes positive youth development). The Search Institute's Developmental Assets for Elementary-Age Children describes these assets as "building blocks of healthy development that help elementary-age children grow up healthy, caring, and responsible" (2004, p. 1). These assets are divided into internal and external assets. *Internal assets* include children's commitment to learning, their acquisition of positive values such as honesty and responsibility, the development of social competences including interpersonal skills and the ability to resist negative peer pressure, and the creation of a positive identity in which children feel they have control over their lives. *External assets*, many of which are provided by the family and community, are seen as the context in which children develop. They include opportunities for the constructive use of time, the establishment of boundaries and expectations through adult role models and organizations, and support in caring environments. These assets can be considered program quality factors, discussed later in this chapter, which out-of-school-time programs can contribute to children's lives.

Because out-of-school-time programs vary in their purposes (e.g., providing a safe environment, promoting academic achievement, and enabling children to develop a range of skills), the expected outcomes for children in these programs will vary extensively. However, the preceding discussion suggests that, to enable children to accomplish their developmental tasks, out-of-school-time programs should focus on social-emotional skills and values and on academic achievement.

> Out-of-school-time programs should focus on both social-emotional skills and academic achievement.

Evaluations of out-of-school-time programs encompass several content areas, including assessments of children who attend programs in specific communities (see table on next page), examinations of academically focused programs, and studies of programs promoting health and mental health in young children. This review presents experimental and quasi-experimental evaluations that targeted programs serving children between six and eight years of age, although in some cases it was not possible to separate findings for first- and second-grade children from those for other elementary grades. The information on many of the programs in this review was identified through the Harvard Family Research Project Out-of-School-Time Program Evaluation Database (Harvard Family Research Project, 2005).

Four studies compared the performance of early elementary age children in a variety of settings in their communities. (see Table 1 on the next page).

ACADEMICALLY FOCUSED PROGRAMS

21st Century Community Learning Centers

Program Characteristics

In 1994, Congress enacted the first large-scale out-of-school-time funding stream, entitled the 21st Century Community Learning Centers, for children in low-performing schools. These centers, located in schools and comparably accessible community locations, are required to include academic activities.

Programs must provide academic enrichment activities to help students meet state and local standards in core content areas, such as reading, math, and science. They also must provide services to families

Table 1   Community Research

Marshall, Coll, Marx, McCartney, Keefe, and Ruh (1997)	Lower-income children in Grades 1 through 4 who participated in afterschool programs exhibited fewer internalizing problems, such as being anxious or shy, than children in other settings (parental care, other adult care, and unsupervised care). However, no differences were found for middle-income children.
Pettit, Laird, Bates, and Dodge (1997)	Lower-income children who had participated in private child care afterschool in first grade, compared to those who had not, displayed higher levels of social competence and had fewer internalizing and externalizing problems in sixth grade.
Mahoney, Lord, and Carryl (2005)	Afterschool arrangements were analyzed to identify the types of settings used by disadvantaged first through third grade children. No type of setting was used exclusively, but four patterns of care were identified: afterschool programs, parent care, parent/non-adult care, and other adult/non-adult care.
	Children in afterschool programs showed higher academic achievement over the course of a school year than children in the other three types of care.
National Institute of Child Health and Human Development [NICHD] (2004)	There was no effect of participation in afterschool programs in kindergarten and first grade on first grade achievement level. However, consistent participation in extracurricular activities was associated with higher math achievement.
	The inconsistency between these findings and those of the other three studies, which found effects in lower-income children, may have been due to the relatively small number of children from less advantaged families in the NICHD study. None of these studies controlled for selection factors, such as socioeconomic status (SES).

of children in the programs. Others services that may be provided include arts and music education activities, tutoring and mentoring, and recreational activities (U.S. Department of Education, Office of Elementary and Secondary Education, 2003). Centers are open four to five days a week for three hours a day.

Evaluation Findings

The national evaluation of the 21st Century Community Learning Centers, which was funded by the Department of Education, used an experimental design for younger children in the program in which researchers randomly assigned children to treatment and control groups at oversubscribed elementary schools. James-Burdumy, Dynarski, Moore, Deke, Mansfield, and Pistorino (2005) reported limited benefits of impact for elementary school participants, who, on average, attended the programs two to three days per week. Moreover, the findings were mixed and varied from year one to year two. In year one, looking only at children in kindergarten to second grade, several positive impacts were found; namely, a smaller percentage of parents of students in the treatment group than the control group reported their children broke something on purpose, a higher percentage of parents reported helping their children with homework frequently, and the children received higher grades in social studies than the control group. However, in year two, early elementary children in the treatment group were more likely than in the control group to be suspended from school and have lower grades in social studies. On a positive note, parents of these children were more likely to have

Target Children	Elementary and middle school children in underperforming schools as defined by the No Child Left Behind legislation.
Program Focus	Academic achievement.
Child-Staff Ratio	Most centers serve about 200 students a year (although fewer attend each day) and employ 12 to 13 staff members.
Funding	Federal (21st Century Learning Centers funding). Appropriations for these programs grew from $40 million in fiscal year 1998 to $991 million in fiscal year 2005 (National Child Care Information Center, 2005; U.S. Department of Education, Office of the Under Secretary, 2003).
Cost	Approximately $1,000 per year per enrolled student.

attended a PTO meeting in year two, but conversely were less likely to have volunteered to help out at school.

The evaluations of three other programs that provided an academically focused program used quasi-experimental designs.

Foundations School-Age Enrichment Program

Program Characteristics

This program provides before-school, afterschool, and summer programs, which are located in public schools, community centers, faith-based organizations, and recreation centers in the eastern United States. Foundations, Inc. uses "a curriculum that involves daily activities emphasizing academic subjects as well as experiences designed to foster physical and emotional development" (Klein & Bolus, 2002, p. 5). The program also promotes parent involvement and coordinates activities with classroom work.

Evaluation Findings

Klein and Bolus (2002) conducted an evaluation of the program that reported findings for first- and second-grade participants for the 2001–2002 school year. Comparisons were made to a national norm group and to students not participating in the Foundations program who had comparable skills and background characteristics. Foundations participants in Grades 1 and 2 had significantly greater mean gain scores in all subjects than nonparticipants. In addition, the effect sizes in math and reading for first- and second-grade students were greater than for those in higher grades. Klein and Bolus (2003) found generally similar results for the 2002–2003 school year.

Target Children	First through fifth grade students, most of whom are from low-income families.
Program Focus	Academic achievement.
Child-Staff Ratio	10:1.
Funding	Federal (21st Century Learning Centers funding), tuition, multiple foundations and other funding entities.
Cost	Approximately $1,900 per year per enrolled elementary student.

Los Angeles' Better Educated Students for Tomorrow Program (LA's BEST)

Program Characteristics

This afterschool program serves elementary school children from disadvantaged public schools and offers services such as help with homework, library activities, field trips, and experiences in the performing arts. Children engage in homework completion and tutoring, as well as participate in clubs, arts, and field trips. Recreational activities include traditional sports and table games.

Evaluation Findings

Using a quasi-experimental design, an evaluation of the program followed students in the second through fifth grades over a five-year period, comparing participants to schoolmates not in the program. "Using path analysis, our results show that higher levels of participation in LA's BEST led to better subsequent school attendance, which in turn related to higher academic achievement on standardized tests of mathematics, reading, and language arts" (Huang, Gribbons, Kim, Lee, & Baker, 2000, p. 7).

Target Children	Elementary school students residing in low-income communities.
Program focus	Safety, academic and educational enrichment, recreation and psychosocial development.
Child-Staff Ratio	Unavailable.
Funding	City of Los Angeles, Los Angeles Unified School District, and private sector.
Cost	Unavailable.

BELL After School

Program Characteristics

The BELL After School program serves children from low-income communities in kindergarten through sixth grade in urban public schools in Boston, New York, and Washington, DC. The program provides tutoring, homework assistance, and weekly enrichment activities. The afterschool program is provided five days per week for 2.5 to 3 hours per week in public schools and community centers. During the 28-week program, children receive tutoring in small groups, work on homework assignments, and participate weekly in arts, music, and drama.

Evaluation Findings

The BELL After School scholars, who began the program below grade level in both reading and math, gained significantly more than the national norm group in math after 28 weeks in the program (BELL, 2003a).

Target Children	Kindergarten to Grade 6 students of color residing in low-income communities who are performing below grade level.
Program Focus	Increased academic achievement and expectations, enhanced self-concept, and development of social and community skills.
Child-Staff Ratio	No more than 7 to 1 in tutoring sessions.
Funding	Foundations, various private sector sources, and parent fees based on a sliding scale.
Cost	$1,500 per program year per enrolled student.

READING AND MATHEMATICS PROGRAMS

Other out-of-school-time programs focus on reading and mathematics programs. The following describes such programs and their evaluation findings.

Meta-Analysis of Programs

Study Characteristics

Lauer et al. (2004) conducted a meta-analysis of out-of-school-time programs that were designed for low-achieving students and focused on reading and mathematics.

Evaluation Findings

They found that programs that served early elementary age children (kindergarten through second grade) had a large positive effect size (.26) in reading compared to programs serving older students. The most effective reading programs lasted from 45 to 210 hours and used one-on-one tutoring (.50 effect size). Conversely, in mathematics, programs were most effective in boosting performance of high school students and did not have a significant effect on early elementary students. The authors suggest that the history of focusing on math reform at the secondary level contributed to the differential findings in mathematics.

TUTORING PROGRAMS

Two studies evaluated afterschool tutoring programs for young elementary students.

Howard Street Tutoring Program

Program Characteristics

This program provides volunteer reading tutors to work with low-achieving second- and third-grade students two afternoons a week from 2:30 PM until 4:00 PM. Children are individually paired with a tutor and receive approximately 50 hours of tutoring during the school year.

Evaluation Findings

The randomized experimental study, which used matched controls, found that students in the treatment group gained more than one grade year in reading during the school year compared to two-thirds of a year for students not receiving tutoring (Morris, Shaw, & Perney, 1990).

Extended-Day Tutoring Program

Program Characteristics

This program was based on the Success for All program, and provided one hour of reading tutoring three days a week after school to Grade 1 through Grade 4 students selected for inclusion because they needed assistance in reading. The program, provided from December through the end of the school year, offered storytelling and retelling, listening comprehension, reading, and other activities. The program, initiated in 1995 and discontinued in 1997, used Title I federal funding.

Evaluation Findings

Using a quasi-experimental matched-pair design for the second through fourth grade participants, the study found significant positive effects on reading on the state standardized achievement test for third grade students only (Ross, Lewis, Smith, & Sterbin, 1996).

SUMMER PROGRAMS

Two evaluations examined summer programs that focused on academic achievement.

BELL Summer Program

Program Characteristics

A companion to the BELL After School program, this program provides an intensive five- to six-week session during the summer to children living in low-income communities in Boston, New York, and Washington, DC. The program operates eight hours a day, and 30% of programming time is dedicated to academic skill development. The cost for the summer program is $1,000 per child, which is generated through private funders and parent fees that are based on a sliding scale.

Evaluation Findings

Employing a quasi-experimental design in which researchers used participants' scores on nationally normed reading and math achievement tests, BELL (2003b) found that second graders advanced six months in their achievement levels. This increase is in contrast to the results of Cooper, Nye, Charlton, Lindsay, and Greathouse (as cited in BELL, 2003b) who reported that, on average, low-income students who have no summer program lose about two to three months in achievement levels during the summer. Overall, the second through sixth grade children moved from the 27th percentile to the 41st in reading and from the 25th percentile to the 44th in math (a score at the 50th percentile indicates average performance).

Teach Baltimore

Program Characteristics

Teach Baltimore provides an eight-week intensive summer program for disadvantaged elementary school children using volunteer university students. The curriculum is offered five days per week from 8:30 to 2:30, focuses on academic achievement, and includes morning education in reading and writing and applied experiences in the afternoon. The program, which is supported through private funders, has a child-staff ratio of eight students to one instructor

Evaluation Findings

The evaluation, which used a randomized experimental design, found significant positive effects only for the 1999 kindergarten cohort after their third year in the program (Borman, Rachuba, Fairchild, & Kaplan, 2002). The findings for the 1999 first grade cohort after three years and the 2000 kindergarten cohort after two years did not show any significant improvement.

MENTAL HEALTH FOCUSED PROGRAMS

Two programs focused on mental health.

Hispanic After School Program (HASP)

Program Characteristics

This program serves Puerto Rican children in kindergarten through sixth grade and seeks to prevent mental health problems using activities, including arts and group discussions, which promote positive ethno-cultural identity.

Evaluation Findings

Using an experimental design in which children were randomly assigned to a program or control group, the evaluation obtained pretest data at the beginning of the program, which covered one academic year, and posttest data three years after the end of the intervention (Garza Fuentes & LeCapitaine, 1990). The children in the program made significant improvements on a scale measuring maladaptive behavior in school, while the maladaptive behaviors of the control group increased. Moreover, the children in the program showed significantly higher gains in self-concept compared to the control group.

Kumba Kids Program

Program Characteristics

Mason and Chuang (2001) evaluated a culturally based afterschool arts program for low-income urban children, designed to promote adaptive behavior and prevent behavioral problems. The program, which uses an African-centered approach, provides 16 two-hour weekly sessions. Specifically, the Kumba Kids program employs African American artists as role models and uses dance and drama to promote the children's cultural awareness, pride, and understanding of their history. In addition to being culturally relevant, the model was designed to be completely arts-focused and not to include any academic components. Furthermore, the program was brief, lasting only one semester.

Evaluation Findings

The quasi-experimental design found that children in the treatment group showed significant improvements in self-esteem, social skills, and leadership competencies relative to the comparison group.

STUDY OF HIGH QUALITY PROGRAMS

Program Characteristics

An ongoing study, the Study of Promising After-School Programs, is focusing on the effectiveness of high quality programs, defined as those that focus on low-income children, provide comprehensive and intensive services, work with the schools, and employ trained staff. (Vandell et al., 2005).

Evaluation Findings

Initial results indicate that elementary school children who attend the high quality programs regularly have positive short-term benefits, based on behavior reported by program staff as well as on teacher-reported classroom behavior.

CHARACTERISTICS OF SUCCESSFUL PROGRAMS

The literature suggests that successful programs are characterized by supportive and educated staff, positive interactions among peers, and environments in which children can exercise choice and learn new skills.

Sufficient data does not exist to conclude what specific practices are causally linked to better outcomes (Harvard Family Research Project, 2003; Mahoney, Larson, Eccles, & Lord, 2005). However, several listings of "key elements" have been identified (Eccles & Gootman, 2002; Hall, Yohalem, Tolman, & Wilson, 2003;

Yohalem, Pittman, & Wilson-Ahlstrom, 2004). For example, Hall and colleagues (2003, p. 21) present the following list of key elements that characterize high quality out-of-school-time programs:

- Safe, stable places
- Basic care and services
- Caring relationships
- Relevant, challenging experiences
- Networks and connections (to expand opportunities)
- High expectations and standards
- Opportunities for voice, choice, and contribution
- Personalized, high quality instruction

Looking specifically at young school-age children, Vandell et al. (2005, p. 2) echo these key elements, identifying four important characteristics of successful programs: (1) "positive relationships with staff" in which staff serve as adult role models and constructively engage children, (2) "positive relationships with peers" in which positive interactions with the other children are encouraged and the children present positive expectations and models, (3) "diverse activities" so that children can learn skills and have new experiences, and (4) "opportunities to exercise choice and autonomy" so that children can engage in activities that interest and challenge them and gain experience in selecting activities in line with their preferences. Another study (Beckett, Hawken, & Jacknowitz, 2001) also identified program flexibility, a favorable emotional climate, and a variety of activities as having the highest level of support for promoting positive outcomes for children.

The C. S. Mott Foundation Committee on After-School Research and Practice (2005) has published a Framework for After-School Programs to assist organizations in developing a "theory of change" to guide after-school program development, implementation, and evaluation efforts. Through this theory of change, programs set goals and define the activities or program elements that will lead to the accomplishment of short-term and long-term outcomes for program participants. This framework assists programs and evaluators in addressing several of the challenges previously identified, such as divergent program purposes and inconsistent program quality.

The Framework identifies four categories of outcome-focused after-school program goals: (1) academic and other learning goals, (2) social and emotional goals, (3) health and safety goals, and (4) community engagement goals. In each of these areas, key program elements such as staff competencies, curricula and other resources, and activities are presented to provide programs with options for program development.

Accompanying desired outcomes for participants and potential perfor-mance measures are also offered.

Characteristics of Quality Reading Programs

Focusing on reading programs, the Lauer and colleagues (2004) meta-analysis found several practices that contributed to program effectiveness. As cited in Lauer and colleagues (2004), several studies (Lauer et al., 2004) identified the use of well-defined reading curricula as key to successful pro-grams. In addition, two studies (Huang et al. and Baker & Witt, as cited in Lauer et al., 2004) found that students with high levels of attendance and engagement in programs demonstrated outcomes that are more positive. Finally, Duffy and Morris et al. (as cited in Lauer et al., 2004) noted that teacher and supervisor quality were important components of successful programs.

Staff Ratios and Education

Research indicates that ratios and staff education also may be critical features. In one study, which observed elementary-age children in 30 pro-grams, those programs with lower adult ratios and less educated teachers had more negative interactions with students, less flexible programming, and fewer activities (Rosenthal & Vandell, 1996). A second study of first-grade children in 38 programs also found that higher adult-child ratios were related to warmer and more supportive interactions with students and to less time in transitions and watching television (Pierce, Hamm, Sisco, & Gmeinder, 1995). Also, staff with higher levels of education were more likely to use positive behavior management strategies and were less likely to be harsh with the children. Findings from the same study also indicated that nonprofit programs had better staff to child ratios and better educated staff. Children in nonprofit programs were less likely to watch television and wander aimlessly, and they experienced fewer nega-tive interactions with staff. Parents also reported higher satisfaction with nonprofit programs than with for-profit programs.

Summary

Overall, successful programs are characterized by having

- supportive staff and positive peer relationships,
- opportunities to exercise choice and learn new skills, and
- educated staff available in sufficient numbers.

In reading programs, quality was associated with well-defined curricula, high levels of student attendance and engagement, and teacher and supervisor quality. Finally, for a program to be effective, it is critical that the program's *activities are aligned with the outcomes* that program developers have identified for the children.

QUALITY ENHANCEMENT TOOLS AND INITIATIVES

To assist out-of-school-time programs in attaining quality, quality enhancement tools and accreditation standards have been developed. Moreover, states are pursuing initiatives to enhance quality in out-of-school-time programs as well as preschool child care.

Quality Assessment Tools

Foundations, Inc. has developed the Quality Assurance System (QAS) for programs to enhance and maintain quality (Weisburd & McLaughlin, 2004). The assessments, which can be done internally or by outside evaluators, are designed to be flexible and provide useful information for program improvement. The two-part program profile assesses (1) "program-basics building blocks," such as staffing, facilities, and health and safety that are common to all programs and (2) "program-focus building blocks," which are specific to programs and have components applicable to academic, recreation, and youth development programs. After an initial assessment, programs can target areas for improvement and conduct a follow-up review to assess changes.

Yohalem and colleagues (2004) identified 15 quality assessment tools used by youth programs and noted that they show "a high degree of consensus regarding specific elements of program quality." Although these tools can be effective in promoting quality, they are also costly to implement: "While mounting evidence shows that quality indeed matters, is measurable, and is malleable, the bottom line is that *quality costs*" (p. 6).

Accreditation

The National AfterSchool Association, formerly known as the National School-Age Care Alliance, has developed a national accreditation system for afterschool programs to "assure parents, children, policymakers, and funders that program quality meets clear development and safety standards" (Carter, 2003, p. 20). The standards are categorized into six groups: (1) human relationships; (2) indoor environment; (3) outdoor environment; (4) activities; (5) safety, health, and nutrition; and (6) administration. Programs engage in self-study, assessing their program on the standards, thus building their capacity to achieve program improvement. They then apply for accreditation, which, if achieved, extends for a three-year period.

Child Care Quality Improvement Initiatives

In the past, child care licensing programs often focused on ensuring that providers met minimal health and safety criteria or overregulated on issues such as facilities and staff-to-child ratios and did not assess characteristics that relate to quality (Quinn, 2005). However, more recently, states have instituted "tiered quality strategies" to promote child care quality through tiered reimbursement, rated licensing, quality rating systems, and a combination of these strategies (National Child Care Information Center, 2004). Of the 36 state child care quality initiatives, 30 include school-age programs as well as preschool programs. In the tiered reimbursement strategy, used by 28 of the 30 states, providers who are participating in the state subsidy program are paid at a higher level if they meet established quality criteria. In rated licensing, which is used only by North Carolina, ratings on quality are part of the state licensing requirements. North Carolina providers in the subsidy system receive different levels of reimbursement based on their rating. Finally, in the quality rating system, used by 10 of these states, child care providers are rated at different quality levels, which providers can use to market their programs and families can use as a consumer guide. Eight states use these strategies in various combinations to promote quality. The more frequently used categories of quality criteria include professional development and training, learning environment and curriculum, licensing status and compliance, and parent and family involvement (Collins, 2004). In Oklahoma, evidence suggests that the state's tiered reimbursement and quality rating system have resulted in higher quality programs (Norris, Dunn, & Eckert, 2003).

CONCLUSIONS AND RECOMMENDATIONS

The paucity of studies, especially experimental studies, makes it difficult to judge the effectiveness of out-of-school-time programs (Fashola, 1998; Hollister, 2003). However, a few tentative conclusions can be made:

- Out-of-school-time programs can produce beneficial effects for children.

- *Studies examining changes in social-emotional behavior consistently found that afterschool programs produced positive outcomes* (Garza Fuentes & LeCapitaine, 1990; Marshall, Coll, Marx, McCartney, Keefe, & Ruh, 1997; Mason & Chuang, 2001; Pettit, Laird, Bates, & Dodge, 1997).
- Programs aimed at improving academic skills varied in their success.
- *Three of the four experimental studies evaluating academically focused programs (Borman et al., 2002; James-Burdumy et al., 2005; Ross et al., 1996) did not find consistent positive effects, although the quasi-experimental studies did (BELL, 2003a; BELL, 2003b; Huang et al., 2000; Klein & Bolus, 2002).* Random assignment to program and control groups has important advantages, especially in voluntary programs such as out-of-school-time programs, because it avoids selection bias—children and their families who are more motivated to participate in out-of-school-time programs are more likely to enroll in these programs than children who have not enrolled (Hollister, 2003; Kane, 2004). Therefore, these quasi-experimental evaluations are not as rigorous tests of the effectiveness of out-of-school-time programs as experimental designs. On the other hand, the disappointing results of the 21st Century program evaluation have been questioned because the design did not relate the quality of program implementation to the level of outcome achievement. Rather, this evaluation was developed to assess the effectiveness of all programs in the sample, regardless of quality. Moreover, the evaluation used the relatively stringent level of effect size (.20) that is expected for standard educational programs, which may have been too high a standard for less intensive out-of-school-time programs (Kane, 2004; Lauer et al., 2004).
- *Early elementary students made greater gains in achievement than older students* (Klein & Bolus, 2002; Lauer at al., 2004), suggesting that out-of-school-time programs, especially for children at risk of educational failure, may be particularly effective at earlier ages.

Out-of-school-time programs provide children with a safe environment in which they can enhance their development in the social-emotional and academic realms, although the research is less consistent for academic outcomes. Moreover, the field is in the early stages of answering the question "what works best and for whom." There is some evidence that early elementary children made greater gains in achievement than older students, which suggests that policymakers should consider early intervention for children at risk of educational failure. Furthermore, the literature indicates that successful programs are characterized by supportive and educated staff, positive interactions among peers, and environments in which children can exercise choice and learn new skills.

To advance the knowledge base for out-of-school-time programs for early elementary age children, the following recommendations are offered:

- *The field should continue to more clearly define each program's goals and expected outcomes so that its "theory of change" can be specified.* Once program activities are aligned with program outcomes, programs can be held more accountable for achieving these outcomes.
- *Clearer specification of suitable evaluation designs is needed before the field can progress in assessing the effectiveness of out-of-school-time programs.* The range of evaluation designs used in assessing out-of-school-time outcomes reflects divisions among policymakers, advocates, researchers, and program professionals on what designs can answer questions about program effectiveness. Furthermore, the findings that children do not spend their time exclusively in any one program but rather are involved in a range of out-of-school-time activities or "sets of experiences" (Mahoney, Lord et al., 2005; Vandell et al., 2005) raise the question of the appropriate comparison group for children in out-of-school-time programs. Therefore, the definition of what constitutes appropriate intervention and comparison groups will have to be reassessed to reflect the reality of children's out-of-school-time experiences.
- *More research is needed to isolate program characteristics and practices that lead to quality.* The field is in the initial stages of defining, assessing, and improving quality. Additional studies should be conducted to identify quality practices that result in better outcomes for children.

REFERENCES

Beckett, M., Hawken, A., & Jacknowitz, A. (2001). *Accountability for after-school care: Devising standards and measuring adherence to them.* Santa Monica, CA: RAND Corporation.

BELL. (2003a). *BASICs (BELL After-School Instructional Curriculum) Program: 2002–2003 national program outcomes.* Dorchester, MA: Author.

BELL. (2003b). *BELL Accelerated Learning Summer Program: 2003 program outcomes.* Dorchester, MA: Author.

Borman, G. D., Rachuba, L. T., Fairchild, R., & Kaplan, J. (2002). *Randomized evaluation of a multi-year summer program: Teach Baltimore, year 3 report DRAFT.* Baltimore: Center for Summer Learning, Johns Hopkins University.

Carter, M. (2003). Evaluating out-of-school-time. *The Evaluation Exchange*, 9(1). Cambridge, MA: Harvard Family Research Project.

C. S. Mott Foundation Committee on After-School Research and Practice. (2005). *Moving towards success: Framework for after-school programs.* Washington, DC: Collaborative Communications Group.

Collins, J. (2004, August). *Exploring the complexities of tiered quality strategies.* Presentation for BUILD Conference Call. (Available from NCCIC, 10530 Rosehaven Street, Suite 400, Fairfax, VA 22030)

Eccles, J. S., & Gootman, J. A. (Eds.). (2002). *Community programs to promote youth development.* Washington DC: National Academy Press.

Fashola, O. S. (1998). *Review of extended-day and after-school programs and their effectiveness* (Report No. 24). Baltimore, MD: John Hopkins University, Center for Research on the Education of Students Placed At Risk.

Garza Fuentes, E., & LeCapitaine, J. E. (1990). The effects of a primary prevention program on Hispanic children. *Education, 110,* 298–303.

Hall, G., Yohalem, N., Tolman, J., & Wilson, A. (2003). *How afterschool programs can most effectively promote positive youth development as a support to academic achievement: A report commissioned by the Boston After-School for All Partnership.* Wellesley, MA: National Institute on Out-of-School-Time.

Harvard Family Research Project. (2003). *A review of out-of-school-time program quasi-experimental and experimental evaluation results.* Cambridge, MA: Author.

Harvard Family Research Project. (2005). *Out-of-School-Time Program Evaluation Database.* Retrieved March 21, 2005, from http://www.gse.harvard.edu/hfrp/

Hollister, R. (2003). *The growth in after-school programs and their impact.* Washington, DC: The Brookings Institution Roundtable on Children.

Huang, D., Gribbons, B., Kim, K. S., Lee, C., & Baker, E. L. (2000). *A decade of results: The impact of the LA's Best After School Enrichment Initiative on subsequent student achievement and performance.* Los Angeles: UCLA Center for the Study of Evaluation, Graduate School of Education & Information Studies, University of California.

James-Burdumy, S., Dynarski, M., Moore, M., Deke, J., Mansfield, W., & Pistorino, C. (2005). *When schools stay open late: The national evaluation of the 21st Century Community Learning Centers Program: Final report.* Washington, DC: U.S. Department of Education, Institute of Education Sciences, National Center for Education Evaluation and Regional Assistance. (Available at http://www.ed.gov/ies/ncee)

Kane, T. J. (2004). *The impact of after-school programs: Interpreting the results of four recent evaluations* (William T. Grant Foundation Working Paper). New York: William T. Grant Foundation.

Klein, S. P., & Bolus, R. (2002). *Improvements in math and reading scores of students who did and did not participate in the Foundations After School Enrichment Program during the 2001–2002 school year.* Santa Monica, CA: Gansk.

Klein, S. P., & Bolus, R. (2003). *Improvements in math and reading scores of students who did and did not participate in the Foundations After School Enrichment Program during the 2002–2003 school year.* Santa Monica, CA: Gansk.

Lauer, P. A., Akiba, M., Wilkerson, S. B., Apthorp, H. S., Snow, D., & Martin-Glenn, M. (2004). *The effectiveness of out-of-school-time strategies in assisting low-achieving students in reading and mathematics: A research synthesis* (Updated ed.). Aurora, CO: Mid-Continent Research for Education and Learning.

Mahoney, J. L., Larson, R. W., Eccles, J. S., & Lord, H. (2005). Organized activities as development contexts for children and adolescents. In J. L. Mahoney, R. W. Larson,

& J. S. Eccles (Eds.), *Organized activities as contexts of development: Extracurricular activities, after-school and community programs* (pp. 3–22). Mahwah, NJ: Erlbaum.

Mahoney, J. L., Lord, H., & Carryl, E. (2005). An ecological analysis of after-school program participation and the development of academic performance and motivational attributes for disadvantaged children. *Child Development, 76*, 811–825.

Marshall, N. L., Coll, C. G., Marx, F., McCartney, K., Keefe, N., & Ruh, J. (1997). After-school time and children's behavioral adjustment. *Merrill-Palmer Quarterly, 43*, 497–514.

Mason, M. J., & Chuang, S. (2001). Culturally-based after-school arts programming for low-income urban children: Adaptive and preventive efforts. *The Journal of Primary Prevention, 22*, 45–54.

Morris, D., Shaw, B., & Perney, J. (1990). Helping low readers in grades 2 and 3: An after-school volunteer tutoring program. *The Elementary School Journal, 91*, 133–150.

National Child Care Information Center. (2004). *State Tiered Quality Strategies (TQS), 2004.* (Available from NCCIC, 10530 Rosehaven Street, Suite 400, Fairfax, VA 22030) Retrieved August 9, 2005, from http://nccic.org

National Child Care Information Center. (2005). *Federal and state funding for early care and education.* Retrieved August 24, 2005, from http://nccic.org

National Institute of Child Health and Human Development Early Child Care Research Network. (2004). Are child development outcomes related to before/after school care arrangements? Results from the NICHD Study of Early Child Care. *Child Development, 75*, 280–295.

Norris, D., Dunn, L., & Eckert, L. (2003). *"Reaching for the Stars" center validation study final report.* Norman, OK: Early Childhood Collaborative of Oklahoma.

Pettit, G. S., Laird, R. D., Bates, J. E., & Dodge, K. A. (1997). Patterns of after-school care in middle childhood: Risk factors and developmental outcomes. *Merrill-Palmer Quarterly, 43*, 515–538.

Pierce, K. M., Hamm, J. V., Sisco, C., & Gmeinder, K. (1995, March). A comparison of formal after-school program types. Poster presented at the biennial meeting of the Society for Research in Child Development, Indianapolis, IN.

Quinn, J. (2005). Building effective practices and policies for out-of-school-time. In J. L. Mahoney, R. W. Larson, & J. S. Eccles (Eds.), *Organized activities as contexts of development: Extracurricular activities, after-school and community programs* (pp. 479–495). Mahwah, NJ: Erlbaum.

Rosenthal, R., & Vandell, D. L. (1996). Quality of care at school-aged child-care programs: Regulatable features, observed experiences, child perspectives, and parent perspectives. *Child Development, 67*, 2434–2445.

Ross, S. M., Lewis, T., Smith, L., & Sterbin, A. (1996). *Evaluation of the extended-day tutoring program in Memphis county schools: Final report to CRESPAR.* Memphis, TN: Center for Research in Educational Policy, University of Memphis.

Search Institute. (2004). *40 developmental assets for elementary-age children.* Retrieved June 7, 2005, from http://www.search-institute.org

Smith, K. (2002). *Who's minding the kids? Child care arrangements: Spring 1997* (Current Population Reports No. P70–86). Washington, DC: U.S. Census Bureau.

U.S. Department of Education. (2004). *Before and after-school care, programs, and activities of children in kindergarten through eighth grade* (NCES 2004–008). Washington, DC: Author.

U.S. Department of Education, Office of Elementary and Secondary Education. (2003). *21st Century Community Learning Centers: Non-regulatory guidance.* Retrieved August 11, 2005, from http//www.ed.gov

U.S. Department of Education, Office of the Under Secretary. (2003). *When schools stay open late: The national evaluation of the 21st Century Learning Centers program, first year findings*. Washington, DC: Author.

Vandell, D. L, Reisner, E. R., Brown, B. B., Dadisman, K., Pierce, K., Lee, D., & Pechman, E. M. (March 2005). *The study of promising after-school programs: Examination of Intermediate Outcomes in Year 2*. Retrieved August 11, 2005, from http://www.wcer .edu/childcare

Weisburd, C., & McLaughlin, R. (2004). Meaningful assessment and continuous improvement using the Foundations Quality Assurance System. *The Evaluation Exchange, 10*, 23.

Yohalem, N., Pittman, K., & Wilson-Ahlstrom, A. (2004). Getting inside the "block box" to measure program quality. *The Evaluation Exchange, X*, 6–7.

PART III

The Future
of the Field

9

Professional Development and Higher Education Systems to Develop Qualified Early Childhood Educators

Gwen G. Morgan and Jeffery Fraser

P rofessional early childhood education/child development specialists are primarily employed in different sectors organized around major funding streams at three levels of government. Public schools are locally funded with property taxes and state aid; Head Start is a federally funded preschool, infant, and toddler initiative; the purchase-of-service system includes private part-day and full-day centers, family child care homes, infant and toddler programs, and school-age programs, licensed and sometimes subsidized through the state.

For many decades, research has shown that quality matters for children (Cost, Quality and Outcomes Study Team, 1995; Morgan et al., l993; Ruopp, Travers, Glantz, & Coelen, 1979) and that the knowledge and abilities of early childhood professionals strongly influence outcomes.

Since the early 1960s, several long-term studies have shown that children from high quality prekindergarten programs continue to do better throughout their school and higher education experiences and in their later work and family lives (Barnett, 1995; Campbell, Ramey, Pungello, Sparling, & Miller-Johnson, 2002; Lazar, Hubbell, Murray, Roache, & Royce, 1977; National Institute of Child Health and Human Development [NICHD], 2001; Reynolds, Temple, Robertson, & Mann, 2000; Schweinhart, Barnes, & Weikart, 1993; Schweinhart et al., 2004).

In the earliest of these research studies, the teachers all had qualifications in early education and care, and the facilities had low staff-child ratios. The studies also identified teacher behaviors that correlated with strong positive results. Future research will reveal whether current qualifications and new programs will result in teacher behaviors and positive effects like those original teachers in these longitudinal studies.

THE CURRENT STATE OF PROFESSIONAL DEVELOPMENT

Today, however, professional development, like the field itself, is largely fragmented. No common infrastructure supports the development of all of the professionals needed to staff early childhood programs (Gallagher & Clifford, 2000). Training exists, but there is no clear career path. Professionals do not move easily from one level or type of program to another. Often, the training individuals have after becoming employed, even with course credit, is not accepted when they apply to a college for a degree, and they will be required to repeat it (Morgan et al., 1993).

Standards for Programs

States license programs, and they also license individuals. Licensing rules for programs are requirements that all programs must meet to obtain or to continue a license to operate in the state. These rules are applied to entire programs or "facilities," including the building and grounds; the equipment; the program of activities; the health and safety policies; the teacher-child, teacher-parent, and child-child relationships; and the qualifications of staff for all roles.

Within these rules, states regulate staff training and qualifications. States may have some or all of three different kinds of required training in their licensing rules: (1) required basic orientation, (2) preservice required qualifications for different roles, and (3) annual hours of training after employment or continuing education. All staff are included in the requirement for annual training, which can deepen the skills of credentialed staff and help noncredentialed staff acquire the skills and college credit to move to more responsible positions.

State licensing rules for programs are not limited to health and safety issues, and their rules for educating children are not limited to teacher qualifications. In almost all states, rules address an educational/developmental program with specific, evidence-based rules for teacher behavior, classroom management, scheduling, and curricula (Lemoine & Morgan, 2005).

Accreditation and Program Evaluation

Two other types of standards are also designed to apply to the entire program, including staff qualifications within that framework. One of these types is the set of voluntary accreditation criteria, such as those set by national organizations for centers, family child care, and school-age programs. These standards define a level of quality above what is required in licensing (Lemoine & Morgan, 2005). To be accredited, programs must be licensed in their state and also meet accreditation standards.

Evaluating programs is also the goal of rating scales and observational measures. Evaluations enable a researcher or a funding monitor to observe teacher and child behaviors. Specific sections of accreditation criteria can be used as observational measures for specific aspects of programs. Rating scales, such as the Early Child Environmental Rating Scale-Revised (ECERS-R; Cryer, Harms, & Riley, 2003), the Infant/Toddler Environmental Rating Scale-Revised (ITERS-R; Cryer, Harms, & Riley, 2004), or the Classroom Assessment Scoring System (CLASS; LaParo, Pianta, & Stulhman, M., 2004) are used to determine the general quality of the entire program.

CREDENTIALS ACROSS EARLY CHILDHOOD SYSTEMS

A credential or a state teacher license is given not to the program or facility but to the qualified individual. As described by the Wheelock College Institute for Leadership and Career Development (Director Credential listserv),

> Credentialing is used to refer to the awarding of a certificate, permit, or other document which certifies that an individual has

mastered a specific set of defined skills and knowledge, and has demonstrated competencies to perform in any early care and education or school-age setting (e.g. Head Start, private non-profit programs, for-profit programs, public and private schools, family child care systems). The body which awards the credential may or may not be the same organization that delivers the training. A credential may be awarded by a professional association, state agency, higher education consortium, or other organization, and signifies a consensus by those groups of the validity of the standards set forth.

More than a decade ago, an overview study of teacher credentials, licensing qualifications, and training (Morgan et al., 1993) had fairly negative findings. At that time, the study found that teacher qualifications specified in states' licensing requirements were inadequate, that some states required no training to work in early childhood programs, and that Department of Education teacher licenses tended to be geared more to kindergarten and early elementary grades than to prekindergarten children.

The study recommended systemic changes. It also recommended that states continue to permit new untrained workers to enter the field in assisting roles and that training be offered and required while they are employed to help them qualify later to become teachers. It further recommended that all staff continue to seek more knowledge and higher degrees rather than considering a single level of higher education to be the terminal qualification for a static role.

Since that study, there have been substantial changes in the direction of systemic improvement in more than half the states, and more change is likely in the future.

Current Credentials in Public Schools

The Department of Education (DOE) focus at the state level is primarily on the role of the teacher. There is a wide divergence in states' policies for teachers working in prekindergarten programs in public schools (Wise, 1994). For example, some states do not require a Department of Education credential for prekindergarten programs. Of those that do, the age ranges covered by a single DOE credential vary widely, including K–8 years, 3–8 years, birth–8 years, or birth–5 years. The amount and content of early childhood preparation required for future teachers varies according to child grades. Very little study has been done to measure the percentage of attention given to the needs of three- and four-year-olds, and even less to infants and toddlers, both periods that are critical to integrated brain development.

Credentials in Head Start

Head Start initially developed the Child Development Associate (CDA) credential for Head Start programs. Today, the CDA is also widely used as a credential in child care programs other than Head Start. But in 2003, Congress mandated that 50% of the Head Start staff have a bachelor's degree by 2010 and that all Head Start teachers have an associate's degree by 2007. As a result, many community colleges have begun to offer credit for the CDA to students who enroll in their associate's degree program. An associate's degree will serve as a credential for some Head Start staff for a few more years. Difficulties in articulation between different levels of higher education are a systemic barrier to professional development in many states.

Specialized Credentials to Work in Private Programs Licensed by the State

A few state licensing offices issue a qualifying certificate to staff who work in licensed programs, making their qualifications portable. Most states' licensing requires the program to employ qualified staff to keep their licenses. A growing number of states have established a central registry process to track the qualifications of individuals (Wheelock College Institute for Leadership and Career Initiatives, 2002).

Basic qualifications for private child care centers and family child care are set by the licensing agency. In states in which part-day programs are not covered by licensing, a few state departments of education have an accreditation based on academic qualifications of staff.

> With a growing number of states now expanding prekindergarten programs in public schools or pursuing universal prekindergarten education and care through public funding (Barnett, Hustedt, Robin, & Schulman, 2005), more emphasis needs to be placed on the qualifications for teachers of three- and four-year-old children.

If the positive effects found in longitudinal studies are expected from large-scale public expenditures, then accountability to the states and local communities will require that credentials for teachers of children younger than kindergarten age assure that the teachers have the knowledge and competencies that can be expected to produce these effects (Phillipsen, Burchinal, Howes, & Cryer, 1997).

Grade-Level Credentials

Very few state departments of education issue teacher credentials that are focused entirely on prekindergarten children, even when the state is expanding its commitment to this age group. For the schools, there are advantages to hiring certified teachers who can be assigned to different grade levels in different years. When a teacher certification includes both the three- and four-year-olds and also the kindergarten up to third graders, states with a new commitment to prekindergarten education should reexamine what percentage of the content of the requirements for certification prepares a teacher to provide the high quality that will result in positive outcomes specifically for prekindergarten children.

Director Credentials

The quality of programs for young children is highly influenced by the competency of the administrator or director, whose responsibilities range from parent relationships, hiring and supervising staff, building community and organizational commitment, goal setting, policy advocacy, and collaborating with other agencies (Cost, Quality and Child Outcomes Team, 1995; Culkin, 1999). An evaluation tool for rating director competencies, Preschool Administrative Leaders, or PAL, has been developed (Bloom & Talen. 2003).

In 2001, one study found that at least 19 states reported that they are implementing a director credential, and 19 others said they are planning to do so (Wheelock College Institute for Leadership and Career Initiatives, 2002). In most of these states, the credential is voluntary, although in some states it may determine compensation rates or state reimbursement rates for programs. Florida and North Carolina require the credential in their licensing rules. Wisconsin's Administrator Credential sets the highest academic standard—one required college course and five voluntary college courses. In Mississippi, the credential is not college based, but requires substantial clock hours. The Penn State Capital Area Early Childhood Training Institute has developed a 30-credit director's certificate program (see Box 9.1).

Family Child Care Credentials

In family child care homes, as in child care centers, high quality child care providers have positive effects on children. Studies suggest (Galinsky, 1994; Galinsky & Howes, 1995; Galinsky, Howes, & Kontos, 1995) that lack of specialized training can diminish positive and lead to negative effects; that caregiver education and training is linked to children's

Box 9.1   Capital Area Early Childhood Training Institute (CAECTI)

The Capital Area Early Childhood Training Institute (CAECTI) is a South Central Pennsylvania training institute that provides regional training in the Harrisburg area to over 1,400 early care and education providers. CAECTI is best known for its innovative Caregiver Mentoring Program that provides intensive on-site technical assistance and mentoring to directors and caregivers. The program has been extensively evaluated, clearly demonstrating its effectiveness in making caregivers more sensitive and responsive to children's cues.

CAECTI is funded with Commonwealth of Pennsylvania and foundation funds and is part of the Commonwealth's Regional Keys to Quality System.

The annual budget for CAECTI is approximately $750,000, which is spent on providing training and technical assistance to 1,400 providers.

CAECTI has trained over 2,000 directors and caregivers throughout Pennsylvania.

CAECTI has mentoring programs in infancy, preschool, special needs, social-emotional development, accreditation, directors, home-based providers, and parents.

performance on standardized cognitive measures; that the more staff training, the better children's outcomes; and that family child care providers who are members of professional associations provide higher quality care than those who are not. Somewhat larger groups of children in family child care were found to have more positive effects than smaller groups, suggesting that, within limits, the stimulation of being with other children and relationships with other children are positive influences in family child care.

Other Credentials

Some states require credentials for other roles in early care and education (Wheelock College Institute for Leadership and Career Initiatives, 2002), often as a funding requirement. These credentials include the following:

- **Infant/toddler credential**. The credential is reported as being established in 18 states.
- **School-age credential**. Twelve states reported that they are implementing a school-age professional credential.
- **Family child care credential**. Ten states reported establishing a family child care credential (Wheelock College Institute for Leadership and Career Initiatives, 2002).

Most of these state credentials are at the certificate level rather than the degree level.

CONTENT OF CREDENTIALS FOR EARLY EDUCATION AND CARE

Findings on the characteristics of effective teachers of prekindergarten children and the quality of the classrooms in which they teach have been remarkably consistent across longitudinal studies from 1979 to today (Campbell et al., 2002; Lazar et al.; 1977; National Center for Early Development and Learning, 2005; NICHD Early Childhood Research Network, 1998 and ongoing; Reynolds et al., 2000; Ruopp et al., 1979; Schweinhart et al, 2004).

Current emphasis at both the state and federal levels is on measuring outcomes for children to determine whether they are progressing in their learning and development. For school children, this measurement takes the form of testing children at intervals in their school careers. The federal testing requirement of the No Child Left Behind Act was created by Congress in 2001; similar state legislation has been evolving, for example in Connecticut (New York Times, 2005).

It is difficult to devise a valid test for what prekindergarten children are learning, since their scope, pace, and individual development varies greatly from one to another (Rothstein, 2004). In the absence of consensus on how to measure progress, federal mandates may encounter disagreement. Controversy over federal standards and mandates is not new. In 1970–1980, for example, battles raged over the Federal Interagency Day Care Requirements, which in the end were abolished (Morgan, 1981). Advocates had never reached agreement on the level at which federal standards should be set.

Demonstration programs have been documented to produce child benefits that have lasted over time. Future prekindergarten programs can be expected to have similar outcomes if they have the same characteristics, or quality, as those that have demonstrated long-term effectiveness.

Teacher Behaviors, Skills, and Characteristics

Since teachers have a strong effect on outcomes, it is useful to examine the behavior and skills of prekindergarten teachers in programs that have long-lasting positive effects on children (Barnett, 1995; Campbell et al., 2002; Lazar et al., 1977; NICHD, 2001; Reynolds et al., 2000; Schweinhart et al., 1993, Schweinhart et al., 2004).

Teacher characteristics that affect outcomes have been described in two categories: structural variables or process variables. Structural variables are those built into the program in advance, such as required credentials for teachers and required ratios, equipment, safe toys, and the like. They can be visualized as input standards. Process variables describe what is actually happening, such as how the teachers or the children are behaving. They can be visualized as "throughput" standards. These process variables can be reliable predictors of program outcomes, if they reflect the processes in the longitudinal programs that have had effective long-term results.

The following is a brief summary of those characteristics that are most frequently found to be significant predictors of long-range positive effects on young children.

1. Structural variables for teachers of prekindergarten children:
   - Have college degrees and specialized early childhood knowledge and skills
   - Maintain low child-staff ratios
   - Are assigned small classes

2. Process variables for teachers of prekindergarten children:
   - Have warmth
   - Are responsive to children
   - Develop relationships with individual child and family
   - Relate to children and interact with them one-on-one or organize children primarily in small groups to interact while teaching
   - Create cognitively stimulating environments
   - Value social and emotional development as an essential readiness factor
   - Allow children to express their feelings
   - Permit and encourage children to talk; extend conversations
   - Work in partnership with parents
   - Are interculturally competent

These characteristics of successful prekindergarten teachers, summarized across a number of longitudinal programs, provide solid information for the content of teacher preparation programs.

Child Development Associate (CDA) Credential

The content of the CDA Credential, for example, is entirely focused on these attributes of teachers who will work with prekindergarten children. Its goals can be viewed as a baseline framework for a curriculum for developing early childhood professionals. They are

- To establish and maintain a safe and healthy learning environment,
- To advance physical and intellectual competence,
- To support social and emotional development and to provide positive guidance,
- To establish positive and productive relationships with families,
- To ensure a well-run, purposeful program responsive to participant needs, and
- To maintain a commitment to professionalism. (This credential is based on demonstrated competencies.)

Teacher Qualifications in Conjunction With Program Quality

It is easy to use teacher qualifications as a stand-in for quality, but, to be sure that our early education programs will have positive results, we must look beyond credentials and observe what is going on in the program. Those competencies that researchers have found to be associated with positive effects must become the content of early childhood teachers' credentials. Even degreed and certified teachers may not all have the skills they need in their roles, unless those that grant the degrees and certifications view these competencies as the content of curricula for preparing early educators.

For example, observers in one major study (NICHD, 2001) expressed doubts about the first-grade teachers the children encountered when they went to school. They concluded that the experiences offered to children in first-grade classrooms vary so much that, taken as a whole, their findings suggested that classrooms may not be meeting children's needs. This example raises a question of whether the school is ready for the children.

Furthermore, a new ongoing study in six states by the National Center for Early Development and Learning (NCEDL) found that the observed quality in prekindergarten classrooms selected for their quality was slightly lower than the classroom quality measured in other large studies, even though the teachers in this study were more qualified. In fact, the findings suggest that superficial task demands, such as giving directions and assigning routine tasks, predominate over activities that promote children's conceptual or skill development (NCEDL, 2005, p. 18). Carolee Howes, one of the study's investigators, suggests that these teachers may never have received professional training that emphasizes how to move children from rote activities to more complex ones. An alternative explanation, she suggested, is that "teachers may be confused about what is expected now that their programs are 'real school'" (Ritchie, Howes, Kraft-Sayre, & Weisner, 2001). This example raises questions about whether children in all prekindergarten programs are going to be ready for school.

Content for Other Credentials and Degrees

Core knowledge and competencies are the heart of credentials and training at all levels. The findings of research studies can influence all the community-based training and all the specialized early education certifications and degrees offered in community colleges by focusing attention on teacher characteristics associated with quality, as reported previously. Some of these characteristics, such as warmth, may be thought to be innate characteristics, but most of them can be, and need to be, taught. For example, responsive interactions with children are difficult to develop in new teachers if not a part of their professional preparation.

EMERGING ISSUES

Recently, there are emerging issues in teacher education.

None of these is a new issue, but all are overshadowed by a current emphasis almost exclusively on literacy through reading. Nevertheless, now they are receiving more attention as teacher competencies receive more attention, and early childhood personnel preparation curricula need to be up-to-date on these issues.

> **Emerging Issues in Teacher Education**
>
> Parent relationships, family-friendly practice, readiness, diversity, inclusion, bilingual education, language development, child subject matter content, and technology are a few of these issues.

Parent Relationships

Teachers need to have some understanding of the lives children and their parents lead. Mothers living in poverty whose infants were in full-time, high quality child care showed more positive involvement with their 6-month-old children compared with poor mothers raising their children at home or those using full-time, lower quality infant care (Fuller & Kagan, 2000).

Family-Friendly Practice

While many programs have developed the ability to involve parents in their programs, fewer have developed the ability to involve their program as a support to the life of the family (Copeland, 1997). The fundamentals of family-centered care have not been clearly defined for practitioners. In 1996, the National Child Care Information Center and the Child Care Bureau brought together approximately 150 child care experts to agree

The Penn State Capital Area Early Childhood Training Institute has implemented a successful parent mentoring program in which seasoned early childhood professionals mentor parents in their own homes or at their child's child care program (Fiene, 2002). (See Box 9.1 on page 165 for more information on this Institute.)

on the basic features of a family-centered child care center. The experts agreed that the features should focus on the family as a true partner in providing care. Centers that add a family-friendly component to existing elements of high quality education and care offer parents what they most want: a strong collaboration between families and staff with a common interest in children. A family-friendly audit tool has been developed by Work/Family Developments (WFD Consulting, 2004).

Readiness

Testing children is a major strategy in school reform for measuring whether children are learning at grade level and whether some children are more consistently at risk of failure. This concept is part of a view that sees schooling as organized in graded norms, in which each level's major purpose is preparing for the next level.

For children three to five years old, the goal of assessment is not performance at grade level, but "readiness" to learn successfully when the children move into kindergarten and the elementary grades. One major study on readiness was conducted in 17 states, with the purpose of identifying a core set of common indicators to measure progress toward school readiness and early school success (National School Readiness Indicators Report, 2005). This study provides important guidance to states and localities for measuring and tracking readiness. Indicators of child readiness are included, but the study makes it clear that the indicators and potential solutions for readiness are not measured in the child alone. For example, the indicators are grouped in five categories: Ready Children, Ready Families, Ready Services, Ready Communities, and Ready Schools.

Brain Development Research

Brain research is increasingly being cited as the rationale for promoting early childhood development because it shows that early childhood is a critical period for learning. New knowledge about the brain stresses the importance of infant/toddler and prekindergarten settings, where most children first learn to interact with other children on a regular basis, establish bonds with adults other than their parents, form or fail to form important relationships for early learning and language development, and experience their first encounter with a school-like environment (Shonkoff & Phillips, 2000). Findings from brain development research, consistent with child development research, show that different aspects of development occur simultaneously, rather than separately.

> "The human brain is a highly integrated organ, and the development of language, intelligence, emotions and social skills is deeply interrelated" (Shonkoff, 2005).

In general, researchers in brain development (Shonkoff, 2005) verify that children are born ready to learn, but that vulnerability to harm during the early years can compromise this innate potential. Beginning even before birth, the brain is greatly influenced by environmental conditions, including the child's care, relationships, culture, and surroundings as well as the stimulation received. After birth, relationships with parents and other caregivers are the "active ingredients" of environmental and cultural influence on early brain development. Adults in early education and care can have a lasting impact on how children develop, learn, and behave.

> The single most important component of school readiness and resilience is a child's social-emotional development, formed through interactions and relationships (Kaufman Foundation, 2002; Shonkoff & Phillips, 2000).

Diversity

American families are rapidly becoming increasingly diverse. The 2000 U.S. Census provides data on today's children and families in the United States. In some communities, there is no longer a white majority. The greatest growth has been in the Latino population. The younger the children, the more diversity there is among them (Andrews & Washington, 2001).

Teacher preparation in the United States may not be adequate to meet the multiple needs of an increasingly diverse population of children and families. While culturally diverse materials exist (Ballinger, 1999; Collins & Ribero, 2004; Delpit, 1995; Far West Laboratory for Child and Family Studies, 1993; Kendall, 1995), they are not widely used by teachers.

Today, the teachers with bachelor's degrees are not from as diverse backgrounds as the prekindergarten children. States are beginning to offer current workers without degrees opportunities for further academic advancement. Otherwise, replacing current workers with younger, less experienced, and Caucasian teachers can have the negative effect of reducing the ethnic and racial diversity of teachers just as children are becoming more diverse (National Black Child Development Institute Cross Cultural Partnership Project, 2004).

Inclusion

In 1972, federal law required that services be given in the states' education systems to children with special needs. But progress in the states has not been rapid. If all children are to be included, teachers need to be prepared to teach all children (Miller, Fader, & Vincent, 2000). However, states and localities resist unfunded mandates from the federal government. There are still communities in which these children are excluded from regular classrooms (Klein & Gilkerson, 2000). Credentialed teachers often lack confidence in their own knowledge of practical teaching techniques to work with all children.

Early Literacy and Other Subject Matter Content for Young Children

Reading is a fundamental building block of school success, and pre-reading efforts to enhance early literacy are gaining attention throughout the nation. Recent brain research provides further evidence that children learn reading and other cognitive tasks through their close relationships with parents and teachers.

The importance given to reading in the nation's goals indicates a need to disseminate knowledge about early literacy to communities who need it, and to include it in professional development (Bryant, 2000; Copple & Bredekamp, 2000). Counting, science, art, and drama are other important learning areas that are stimulating to the eager curiosity of three- and four-year-olds and should be part of teacher preparation curricula (National Center for Early Development and Learning, 2005).

Technology

Seventy-two percent of higher-income children between kindergarten and first grade are using computers for educational purposes, compared to 32% of lower-income children (U.S. Department of Education, National Center for Education Statistics, 2003). The percentage of high-income children using computers for playing games was 44%, and, among low-income children, it was 50%, an indication of growing access. Despite national concern over the divide between poor and affluent children in access to and use of technology, teachers at all levels are resistant to bringing computers into classrooms (U.S. Department of Education, National Center for Education Statistics 2003). Teachers of children younger than kindergarten age are especially lacking in knowledge of the appropriate use of computers along with other classroom teaching materials with preschool children, of the benefits of computers to children, and of how to choose software. In the last several decades, high quality software has been developed for preschool children, including literacy software, but teachers tend not to use this technology even when it is available (Clements, 1987; Wright & Shade, 1994).

CHANGES AT THE COLLEGE LEVEL

Early care and education call for some approaches to professional development that are not always customary in colleges and universities.

Older Students

Colleges and universities today are more likely to see older "returning" students in this field who have taken time to gain work experience before completing a degree. Younger students in the 18- to 22-year-old age range and many graduate students may now be working full time with children while attending school and applying what they learn through employment to what they learn in their courses. Some four-year colleges' early childhood programs may also have larger numbers of junior transfers entering with work experience, prior credit, or a CDA or associate degree (Morgan et al., 1993).

These older students may not "fit in" to an organizational culture geared to the needs of 18- to 22-year-old residential students. Some of today's degree candidates may have nontraditional needs that may affect the way colleges and universities approach their instruction (Klein & Gilkerson, 2000). These older students bring with them knowledge gained from experience, but they may need initial academic support.

Students Currently Working in Child Care

Another example of today's differences is the fact that colleges and universities need to offer coursework—often in community settings—for the staff already employed in child care programs. Colleges need to market their courses and degrees not just to high school students but also to the staff of direct service community programs for children.

A college or university may set up a special entry-level course or a special cohort to facilitate the movement of low-income women into the field. Many of these women will not be engaged or inspired in entry-level coursework if it is designed only to make up for their perceived deficiencies. They are already engaged in learning more about working with children. They may need counseling to help them see opportunities beyond the entry-level role and encouragement to continue their education if they are to advance. They may need academic supports during their first year or two of college work. Many of them will encounter hardships while going to school, such as juggling family, housing, health, and budget problems, and they may need personal support. Such support can come through a cohort group and from mentors and faculty who see their roles as including personal as well as academic support.

Faculty Training Institutes

The Head Start Bureau set up faculty training institutes for colleges offering associate's programs, anticipating that those teachers with the CDA credential would be applying to get associate's degrees and beyond. Similar faculty institutes could share what is known about best practices and effective teaching with already employed workers in the early childhood field while programs, like Head Start, raise the bar and expect teachers working in early education programs to move to four-year degrees.

The need for faculty training institutes has also been identified in the development of director credentials because the content of that training spans early childhood theory and practice, organizational psychology theory and practice, financial management, operations, law, and community leadership. Colleges offering early education degrees may lack faculty with the knowledge to span these different disciplines and adapt this knowledge to the early education field.

PROFESSIONAL DEVELOPMENT PLANNING GROUPS

For the last 10 or 15 years, career and professional development planning groups in the states have identified barriers to needed solutions. During that time, the importance of a systems perspective and cross-sector alliances has led to policy changes and more effective systems. Today, professional development planning is gathering strength and going forward in most states, much of it dating back to the early 1990s.

Results to Date

By 2002, state and local planning groups were reporting the following gains, as well as setbacks and obstacles (Wheelock College Institute for Leadership and Career Initiatives, 2002):

Systemic Planning. A common base of core competencies and knowledge has been established in 34 states.

Effective Quality Controls. Two examples of quality controls are training approval and tiered rating processes. In 26 states, a training approval process is in place through which courses offered in different colleges are approved as covering aspects of the necessary core knowledge. Half the states have a tiered or differentiated rating process to move child care centers toward excellence, beyond the basic level required by licensing.

Progressive, Role-Related, Articulated Training. The professional development planning groups are identifying all the roles in the early education and care field across different funding systems and organizing progressive credit-bearing qualifications for different roles, qualifications related to career advancement, and salary expectations. Twenty-nine states report having a career ladder, and nearly all of the others are planning one. Entry-level credit-bearing training has been developed in 27 states as the first stage of professional development. In 33 states, colleges assign credit to the CDA credential. Mentoring programs are found in 24 states, bilingual early childhood courses are offered in 13 states, and early childhood courses in a language other than English are offered in 13 states. Modularized training is found in 21 states, enabling colleges to better understand the relationship between knowledge of the field and the credits that students are attempting to transfer into the core competencies. All these strategies help individuals already working in the field to advance their careers through gaining more college-level qualifications for more responsible roles.

> Rigorous credit definition is the currency for professional development systems.

Recognition and Reward Systems. Twenty-seven states have developed ways to document training of individuals, and 21 of them have computerized registries. Twenty-one states have implemented improvements in compensation tied to improved qualifications. States have developed credentials for directors, infant/toddler teachers, school-age leaders, and family child care providers. All states have implemented an apprenticeship program of the Department of Labor that results in a credential for early childhood teachers based on substantial college training.

Expanded and Coordinated Funding. Seventeen states have implemented a Teacher Education and Compensation Helps (T.E.A.C.H.) Early Childhood Scholarship Program, and 17 others are planning one. Many of the states have succeeded in uniting Head Start and child care in the same training. Many of these planning groups initially organized with little or no staff, relying on volunteers, but by 2001, many of them had paid directors.

A good resource for the most up-to-date information on these issues is the National Child Care Information Center. (See the Center's Web site at www.nccic.org.) An important ingredient in the success of these planning efforts has been the participation of different governmental and nongovernmental sectors, including licensing, departments of education, resource and referral networks, health departments, and departments of labor.

THE ROLE OF PROFESSIONAL ASSOCIATIONS

Professional associations are a nongovernmental element of the common infrastructure for a professional development system. The largest such association is the National Association for the Education of Young Children (NAEYC). NAEYC develops standards for colleges and universities and participates in the accreditation of bachelor's degree programs that specialize in early childhood. NAEYC has developed standards for the accreditation of colleges offering the bachelor's degree, associate's degree, and, more recently, new standards for graduate education in early care and education. In addition, NAEYC has established a code of ethics. NAEYC has state and local chapters.

Strong national associations that offer accreditation, as NAEYC does, play an important role, since their accreditation criteria, agreed on by professional leaders across all the states, are, in fact, a leadership consensus on what are national standards, even though not federal standards.

In 2005, the National Association of Elementary School Principals recognized the critical role principals can play in early learning by creating standards for what principals should know and be able to do in early childhood education.

There are also national associations for elementary school principals, family child care providers, school-age programs, infant/toddler programs, and child care directors.

The National Association for Family Child Care and its local affiliates offer a credential for family child care homes. The National AfterSchool Association (formerly the School-Age Child Care Association) and its local affiliates offer an accreditation for school-age programs.

The National Black Child Development Institute is a national association with local affiliates that has a strong interest in leadership development and early childhood professional development. There are several national associations of directors, one of which, the National Child Care

Association, offers a 30-hour credential for directors. Director associations are strong at the state and local level, often stronger than the national associations, but some are divided between for-profit and not-for-profit early education programs.

CONCLUSIONS AND RECOMMENDATIONS

The systemic changes made in the past 10 years are dramatic, but this work needs to continue. Strategies and next steps include the following:

- Assess both teacher qualifications in child care licensing requirements and state certification for teachers to determine whether the requirements reflect what is known about effective teaching for children younger than kindergarten age.
- Explore offering other credentials, such as infant/toddler, family child care, and school-age credentialing.
- Assure that training for those already employed in early childhood programs offers the option of course credit toward a degree to help them advance their careers.
- Encourage college faculty to work together, internally and externally to their own schools, to compare courses, build core knowledge into degree programs, and develop articulation among different levels of education.
- Offer faculty institutes opportunities to broaden the abilities of teachers to teach children younger than kindergarten age and to update their knowledge of new issues in the field.
- Encourage the recruitment and training of teachers from the children's own community, especially for younger children, thereby promoting diversity in faculty. We should welcome and value these teachers as major assets.
- Agree on a statewide career ladder and make recommendations to the states regarding pathways for advancement toward degrees and compensation policies linked to level of advancement.
- Use NAEYC standards for higher education programs in early childhood to assure that colleges and state decision makers are familiar with the expectations of the early childhood field.

REFERENCES

Andrews, J. D., & Washington, V. (2001). *The children of 2010.* Washington, DC: National Association for the Education of Young Children.

Ballinger, C. (1999). *Teaching other people's children.* New York: Teachers College Press.

Barnett, W. S. (1995). Long-term effects of early childhood programs on cognitive and school outcomes. *The Future of Children, 5*(3), 25–50.

Barnett, W. S., Hustedt, J. T., Robin, K. B., & Schulman, K. L. (2005). *The state of preschool: 2004 state preschool yearbook*. New Brunswick, NJ: Rutgers University, The National Institute for Early Education Research (NIEER).

Bloom, P. J., & Talen, T. N. (2003). *Preschool Administrative Leaders (PAL)*. Wheeling, IL: National-Louis University Center for Early Childhood Leadership.

Bryant, D. (2000, Spring). Linking literacy and language with social and emotional learning. *Prevention Update*. (Available from the Committee for Children Web site: http://www.cfchildren.org/cfc/)

Campbell, F. A., Ramey, C. T., Pungello, E., Sparling, J., & Miller-Johnson, S. (2002). Early childhood education: young adult outcomes from the Abecedarian Project. *Applied Developmental Science, 6*(1), 42–57.

Clements, D. (1987). Research in review. Computers and young children: A review of research. *Young Children 43*, 34–44.

Collins, R., & Riberro, S. (2004). Toward an early care and education agenda for Hispanic children. *Early Childhood Research Practice, 6*(2). Retrieved January 25, 2006, from http://ecrp.uiuc.edu/v6n2/collins.html

Copeland, M. (1997). *Tracing our family friendly history*. Unpublished course material, Wheelock College, Boston, MA.

Copple, C., & Bredekamp, S. (2000). *Learning to read and write: Developmentally appropriate practices for young children*. Washington, DC: National Association for the Education of Young Children.

Cost, Quality and Child Outcomes Study Team. (1995). *Cost, quality and child outcomes in child care centers* (2nd ed). Denver: University of Colorado, Economics Department.

Cryer, D., Harms, T., & Riley, C. (2003). *All about the ECERS-R*. Lewisville, NC: Kaplan PACT House Publishing.

Cryer, D., Harms, T., & Riley. C. (2004). *All about the ITERS-R*. Lewisville, NC: Kaplan PACT House Publishing.

Culkin, M. (1999). *Managing quality in young children's programs: The leader's role*. New York: Teachers College Press.

Delpit, L. (1995). *Other people's children: Cultural conflict in the classroom*. New York: New Press.

Far West Laboratory for Child and Family Studies. (1993). *Essential connections: Ten keys to culturally sensitive care* [Video]. San Francisco, CA: Far West Laboratory.

Fiene, R. (2002). Improving child care quality through an infant caregiver mentoring project. *Child and Youth Care Quarterly, 31*(2), 79–87.

Fuller, B., & Kagan, S. L. (2000). *Remember the children: Mothers balance work and child care under welfare reform. Growing up in poverty project, Wave 1 findings*. Berkeley: University of California.

Galinsky, E. (1994). *The family child care training study*. New York: Families and Work Institute.

Galinsky, E., & Howes, M. A. (1995). *The family child care and relative study*. New York: Families and Work Institute.

Galinsky, E., Howes, M. A., & Kontos, S. (1995). *The family child care training study: Highlights of findings*. New York: Families and Work Institute.

Gallagher, J., & Clifford, R. (2000). The missing support infrastructure in early childhood. *Early Childhood Research and Practice, 2*(1). Retrieved January 25, 2006, from http://ecrp.uiuc.edu/v2n1/gallagher.html

Kaufman Foundation. (2002). *Set for success: Building a strong foundation for school readiness based on the social-emotional development of young children.* Kansas City, MO: Author.

Kendall, F. (1995). *Diversity in the classroom.* New York: Teachers College Press.

Klein, N. K., & Gilkerson, L. (2000). Personnel preparation for early childhood intervention programs. In J. P. Shonkoff & S. J. Meisels (Eds.), *Handbook of early intervention.* New York: Cambridge University Press.

LaParo, K. M., Pianta, R. C., & Stulhman, M. (2004). The Classroom Assessment Scoring System: Findings from the prekindergarten year. *The Elementary School Journal, 104*(5), 409–426.

Lazar, I., Hubbell, V. R., Murray, H., Roache, M., & Royce, J. (1977). *The persistence of preschool effects: A long-term follow-up of fourteen infant and preschool experiments. Final report* (Grant No. 18-76-0783 ACYF). Denver, CO: Education Commission for the States.

Lemoine, S., & Morgan, G. (2005). *Developmental rules for licensed centers* (Report Nos. 1–5). Vienna, VA: National Child Care Information Center. (Available from the Center's Web site: http://www.nccic.org)

Miller, P., Fader, L., & Vincent, L. J. (2000). Preparing early childhood educators to work with children who have exceptional needs. In D. Horm-Wingerd & M. Hyson (Eds.), *New teachers for a new century: The early childhood professional preparation* (pp. 91–112). Washington, DC: National Institute on Early Childhood Development and Education. (Available from the U. S. Department of Education Web site: http://www.ed.gov)

Morgan, G. (1981). *The FIDCR Fiasco.* Unpublished course material, Wheelock College, Boston, MA.

Morgan, G., Azer, S. L., Costley, J. B., Genser, A., Goodman, I. F., Lombardi, J., & McGimsey, B. (1993). *Making a career of it: The state of the states report on career development in early care and education.* Boston, MA: Wheelock College Center for Career Development in Early Care and Education.

National Association of Elementary School Principals. (2005). *Leading early childhood learning communities: What principals should know and be able to do.* Alexandria, VA: Author.

National Black Child Development Institute Cross Cultural Partnership Project. (2004, July). *Universal prekindergarten in New Jersey: Teacher preparation and professional development in New Jersey's Abbott districts* (Policy brief). Washington, DC: Author.

National Center for Early Development and Learning. (2005). Who are the pre-k teachers? What are pre-k classrooms like? How is the pre-k day spent? *Early Developments, 9(1),* 15–28.

National Institute of Child Health and Human Development (NICHD). (2001). *First grade classrooms may not be ready to meet children's needs.* (Released April 20, 2001 at the Society for Research in Child Development.) Bethesda, MD: Author.

National Institute of Child Health and Human Development (NICHD) Early Childhood Research Network. (1998, 2000, 2001). *Study of child care.* Bethesda, MD: Author.

National School Readiness Indicators Report. (2005, February). *Getting ready: Findings from the National School Readiness Indicators initiative—A 17 state partnership.* (Available online at http://www.gettingready.org)

New York Times. (2005, April 8). *The New York Times,* pp. A1, A16.

Phillipsen, L. C., Burchinal, M. R., Howes, C., & Cryer, D. (1997). The prediction of process quality from structural features of child care. *Early Childhood Research Quarterly, 12*(3), 281–303.

Reynolds, A. J., Temple, J. A., Robertson, D., & Mann, E. (2000). *Long-term benefits of participating in Title I Chicago child-parent centers.* Presentation at the biennial meeting of the Society for Research on Adolescence, Chicago, IL.

Ritchie, S., Howes, C., Kraft-Sayre, M., & Weisner, B. (2001). *Emerging academics snapshot.* Unpublished measure, University of California at Los Angeles.

Rothstein, R. (2004, November). Too young to test: Why we need a better means of evaluating our nation's youngest children. *The American Prospect, 15*(11), Article 8774. Retrieved January 26, 2006, from http://www.prospect.org/web/index.ww

Ruopp, R., Travers, J., Glantz, F., & Coelen, C. (1979). *Children at the center: Final report of the national day care study.* Cambridge, MA: Abt Associates.

Schweinhart, L. J., Barnes, H. V., & Weikart, D. P. (1993). Significant benefits: The High/Scope Perry Preschool study through age 27. Ypsilanti, MI: High/Scope Press, 233-235.

Schweinhart, L. J., Montie, J., Xiang, Z., Barnett, W. S., Belfiend, C. R., & Nores, M. (2004). *Lifetime effects: The High/Scope Perry Preschool study through age 40.* Ypsilanti, MI: High/Scope Press.

Shonkoff, J. P. (2005, December 31). *Using science to design an early education and care system for Massachusetts.* Presentation to the Massachusetts Legislative Children's Caucus, Brandeis University, The Heller School for Social Policy and Management, Waltham, MA.

Shonkoff, J. P., & Phillips, D. A. (Eds.). (2000). *From neurons to neighborhoods: The science of early childhood development.* Washington, DC: National Academy Press.

U. S. Department of Education, National Center for Education Statistics. (2003). *Young children's access to computers in the home and at school in 1999 and 2000.* Washington, DC: National Center for Education Statistics.

WFD Consulting. (2004). *Family friendly audit tool.* Watertown, MA: Author.

Wheelock College Institute for Leadership and Career Initiatives. (2002). *Report on 2001 early childhood/school-age career development survey.* Boston, MA: Author.

Wise, A. (1994). The coming revolution in teacher licensure: Redefining teacher preparation. *Action in Teacher Education, 16*(2), 1–13.

Wright, J., & Shade, D. (1994). *Young children: Active learners in a technological age.* Washington, DC: National Association for the Education of Young Children.

Index

Abelson, W. B., 118, 119n 1, 122
Accreditation, 95, 109, 149–150,
     161, 163, 176
Ackerman, D., 14
Adelman, S., 109
Administration on Children, Youth and
     Families (ACYF), 36, 68, 69, 70, 71
Adult-child ratios, 30, 148, 150, 167
   demonstration programs and, 90, 92,
     94, 95, 96
Adult Education Act, 72
African Americans, 70, 89, 91,
     93, 120, 146
Akiba, M., 142
Alarcon, R., 36
Alcohol problems, 15 (Box), 97
Alexander, K. L., 116
Americans With Disabilities Act, 42
Andrews, J. D., 171
Aos, S., 93
Apfel, N. H., 118, 122
Apthorp, H. S., 142
Arts, 136, 137, 141, 145, 146, 172
Atkins, M. S., 38
Attention difficulties, xxi, 12, 14
August, D., 34, 35, 37
Autism. *See* Developmental disabilities
Axinn, W. G., 13
Ayankoya, B., 38
Azer, S. L., 159

Bagnato, S. J., 28, 95, 96, 107, 108
Bailey, D. B., 43
Baker, E. L., 141, 148
Ballinger, C., 171
Barber, J. S., 13
Barnes, H. V., 27, 90, 160
Barnett, W. S., 27, 90, 114, 121, 131,
     160, 166
Barnoski, R., 93
Barrera, I., 34

Barrett, B. J., 69
Basa, F., 12
Basile, K. C., 74
Bates, J. E., 138, 151
Becker, W. C., 118, 122
Beckett, M., 147
Behavior management, 19, 148
Belfield, C. R., 90, 160
BELL After School program,
     141–142, 144
Belsky, J.
Bergsten, M., 103
Berlin, L. J., 25, 27
Berrueta-Clement, J. R., 90
Bezruczko, N., 124
Bigelow, J. H., 67, 90
Blank, M., 8
Bloom, P. J., 164
Bohan-Baker, M., 61, 62
Bolus, R., 140, 151
Boocock, S. S., 98
Borman, G. D., 145, 151
Bos, J., 13
Boston, 141, 144
Bowe, F. G., 26
Bowman, B. T., xix, 17, 26,
     27, 28, 29, 30, 31, 38
Brady, C., 13
Brain development, 3, 10, 170–171, 172
Brandon, R. N., 106, 109
Brayfield, A., 102
Bredenkamp, S., 5, 60, 62, 172
Brezausek, C. M., 57 (Box),
     119, 126, 128
Brickley, D., 28, 95
Bridge-to-Reading, 92
Britto, P. R., 13
Bronfenbrenner, U., 28
Bronson, M. B., 94
Brookline Early Education
     Project (BEEP), 93–95

Brooks-Gunn, J., 11, 13, 16, 25, 26, 27, 28, 32
Brown, B. B., 146
Brown, W. H., 43
Bruner, C., 4, 11, 18, 19, 20
Bryant, D. M., 29, 127, 172
Buka, S., 42
Burchinal, M. R., 29, 30, 118, 121, 127, 163
Burkam, D. T., 3, 16
Burns, M. S., xix, 17, 26, 27, 29, 30, 36
Bush, G. W., 4
Buysse, V., 43

C. S. Mott Foundation Committee on After-School Research and Practice, 147
Cabezas, M. C., 11
Campbell, F. A., 27, 91, 118, 120, 127, 131, 160, 166
Campos, M. M., 37
Cannon, J. S., 90
Capital Area Early Childhood Training Institute (CAECTI), 164, 165 (Box)
Carl, B., 103
Carolina Abecedarian Project (ABC), 27, 91–92, 116, 117 (Table), 118 (Table), 119n 2, 120–121
Carryl, E., 138
Carter, M., 149
Castro, G., 40
Caulkins, J. P., 90
Certification, 7, 177
Chan, E., 94
Chanana, N., 79
Chandler, L. K., 43
Chiesa, J., 27
Child abuse, xxi
Child care, 15 (Box), 49
    center-based, 102, 103, 104, 108, 109, 110
    demonstration programs and, 97
    out-of-school-time programs and, 136
    poverty and, 30
    school readiness and, 13, 14–16
    See also Home-based child care
Child Development Associate (CDA), 163, 167–168
Child Development Program (CCDP), 58
Child-Parent Center (CPC), 80–82
Child-staff ratios, 30, 148, 150, 167
    demonstration programs and, 90, 92, 94, 95, 96

Child Trends, Inc., 11, 12, 13
Children's Defense Fund, 26
Chuang, S., 145, 151
Clarke-Stewart, K. A., 41
Class size, 7, 14, 30, 58
Clayton, S. L., 13
Clements, D., 173
Clifford, R. M., 11, 30, 104, 160
Coelen, C., 159
Cognitive development, xix
    curriculum and, 31
    demonstration programs and, 88, 90, 91, 93, 94, 95–96, 98
    emotional development and, 13
    environmental toxins and, 12
    extended intervention programs and, 114, 120
    Head Start and, 69
    kindergartners and, 10
    nurturing environments and, 3–4
    poverty and, 13, 29
    preschools and, 68, 74, 76, 89
    protective factors and, xxii
    school readiness and, 4, 5, 9 (Box), 11, 20–21
    transitions and, 58
Cohen, N. E., 14
Coiro, M. J., 13
Colbert, K., 127
Cole, R. E., 29
Coll, C. G., 138, 151
Collier, V. P., 34, 35
Collins, R., 150, 171
Committee for Economic Development, xx, 4
Condelli, L., 69
Congress, 69, 70, 137, 163, 166
Connor, R., 43
Conrad, K. J., 125
Copeland, M., 169
Copeman, A., 4, 11, 18
Copple, C., 60, 62, 172
Cost, Quality and Child Outcomes Study Team, 159, 164
Costley, J. B., 159
Cox, M. J., 58, 59, 62, 89
Credentials, 161–166, 177
Crnic, K., 27, 29
Croan, T., 10
Crosby, D., 13
Cryer, D., 110, 161, 163
Culkin, M. L., 30, 164

Culture, xxii, 5, 14, 33, 34, 35, 36, 146, 171
Currie, J., 70, 88, 114, 123, 131

Dadisman, K., 146
Darlington, R., 28, 92
Deal, A. G., 41
DeBlasi, C. L., 118, 122
Deck, C., 72
Deitch, S., 102
Deke, J., 139
DeKlyen, M., 43
Delpit, L., 171
Dental care, 11, 68
Denton, K. L., 62
Department of Education (DOE), 162
Depression, 13–14, 25, 95
Dettore, E., 28, 95
Developmental disabilities, 25, 39–49, 40, 43, 45–48 (Tables)
DEC and, 45–48 (Table)
ELLs and, 38, 39
inclusion and, 42–43
retardation and, 120, 128
Días, R. M., 36
Dichtelmiller, M. L., 18
Disabilities, xxii, 26, 42, 69, 110, 127
Division for Early Childhood (DEC), 43–44, 45–48 (Table)
Dockett, S., 58, 60, 61
Dodge, K. A., 138, 151
Donovan, M. S., xix, 17, 26, 27, 29, 30
Dorchester, M. A., 144
Dore, T., 109
Dorfman, A. B., 18
Doyle, S., 106, 109
Duncan, G. J., 13, 16, 26, 28
Dunn, L., 150
Dunst, C. J., 41
Dynarski, M., 139

Early, D. M., 58, 59, 62
Early, Periodic Screening, Diagnosis, and Treatment (EPSDT), 11
Early Childhood Environment Rating Scale (ECERS), 104, 104 (Figure), 110–112
Early Childhood Initiative (ECI), 95–96
Early Childhood Program Aid (ECPA), 77
Early Learning Improvement Consortium, 77

Eash, M. J., 125
Eccles, J. S., 136, 146, 147
Eckenrode, J. J., 29
Eckert, L., 150
Economic Opportunity Act, 42
Education Commission of the States, 61, 78
Education of All Handicapped Children Act, 42
Education of the Handicapped Act Amendments, 39
Emotional development, 12
credentials and, 168
demonstration programs and, 88, 98
extended intervention programs and, 122
kindergartners and, 10
nurturing environments and, 3–4
out-of-school-time programs and, 136, 140, 147
preschools and, 68
process variables and, 167
school readiness and, 4, 5, 9 (Box), 12–13, 20–21
English language learners (ELL), 32–39, 44, 45, 49
See also Language development
English-Romanian Adoption Study Team, 38
Entwisle, D. S., 114, 116
Epstein, A. S., 27, 90
Espinosa, L., 36
Ethnicity, xx, 10, 14, 33, 35, 59, 92
Even Start program, 59, 71–73
Everingham, S. S., 27

FACES Project, 69
Fader, L., 172
Fairchild, R., 145
Faith-based organizations, 140
Family Child Care (FCC), 104, 105
Family Day Care Environmental Rating Scale (FDCRS), 103, 104, 104 (Figure), 106, 107 (Figure), 110–112
Family Development Research Program (FDRP), 93
Family services, xxii
Far West Laboratory for Child and Family Studies, 171
Farran, D. C., 25, 27, 29, 31, 32, 40
Fashola, O. S., 136, 150
Fegley, C., 103

Fewell, R., 40
Fiene, R., 103, 104, 105, 106,
    108, 110, 170
Fiese, B. H., 28
Filer, J., 42
Floyd, S., 4
Food Stamps, 11
Forness, S. R., 119, 128
Foundations, Inc., 140, 149
Fowler, S. A., 43
Frank Porter Graham Child
    Development Center, 14
Frede, E. C., 30, 31, 32
Frelow, V. S., 10, 11, 16, 17, 18
Fuerst, D., 118, 125
Fuerst, J. S., 118, 125
Fuligni, A. S., 25, 27
Fuller, B., 169
Funding, xx, 159
    demonstration programs and, 90, 92,
        94, 95, 96, 98–99
    developmental disabilities and, 44, 49
    Even Start Family Literacy Program
        and, 73
    extended intervention programs and,
        121–122, 126, 127
    Head Start and, 71
    home-based child care and,
        108 (Box), 110
    out-of-school-time programs
        and, 139, 140, 141, 149
    preschools and, 74, 76, 77,
        78, 80, 82, 84
    Title I and, 123, 143
Funk, S., 110

Galinsky, E., 103, 107, 109, 110, 164
Gallagher, J., 160
Galper, A. R., 127
Ganson, H., 69
Garces, E., 70
Garcia, E., 34, 35, 36
Gardner, D. M., 118, 121
Garza Fuentes, E., 145, 151
Gayer, T., 76
General Accounting Office (GAO), 69
Genser, A., 159
Gersten, R., 118, 122
Gibbons, L., 103
Gibson, C., 13
Gilkerson, L., 172, 173
Gilliam, W. S., 74, 89
Girolametto, L., 41

Glantz, F., 159
Glennen, S., 38
Glick, M., 40
Gmeinder, K., 148
GOAL math program, 92
Goelman, H., 103
Goode, S., 38
Goodman, I. F., 159
Gootman, J. A., 27, 30, 31, 147
Gordon, C. S., 75
Gormley, W. T., 76
Gottman, J. M., 43
Gould, H., 11
Gould, M., 11
Grade retention, 68, 70, 74,
    81, 121, 123, 125
Graduation rates, 28, 125
Granger, R., 13
Grantham-McGregor, S., 11
Greathouse, 144
Greenberg, M. T., 103, 115
Greene, A. D., 13
Greenwood, P. W., 27
Gribbons, B., 141
Gross, R. T., 11
Groza, V., 38
Gruenwald, R., 4
Gunnar, M., 38
Guralnick, M. J., 26, 27,
    39, 40, 42, 43, 114

Hagemann, M., 124
Hair, E. C., 10
Hakuta, K., 34, 35, 36–37
Hall, G., 147
Halle, T., 13
Halpern, R., 25
Hamm, J. V., 148
Hammond, M., 43
Hamre, B. K., 56, 58, 61
Hanson, M. J., 38
Harms, T., 104, 161
Harvard Family Research
    Project, 137, 146
Haskins, R., 10
Hauser-Cram, P., 94
Hausner, 148
Hawken, A., 147
Hayes, C., 103, 105
Head Start, 11, 49
    credentials and, 162, 163
    funding and, 159
    Georgia and, 75

home-based child care and,
104, 105, 106 (Figure)
migrants and, 36–37
preschools and, 68–71, 79, 83
school readiness and, 6
training and, 173, 174, 175–176
transitions and, 59, 60
Head Start Child Outcomes
Framework, 4, 8, 9 (Box)
Head Start/Follow Through (FT),
116, 117 (Table), 118 (Table),
121–123, 126
Head Start Transition Study,
56, 57 (Box), 64n 1
Health, 160, 161
demonstration programs and, 93, 95
extended intervention programs and,
122, 123, 124, 127
Head Start and, 69
home-based child care and, 109
kindergartners and, 10
out-of-school-time programs and,
136, 137, 147, 149, 150
poverty and, 13
school readiness and, 4, 5, 7, 8,
9 (Box), 10, 11–12, 20–21
services and, 19, 127, 130
transition programs and, 57 (Box)
Health care, xx, 3–4, 68, 121
Health problems, 25, 26
Heckman, J. J., 130
Hegland, S. M., 127
Helburn, S. W., 110
Helms, R., 120
Hemmeter, M. L., 41, 44, 48
Henderson, Jr., C. R., 29
Henderson, L. W., 74
Henry, G. T., 74, 75
Hofferth, S. L., 102
Holcomb, P., 102
Hollister, R., 150, 151
Holmes, D. L., 12
Home-based child care:
characteristics of, 105
environmental quality of, 106 (Figure)
illegally operating and, 102, 103
intentional providers and, 106, 110
legally unregulated and, 102, 103
mentoring/training and, 107–109,
108 (Box)
quality of, 103–105
regulated providers and, 102–103,
105, 109, 110

relatives/neighbors and, 109
See also Child care
Home visits, xxii
demonstration programs and, 89, 94
Even Start Family Literacy Program
and, 72
Head Start and, 71
poverty/early interventions and, 28
school readiness and, 8, 11
Honig, A., 93
Hopkins, B., 43
Horton, C., 18
Hoube, J., 27
Hough, S., 38
Howes, C., 30, 61, 103, 107,
109, 110, 163, 168
Howes, M. A., 164
Huang, D., 141, 148, 151
Hubbell, V. R., 160
Human services, 93
Hundert, J., 43
Hustedt, J. T., 163
Huston, A. C., 13
Hyperactivity, 12

Ileana, D., 38
Illinois, 80–82
Immunizations, 11
Incomes, 21, 28, 95, 138
Individuals With Disabilities
Education Act, 12, 42
Infant Health and Development
Program (IHDP), 16
Infants, 29
Ingram, A., 96
Innes, F. K.
Iutcovich, J., 110

Jablon, J. R., 18
Jacknowitz, A., 147
Jaeger, E., 110
James-Burdumy, S., 139, 151
Jodry, W., 41
Joesch, J. M., 106, 109
Johnson, J., 110
Joseph, G. E., 44
Juvenile delinquency, xxii, 19, 68,
81, 89, 90, 125

Kabbani, N., 116
Kagan, S. L., 5, 10, 14, 16,
30, 58, 62, 169
Kahn, A., 103

Kamerman, S., 103
Kane, T. J., 151
Kaplan, J., 145
Kappel, A., 40
Karoly, L. A., 27, 28, 67, 90
Katholi, C. R., 57, 119, 126
Kauffman Foundation, 12–13, 13, 171
Kavale, K.A., 119, 128
Keefe, N., 138, 151
Kendall, F., 171
Kennedy, E. M., 122
Kilburn, M. R., 27, 90
Kim, K. S., 141
Kinnish, K., 43
Kitzman, H., 29
Klebanov, P. K., 16
Klein, L. G., 20
Klein, N. K., 172, 173
Klein, S. P., 140, 151
Kochanek, T., 42
Kontos, S., 103, 107, 109, 164
Koppel, R., 110
Korenman, S., 11
Kraft-Sayre, M. E., 6, 58, 62, 168
Kreider, H., 59
Kulieke, M. J., 16

Laird, R. D., 138, 151
Lally, J. R., 93
Lamb, M. E., 29
Landmark Elementary and Secondary
     Education Act, 123
Langan, F., 110
Language development:
     assessments and, 18
     brain research and, 170–171
     class sizes/teacher-child ratios and, 30
     early child care and, 14
     ELLs and, 32–39, 44, 45
     emotional development and, 13
     extended intervention programs and,
          120, 124, 128
     home-based child care and, 110, 111
     out-of-school-time programs and, 141
     preschools and, 76, 77, 79, 81
     school readiness and, 4, 5, 6, 9 (Box),
          11, 20–21
Lanzi, R. G., 57 (Box), 119, 127
LaParo, K. M., 161
Larsen, L., 96
Larson, R. W., 136, 146
Lauer, P. A., 142, 148, 151
Lawrence, F., 57 (Box), 119, 126

Lazar, I., 28, 92, 160, 166
Le Menestrel, S., 13
Leadership, 7–8, 108, 127,
     128, 129, 146
LeCapitaine, J. E., 145, 151
Lee, C., 141
Lee, D., 146
Lee, V. E., 3, 16, 114, 131
Lemoine, S., 161
Lewis, T., 144
Liaw, F. R., 11
Licensing, 150, 160, 162, 163–164, 177
Lieb, R., 93
Light, R.J. (Eds.), 88
Literacy development:
     assessments and, 18
     demonstration programs and, 92
     emotional development and, 13
     Even Start Family Literacy Program
          and, 72, 73
     extended intervention programs and,
          120, 130
     Head Start and, 69
     home-based child care and, 105
     preschools and, 79
     school readiness and, 4, 5, 9 (Box), 11
Literacy Involves Families
     Together (LIFT), 71
Little, P., 61, 62
Loeb, S., 114
Logue, M. E., 58
Lombardi, J., 159
Lopez, M., 15
Lord, H., 136, 138, 146, 152
Love, J. N., 58
Low-achieving students, 142, 143
Low birth weight, 5, 11, 25
Lubeck, R. C., 43
Lynch, R., 20

MacLean, K., 38
Magnuson, K., 13
Maher, E. J., 106, 109
Mahoney, B., 43
Mahoney, G., 41, 43
Mahoney, J. L., 136, 138, 146, 152
Mandates, 166, 172
Mangione, P. L., 60, 93
Manlove, J., 13
Mann, E. A., 81, 119, 125, 131, 160
Mansfield, W., 139
Marfo, K., 41
Mariner, C., 13

Marsden, D. B., 18
Marshall, N. L., 138, 151
Martin-Glenn, M., 142
Marx, F., 138, 151
Maryland State Department
    of Education, 11
Mashburn, A. J., 75
Mason, M. J., 145, 151
Masse, L. N., 91, 121
Masters, M., 38
Mastroprieri, M. A., 40
Mavrogenes, N. A., 124
McCall, R. B., 96, 98
McCartney, K., 30, 138, 151
McCarton, C., 11
McCollum, J. A., 41
McConkey, C., 69
McConnell, S. R., 43
McCormick, M. C., 11
McEvoy, M. A., 43
McGimsey, B., 159
McKay, M. M., 38
McKey, R. H., 69
McLaughlin, R., 149
McLean, M. E., 33, 43, 44, 48
McLelland, M. M., 12
McLoyd, V., 13
McWilliam, R. A., 43
Medicaid, 11, 125
Meisels, S. J., 18, 26, 27, 61
Melnick, S., 103, 104
Mental health:
    adopted ELLs and, 38
    demonstration programs and, 97
    extended intervention
        programs and, 127
    out-of-school-time programs
        and, 137, 145–146
    parents and, 13–14
    poverty/early interventions
        and, 28
    retardation and, 120, 128
    risk factors and, xxi
    school readiness and, 13
Mentoring, 175
    demonstration programs and, 95
    home-based child care and, 105,
        107–109, 110
    out-of-school-time programs
        and, 136, 137
    parents and, 170
    school readiness and, 6–7
Mersky, J. P., 125

Michigan School Readiness
    Program (MSRP), 79
Miedel, W. T., 81
Migrant and Seasonal Head
    Start (MSHS), 36–37
Miller, J. E., 11
Miller, P., 172
Miller-Johnson, S., 91, 118, 121, 160
Minorities, 3, 11–12, 145
    See also African Americans
Mistry, R., 13
Mitchell, A., 79, 82
Montessori, 75
Montie, J., 90, 160
Moore, E., 5
Moore, K., 13
Moore, K. A., 10
Moore, M., 139
Morgan, G., 159, 161, 162, 166, 173
Morris, D., 143, 148
Morrison, D. R., 13
Morrison, F. J., 12
Morrison & Coiro, 13
Motor development, 5, 9 (Box),
    20–21, 76, 91
Murray, H., 28, 92, 160
Murray, S., 72

National AfterSchool
    Association, 149, 176
National Association for the
    Education of Young Children
    (NAEYC), 33, 34, 59, 74,
    95, 108–109, 176
National Association of Early
    Childhood Specialists in State
    Departments of Education
    (NAECS/SDE), 33, 34
National Black Child Development
    Institute, 171, 176
National Center for Early Development
    and Learning (NCEDL), 62, 166,
    168, 172
National Center for Education Statistics
    (NCES), 33, 172
National Child Care Association,
    176–177
National Child Care Information Center,
    150, 169, 176
National Education Goals Panel (NEGP),
    4–8, 9 (Box), 14, 16, 17
National Head Start Association
    See Head Start

National Head Start Early Childhood
Transition Demonstration Project,
57 (Box), 116, 126–127
National Institute for Early Education
Research, 67, 68, 73, 82
National Institute of Child Health and
Human Development (NICHD),
14, 30, 138, 160, 166, 168
National Research Council, 17, 27, 40
National School Readiness Indicators
Report, 170
National Survey of America's Families
(NSAF), 109
Neglect, 26
Newman, M. J., 58, 59, 62
No Child Left Behind Act (NCLB), 3, 4, 15,
30, 71, 166
Nores, M., 90, 160
Norris, D., 150
Nursery schools, 104, 105, 106 (Figure)
Nutrition:
demonstration programs and, 93
extended intervention programs and,
123, 124, 126, 127
nurturing environments and, 3–4
out-of-school-time programs and, 150
school readiness and, 8, 11

Oden, S., 69
Odom, S. L., 43
Office of Elementary and Secondary
Education, 139
Office of School Readiness, 74
Olds, D. L., 29
Orfield, A., 12
Ou, S., 116, 125

Palfrey, J. S., 94, 95
Palmer, J., 103
Pechman, E. M, 146, 147, 152
Peisner-Feinberg, E. S., 30, 61
Pence, A., 103
Pennsylvania Partnerships
for Children, 39
Perney, J., 143
Perry, B., 58, 60, 61
Peters, B. R., 38
Peters, S., 59
Pettit, G. S., 138, 151
Phillips, 32, 127, 128, 171
Phillips, D. A., xxii, 4, 13, 17, 26, 27, 28,
29, 30, 31, 32, 40, 171
Phillips, M. M., 57, 119, 126, 127, 128

Phillipsen, L. C., 61, 163
Phipps, P., 93
Phonics, 92, 130
Physical development, 3–4, 5, 8,
9 (Box), 11, 12, 13–14, 136, 140
Pianta, R. C., 6, 56, 58,
59, 61, 62, 89, 161
Pierce, K. M., 97, 98, 146, 148
Pistorino, C., 139
Pittman, K., 147
Plantz, M. C., 69
Platt, L. J., 11
Play, 5, 30, 43, 58, 60, 80, 112
Ponder, B. D., 75
Powell, A., 41
Pregnancies, 90, 91
Prekindergarten *See* Preschools
Prereading skills, 10, 42, 60,
70, 72, 74, 83, 106 (Figure)
Preschool Administrative
Leaders (PAL), 164
Preschools:
diversity and, 59
expulsion rates and, 89
federal programs and, 68–73
funding and, 159
kindergarten and, 77, 79, 82
percentage of children
enrolled in, 67–68
school readiness and, 14
state programs and, 68, 73–82
Psychosocial development,
13, 136, 141, 174
Pungello, E., 91, 118, 121, 160

Quality and Child Outcomes Team, 164
Quality Assurance System (QAS), 149
Quinn, J., 150

Rachuba, L. T., 145
Ramey, 27, 56, 58, 60, 62, 97
Ramey, C. T., 27, 56, 60, 62, 91, 97,
118, 121, 126, 160
Ramey, S. L., 56, 60, 62,
91, 97, 118, 126
Ramsey, A. B., 44
Raver, C. C., 12, 49
Readiness skills, 75, 79, 81, 170–171
Reading:
demonstration programs
and, 91, 94
emotional development and, 12
environmental toxins and, 12

Even Start Family Literacy Program
and, 72
extended intervention programs and,
121, 124, 125
home-based child care and, 111
out-of-school-time programs and, 137,
140, 141, 142–143, 144, 148
poverty/early interventions and, 28
prephonics and, 92
prereading skills and, 60
preschools and, 74, 81
success and, 172
transition programs and, 57 (Box)
Redden, S. C., 119, 128
Redshirting, 7
Rehabilitation Act, 42
Reidinger, S. A., 59
Reisner, E. R., 146
Residential placements, 40
Retardation, 120, 128
See also Developmental disabilities;
Mental health
Retentions, grade, 7, 28, 89,
91, 92, 95–96
Reynolds, A. J., 28, 81, 116,
118, 124, 129, 160, 166
Rhode Island Kids Count, 12, 16
Riberro, S., 171
Rice, M. L., 38
Richter, K., 13
Rickman, D. K, 75
Riley, C., 161
Rimm-Kaufman, S. E., 58, 89
Ringwalt, S., 38
Ripple, C., 79
Ritchie, S., 168
Roache, M., 160
Robertson, D. L., 81, 119, 125, 131, 160
Robin, K. B., 163
Rock, D. A., 19
Rodríguez, J., 36
Rolnick, A., 4
Romano, A., 13
Romano Papillo, A., 15
Romich, J., 13
Rosenbaum, J. E., 16
Rosenbaum, L. K., 118, 122
Rosenberg, F., 37
Rosenthal, R., 148
Ross, S. M., 144, 148, 151
Rothstein, R., 3, 8, 12, 166
Rouse, C., 10
Royce, J., 28, 92, 160

Rubinowitz, L. S., 16
Ruh, J., 138, 151
Ruopp, R., 159, 166
Rutter, M., 38
Ryan, R. H., 13, 36
Rydell, C. P., 27

Safety, 160, 161
credentials and, 168
demonstration programs
and, 93
home-based child care and, 109
out-of-school-time programs and, 136,
137, 147, 149, 150
Saluja, G., 11, 18
Sameroff, A. J., 28
Sandall, S., 43, 44, 48
Sanders, M., 27
Sazer O'Donnell, N., 15
Scarr, S., 30
Schacht R., 42
Schulman, K. L., 163
Schweinhart, L. J., 27, 69, 79, 90, 118,
119n 1, 122, 160, 166
Scott-Little, C., 10, 11, 16, 17, 18
Sealand, N., 16
Seefeldt, C., 127
Seitz, V., 118, 122
SERVE, 60
Shade, D., 173
Shaw, B., 143
Shaw, E., 38
Shinn, M., 103, 109
Shonkoff, J. P., xxii, 4, 13,
17, 25, 31, 32, 40, 171
Shore, R., 6
Sirin, S., 94
Sisco, C., 148
Sjaastad, J. E., 11
Skinner, M. L., 118, 121
Smith, B. J., 43, 44, 48n
Smith, K., 135
Smith, L., 144
Smith-Jones, J., 28, 95
Smolensky, R., 27, 30, 31
Snipper, A., 28
Snow, D., 142
Snyder, K., 109
Snyder, S., 57, 119, 126
Social development, xix
brain research and, 171
credentials and, 168
curriculum and, 31

demonstration programs and, 88, 91,
    93, 94–95, 96, 98
developmental disabilities and, 41, 43
emotional development and, 12
extended intervention programs and,
    120, 122, 126, 127, 128
Head Start and, 69, 70
home-based child care and, 111
kindergarteners and, 10, 61, 62
nurturing environments and, 3–4
out-of-school-time programs and, 136,
    137, 138, 142, 146, 147, 151
poverty and, 28, 29
preschools and, 68, 79, 84
process variables and, 167
protective factors and, xxii
risk factors and, xxi, xxii
school readiness and, 4, 5,
    9 (Box), 11, 20–21
Social services, 78, 90, 91, 122, 130
Socioeconomic status (SES),
    16, 21, 26, 138
Sontag, J. C., 42
Spanish-speaking children, 36–37
Sparling, J .J., 91, 118, 120, 121, 160
Special education:
    assessments and, 17–18
    demonstration programs
        and, 91, 92, 96
    developmental disabilities
        and, 39, 40, 42
    extended intervention programs and,
        121, 123
    Head Start and, 69
    poverty/early interventions and, 28
    preschools and, 68, 81, 89
    school readiness and, 6, 19, 20
    transitions and, 58
SPECS Program Evaluating Team, 107
Speech impairment, 128
Speth, T., 60
Spiker, D., 11
Sports, 136, 141
Sprague, P., 15
St. Pierre, R. G., 72
Staff-to-child ratios, 30, 148,
    150, 167
    demonstration programs and, 90, 92,
        94, 95, 96
Stahl, D., 15
Standards, 160–161
    credentials and, 162, 166
    early child care and, 15–16

home-based child care and, 102, 103,
    108, 109
MSHS and, 36
NAEYC and, 176, 177
NCLB and, 30
out-of-school-time programs and,
    137, 147, 149, 150
preschools and, 83, 84–85
school readiness and, 8
tests and, 61, 141, 144
State Child Health Insurance Programs
    (SCHIP), 11
Stechuk, R. A., 36
Stenner, A. J., 19
Sterbin, A., 144
Stipek, D. J., 13, 36
Stormshak, E., 27, 29
Storytelling, 111, 143
Stress, xxi, 6, 29, 56, 97, 103
    demonstration programs and, 97
    home-based child care and, 103
    risk factors and, xxi
    school readiness and, 6
Stulhman, M., 161
Suen, H. K., 28, 95
Sullivan, L. M., 130
Surveys, 18, 62
Swartz, J. P., 72
Synder, P., 44

Tabors, P. O., 37, 38
Talen, T. N., 164
Tatelbaum, R. C., 29
Taylor, K. B., 127
Taylor, L., 59
Teacher aides, 122, 124
Teacher-child ratios, 30, 148, 150, 167
    demonstration programs and, 90, 92,
        94, 95, 96
Teacher Education and Compensation
    Helps (T.E.A.C.H.), 175
Technology, 169, 172–173
Teenage pregnancies, 90, 91
Temple, J. A., 28, 81, 118, 119, 125,
    131, 160
Thayer, K., 58
Thomas, D., 70, 114, 131
Thomas, W. P., 34, 35
Thornton, A., 13
Title I, 80, 123, 143
Tivnan, T., 94
Tolman, J., 147
Tonascia, J., 11

Topitzes, J. D., 116, 125
Tout, K., 15
Travers, J. R., 88, 159
Trivette, C. M., 41
Trudeau, J. V., 58
Tutoring, 136, 137, 141, 142, 143–144

U.S. Census Bureau, 33
U.S. Department of Education, 59, 67,
    72, 135, 139
U.S. Department of Education,
    National Center for Education
    Statistics, 33, 172
U.S. Department of Health and Human
    Services, 8, 12, 68, 70, 74, 126
U.S. General Accounting Office (GAO), 69

Vandall, D., 26, 30, 31
Vandell, D. L., 29, 97, 98,
    146, 147, 148, 152
Vandivere, S., 15
Ventura, A., 13
Vincent, L. J., 172
Vocabulary, 69–70, 75, 81

Wagner, M. M., 13
Walberg, H. J., 119, 129
Wallgren, C. R., 118, 119n 1, 122
Wang, M. C., 119, 129
Warfield, M. E., 94
Wasik, B. H., 29
Watkins, S., 40
Webb, M. B., 127

Weikart, D. P., 27, 69, 90, 160
Weikert, D. P., 90
Weisburd, C., 149
Weisner, B., 168
Weissberg, R. P., 115
Welfare, 20, 28, 130
Wertheimer, R., 10
Wesley, P. W., 60
West, J., 62
Wheelock College Institute for Leadership
    and Career Initiatives, 161, 163,
    164, 165, 176
Wilcox, K. A., 38
Wilkerson, S. B., 142
Wilson, A., 147
Wilson-Ahlstrom, A., 147
Winsler, A., 36
Wise, A., 162
Women, Infants, and Children (WIC), 11
Wright, J., 173

Xiang, Z., 79, 90, 160

Yazejian, N., 30
Yohalem, N., 147, 149
Yoshikawa, H., 28
Younoszai, T. M., 127
Yun, J., 12

Zaslow, M., 13, 15, 103
Zigler, E. F., 74, 118, 122, 127
Zigmond, N., 40
Zinsser, C., 105

**CORWIN
PRESS**

The Corwin Press logo—a raven striding across an open book—represents the union of courage and learning. Corwin Press is committed to improving education for all learners by publishing books and other professional development resources for those serving the field of PreK–12 education. By providing practical, hands-on materials, Corwin Press continues to carry out the promise of its motto: **"Helping Educators Do Their Work Better."**